The Complete Guide to DAZ Studio 4

Bring your 3D characters to life with DAZ Studio

Paolo Ciccone

BIRMINGHAM - MUMBAI

The Complete Guide to DAZ Studio 4

First published: October 2013

Production Reference: 1071013

Published by Packt Publishing Ltd.
Livery Place
35 Livery Street
Birmingham B3 2PB, UK.

ISBN 978-1-84969-408-7

www.packtpub.com

Cover Image by Charley S (callad@hotmail.com)

Credits

Author
Paolo Ciccone

Reviewers
Joshua S. Nye

Atausch Paolini

Acquisition Editor
Edward Gordon

Lead Technical Editor
Mayur Hule

Technical Editor
Amit Ramadas

Project Coordinator
Navu Dhillon

Proofreaders
Ting Baker

Bernadette Watkins

Indexer
Priya Subramani

Production Coordinator
Shantanu Zagade

Cover Work
Shantanu Zagade

About the Author

Paolo Ciccone is a software engineer and photographer who lives in Santa Cruz, California. He has been developing software for more than 20 years in a large series of disciplines, including IDEs (JBuilder) and 3D modeling and rendering. His field of expertise is developing multiplatform applications (Mac OS and Windows) that help computer graphics artists achieve photorealistic results.

In 2010, he founded Prêt-à-3D (`www.preta3d.com`), a company dedicated to bringing high-end computer graphics tools to the masses. His Reality software for Poser and DAZ Studio has been used for video game illustration and for the preproduction of Hollywood large budget movies such as Jurassic Park IV and Hunger Games: Catching Fire.

For more than two decades, Paolo has taught all kinds of classes, from training for large corporations to live workshops about 3D graphics.

Paolo's experience with 3D software started in 1999, with the first public version of Blender, and then evolved to include other programs, including DAZ Studio, which he has used since version 1.0. Paolo is very active in the online community and he publishes a weekly blog covering topics about 3D graphics.

I would like to thank my wife Holly for her constant support during the writing of this book.

About the Reviewers

Joshua S. Nye is currently going into the second year of the Studio Art program at the University of Vermont, transferring there following studying Psychology for three semesters at Daniel Webster college. In his coursework, he diligently applies his computer and creative skills he's practiced for his entire life. Ranging from 3D modeling to graphic design and even some dabbling in computer programing, he enjoys the wide skill set he has developed. However, Joshua still finds projects that are purely abstractionist, not very interesting.

Using DAZ Studio for anatomical and still life references, Joshua is currently working on a graphic novel that he plans to publish as well as merchandise.

He spends a fair portion of his time in the northern wilderness of Vermont and when not on his computer (which is more common than one would think), he can be found enjoying fresh air.

I would like to thank my parents for supporting my interests (especially when I changed my major four times); without them, I would not have pursued these interests and consequently not be a better person. I would also like to thank the wonderful people who made DAZ Studio; without them, the author would have had nothing to write, and I would have had nothing to review.

Thank you to the nice people at Packt Publishing; it was a pleasant surprise for me when they approached me to review this book. I would also like to thank one of my art professors, Mr Donald Wellman, for teaching such a wonderful, thought provoking perspective on contemporary art.

Atausch Paolini is a 3D artist, game developer, and game programmer in the world of 3D graphics. As a recognized 3D artist, he has worked on several games in the gaming industry. In his five years as a 3D artist, he's had the opportunity to work for Staltech, Enraged Entertainment, and Hawkeye Games, and a handful of startup companies. Currently, he is the CEO of Xentrium Entertainment working as a one-man team, developing games for mobile devices. Atausch is a contributing artist to several games, including Relic, Liberico, and Iron Pride. You can read more about Atausch at www.atausch.com or learn more about Xentrium Entertainment at www.xentrium.com.

I'd like to thank Navu Dhillon for helping me review this book, as well as for the help that she provided when I encountered a few bugs and errors. I also would like to thank Mayur Hule who I've worked with in reviewing this book.

Last but not least, I would like to send many thanks to Mom and Dad for being the people to look up to, and to my love, Marí, who put up with my grumpiness, as well as with all the lonely nights.

www.PacktPub.com

Support files, eBooks, discount offers and more

You might want to visit www.PacktPub.com for support files and downloads related to your book.

Did you know that Packt offers eBook versions of every book published, with PDF and ePub files available? You can upgrade to the eBook version at www.PacktPub.com and as a print book customer, you are entitled to a discount on the eBook copy. Get in touch with us at service@packtpub.com for more details.

At www.PacktPub.com, you can also read a collection of free technical articles, sign up for a range of free newsletters and receive exclusive discounts and offers on Packt books and eBooks.

http://PacktLib.PacktPub.com

Do you need instant solutions to your IT questions? PacktLib is Packt's online digital book library. Here, you can access, read and search across Packt's entire library of books.

Why Subscribe?

- Fully searchable across every book published by Packt
- Copy and paste, print and bookmark content
- On demand and accessible via web browser

Free Access for Packt account holders

If you have an account with Packt at www.PacktPub.com, you can use this to access PacktLib today and view nine entirely free books. Simply use your login credentials for immediate access.

Table of Contents

Preface

Computer art is today a mature field. Gone are the days when 3D modeling and rendering were arcane arts reserved for software experts who had access to expensive programs. Today, we have 3D software that is both affordable and easy to use.

About 18 years ago, Larry Weinberg, a software engineer working for a Hollywood VFX company, had a vision of a program that would give everybody the means to easily pose and render human figures. That software was, of course, Poser, a 3D program for the masses. Poser spawned a large business of premade content marketed by several companies. One of the companies born from the Poser phenomenon was DAZ 3D. DAZ became famous as the maker of the Victoria and Michael Poser figures, which have been received very well by the market. In fact, Victoria 4 is the most widely used 3D figure of all time. In 2006, DAZ released its own alternative to Poser, dubbed DAZ Studio. DAZ Studio is distributed as freeware, software that is given away for free because DAZ's business model is based on selling premade content. By giving away the software, DAZ provides a great entry point for people who want to explore the fascinating world of 3D computer art.

This book helps you take full advantage of the many features of Studio. You will learn how to pose human figures and how to make your own creature by using morphs. You will learn how to light your 3D scenes and render them as beautiful images that you will be able to share or even sell as illustrations. The cover of this book, for example, was created with DAZ Studio.

With concrete and hands-on examples, you will be able to become familiar with DAZ Studio and use it for both personal and professional applications.

What this book covers

Chapter 1, Quick Start – Our First 3D Scene, introduces some of the main Studio features by creating a simple scene, showing how to position the camera and how to render the scene to an image file.

Chapter 2, Customizing Studio, shows how to personalize Studio by simplifying the user interface and configuring special keystrokes to make us work faster and with less effort.

Chapter 3, Posing Figures, explains how to use premade poses and create our own pose for a human character.

Chapter 4, Creating New Characters with Morphs, introduces the power of morphs, showing how we can create whole new characters from a regular human figure.

Chapter 5, Rendering, explains the rendering options in detail, including what graphic file format provides the best results.

Chapter 6, Finding and Installing New Content, describes in detail where we can find additional content and how we can install it on both Macintosh and Windows PCs.

Chapter 7, Navigating the Studio Environment, explains how to organize the Studio library and how to use the scene manipulation tools of Studio. This chapter also gives information about the building block of geometry objects.

Chapter 8, Building a Full Scene, shows how to create a full scene with a character, clothing, and creative use of props to build an environment. We also see how to solve common clothing issues.

Chapter 9, Lighting, delves deep into the magic of lighting.

Chapter 10, Hyper-realism – the Reality Plugin, introduces an alternative rendering system that gives you the highest level of realism with Studio.

Chapter 11, Creating Content, describes how to create clothing for a figure and how we can sell it on the Internet.

Chapter 12, Animation, covers the principles of animation, from its building blocks all the way to the finished product available for playback.

Appendix, Installing DAZ Studio, shows how to install DAZ Studio on your computer.

What you need for this book

For most of this book the only thing that you need is DAZ Studio 4.6 or above. For *Chapter 11, Creating Content*, you will need to download the evaluation version of modo. It's best if you wait until you reach *Chapter 11, Creating Content* before downloading modo (instructions and links are found in the chapter), as the evaluation period starts from the moment you download the program.

Who this book is for

This book is for all users of DAZ Studio. If you have just started using Studio and you need to figure out how to use the program, this book is for you. If you have used Studio for some time and you want to learn more about lighting, rendering, content creation, and installation, this book is for you.

Conventions

In this book, you will find a number of styles of text that distinguish between different kinds of information. Here are some examples of these styles, and an explanation of their meaning.

File names in text are shown as follows: "You can find the scene in the projects files inside the `Project Files` directory."

Any command-line input or output is written as follows:

```
cd Documents Return
```

New terms and **important words** are shown in bold. Words that you see on the screen, in menus or dialog boxes for example, appear in the text like this: "Click on the **Accept** button to save your choice."

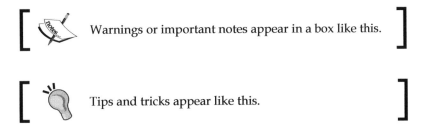

Warnings or important notes appear in a box like this.

Tips and tricks appear like this.

Reader feedback

Feedback from our readers is always welcome. Let us know what you think about this book—what you liked or may have disliked. Reader feedback is important for us to develop titles that you really get the most out of.

To send us general feedback, simply send an e-mail to feedback@packtpub.com, and mention the book title via the subject of your message.

If there is a topic that you have expertise in and you are interested in either writing or contributing to a book, see our author guide on www.packtpub.com/authors.

Customer support

Now that you are the proud owner of a Packt book, we have a number of things to help you to get the most from your purchase.

Downloading the example code

You can download the example code files for all Packt books you have purchased from your account at http://www.packtpub.com. If you purchased this book elsewhere, you can visit http://www.packtpub.com/support and register to have the files e-mailed directly to you.

Downloading the color images of this book

We also provide you a PDF file that has color images of the screenshots/diagrams used in this book. The color images will help you better understand the changes in the output. You can download this file from http://www.packtpub.com/sites/default/files/downloads/4087OT_Graphics.pdf.

Errata

Although we have taken every care to ensure the accuracy of our content, mistakes do happen. If you find a mistake in one of our books—maybe a mistake in the text or the code—we would be grateful if you would report this to us. By doing so, you can save other readers from frustration and help us improve subsequent versions of this book. If you find any errata, please report them by visiting http://www.packtpub.com/submit-errata, selecting your book, clicking on the **errata submission form** link, and entering the details of your errata. Once your errata are verified, your submission will be accepted and the errata will be uploaded on our website, or added to any list of existing errata, under the Errata section of that title. Any existing errata can be viewed by selecting your title from http://www.packtpub.com/support.

Piracy

Piracy of copyright material on the Internet is an ongoing problem across all media. At Packt, we take the protection of our copyright and licenses very seriously. If you come across any illegal copies of our works, in any form, on the Internet, please provide us with the location address or website name immediately so that we can pursue a remedy.

Please contact us at copyright@packtpub.com with a link to the suspected pirated material.

We appreciate your help in protecting our authors, and our ability to bring you valuable content.

Questions

You can contact us at questions@packtpub.com if you are having a problem with any aspect of the book, and we will do our best to address it.

1

Quick Start – Our First 3D Scene

While preparing for a real-life photo shoot, let's say a fashion shoot, a photographer will have to hire a model, pose her in front of a background, position some lights, and then take a few photos. This workflow is pretty much what we will follow to create a scene in DAZ Studio, except that we will work with 3D objects. These objects have been designed by 3D modelers and are prepared in a way that Studio can easily add them to a scene. Because these are 3D objects, instead of simple bidimensional images, we can move around them and photograph them from any point of view. Welcome to the fascinating world of 3D art!

In this chapter you will learn the following topics:

- Adding a human figure to the scene
- Positioning the camera
- Moving objects in the scene
- Rendering an image

Stepping into DAZ Studio

With DAZ Studio you can create 3D scenes filled with all kinds of objects, such as people, cars, buildings, animals, and plants. As the best way to learn is by doing, we are *not* going to spend any time at this point discussing 3D concepts and ideas. Instead, we are going to dive into the program and start doing something interesting with it.

Let's start!

Studio uses 3D assets

A program like Studio allows you to create a scene using 3D assets. Think of Studio as your own virtual, potentially infinite, photographer's studio. In it you can pose models, add objects, pose lights, and then take a photograph. While using Studio you pick from a library of premade 3D assets, such as people, clothing, cars, buildings, weapons, and so on. Once you select an object, you place it in the scene and change its place until you find an arrangement that works for the image that you have in mind. Throughout this book, we will see many different types of 3D assets. Some of these assets come with Studio; they are installed with the program so that you can start getting results within minutes after finishing the installation. Other assets can be added by either purchasing them or by downloading them from free repositories on the Web.

Refer to *Appendix, Installing DAZ Studio,* for step-by-step instructions on how to install DAZ Studio on your computer.

Customizing Studio

After you install Studio, the program presents itself with a predefined scene that shows a gray human figure standing in the standard T pose.

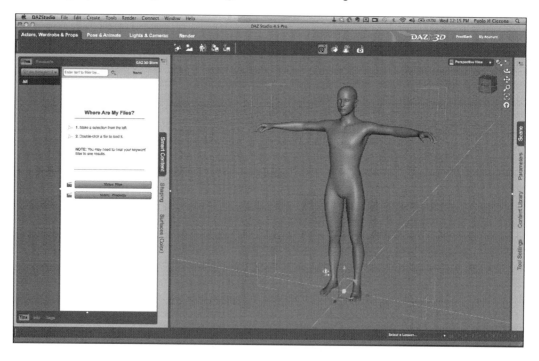

This configuration is not optimal. Most of the time, we will end up deleting the default figure to start your scene with something that you want. In addition, the loading of that figure adds to the time that it takes to start Studio, and we all know how much fun it is to wait for a program to become ready. So, let's make a few changes that will help us work faster.

First of all we delete the figure from the scene. To do this, we double-click on the figure's pelvis and then press the *Delete* key.

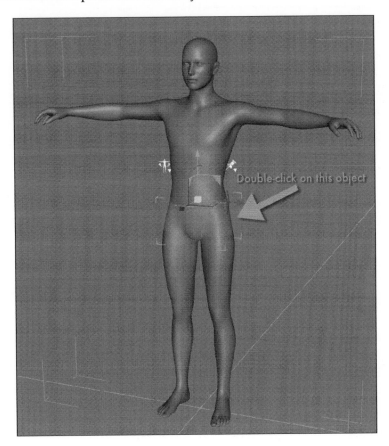

Downloading the example code

You can download the example code files for all Packt books you have purchased from your account at http://www.packtpub.com. If you purchased this book elsewhere, you can visit http://www.packtpub.com/support and register to have the files e-mailed directly to you.

This action will get rid of the figure and give us a clear scene. Of course, repeating this operation every time we start Studio becomes very tedious very quickly. There is a much better way. We can configure Studio to start with an empty scene.

1. Call the Studio configuration window by navigating to **DAZStudio | Preferences** (in Mac) or **Edit | Preferences** (in Windows).
2. Click on the **Startup** tab.
3. Uncheck the option labeled **Load file**.
4. Click on the **Accept** button to save your choice.

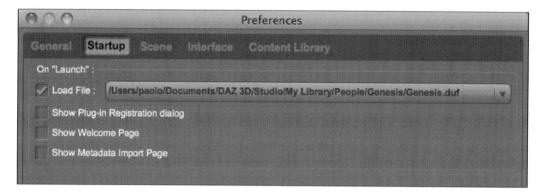

Now, every time you start Studio, it will come up with an empty scene and it will load faster.

Now if we look at the User Interface (UI) of Studio, we can see a couple of areas where we can apply some streamlining. Studio's UI comes with a default style, but that style, the way the UI elements are drawn on the screen, can be changed. This is useful, for example, to make Studio take less screen surface to draw some widgets such as buttons and tabs. The default style used by Studio is called **Main Street** and it uses large widgets that take a lot of screen space. Even with a very high screen resolution this style can be a bit invasive. I strongly believe that the UI of a program should stay as essential as possible, and this is even truer for programs used for artistic expression. We need a large canvas and as few distractions as possible. To change the style of Studio, navigate to **Window | Style | Select Style**. A window will appear where you can select the style for the UI. From the **Select a Style** window, click on the drop-down list at the top and select **Highway**.

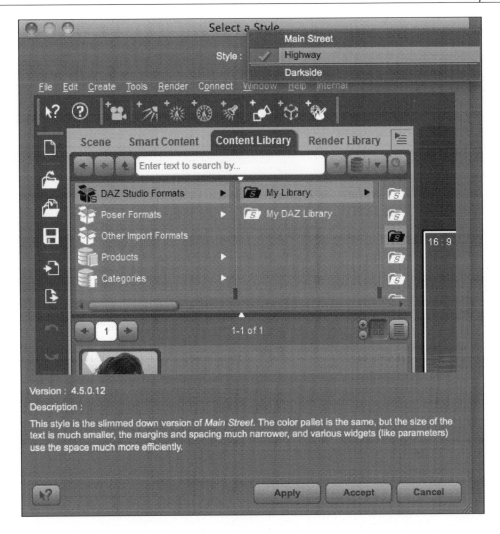

The **Highway** style is similar to the default one, but it takes a lot less screen real estate to be drawn. Click on the **Accept** button to confirm your choice.

Let's take a break for a moment and consider what we have done up to this point. Right now the screen of Studio looks a little tidier, the UI is not as predominant, and we get a clean slate every time we start. These little steps make the experience of using Studio better and faster. A few seconds saved every time you run the program really add up at the end of the year. In addition, the customization of the environment is the first step in making the program your own. It also shows you that you are in control of the program and not the other way around.

Lastly, we need to fix the orientation of the tabs. While having the tabs arranged vertically might seem like a good way of saving screen space, the orientation makes it very hard to read the text of the tabs and it forces us to tilt our heads sideways. To fix this issue, navigate to **Window | Workspace | Orient Tabs Along Top**. Refer to the following screenshot to see exactly where the menu option is:

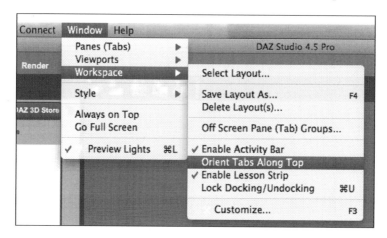

Once you perform this last change, you will see the right pane of the window collapse to almost nothing. Don't worry about it. We will do some more rearranging of the layout later on. For now, be assured that you will be able to get access to the pane by simply clicking on the disclosure arrow.

Every now and then we will see elements of the UI using small triangles, usually black, that are employed to open up or close down parts of the interface. These triangles, or arrows, are visible in the menus in the edges of panels and other UI elements. While the term *disclosure triangle* can be a mouthful, that's how those elements are named. Having a bit of common terminology helps us understand each other while communicating via e-mail, online forums, and social media.

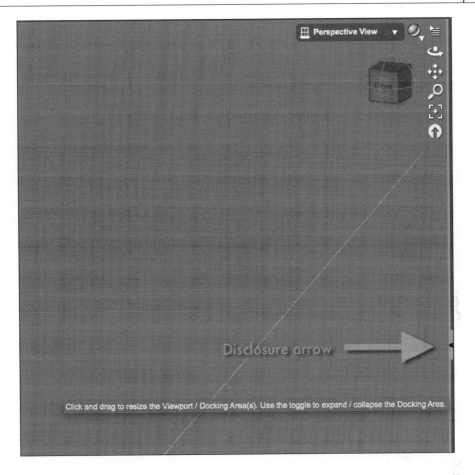

Now that we have configured Studio with a much more comfortable layout, we can start putting together the elements of our first scene.

Introducing Genesis – a shapeshifter

If you have installed Studio as described in *Appendix, Installing DAZ Studio,* you should have several 3D assets ready to use. One of these assets is the Genesis figure. Genesis is a base humanoid figure that can be altered to assume all kinds of shapes. It can be a woman, a man, a giant, a monster, or a baby. It can even be altered to assume shapes that are radically different from the basic human form. For example, you can have a creature with the head of Anubis, the jackal-headed god of ancient Egypt. We'll see more of this in *Chapter 4, Creating New Characters with Morphs,* but for now let's locate Genesis and add it to our scene.

In the **Smart Content** tab, which should be at the left of your monitor, you can find a series of vertical labels that indicate the groups of 3D assets available in Studio.

Click on the People category, where there are four actors available: **Basic Child**, **Basic Female**, **Basic Male**, and **Genesis**. If this is a fresh installation, all the icons will have a **New** label to indicate that the asset has never been used before.

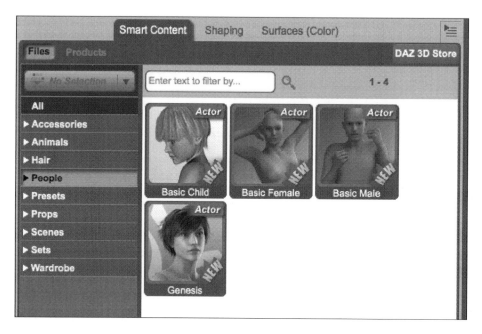

It would seem that the icon labeled **Genesis** would add a female figure to the scene, complete with hair. That icon actually loads the same androgynous gray figure that we deleted from the scene.

Instead, let's double-click on the **Basic Female** icon. This action will cause the 3D model of a woman to be added to your scene. The model will appear in the **3D Viewport**. Notice that the **Basic Female** icon doesn't have the **New** label anymore.

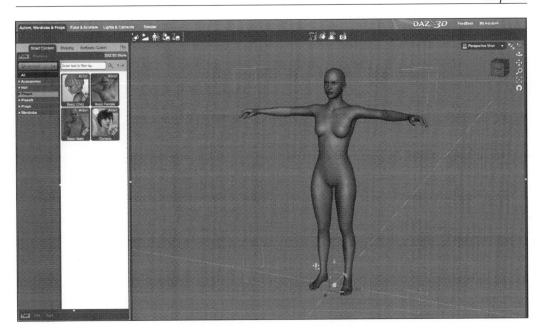

The figure comes in the scene with the typical T pose, a neutral pose that is common to most characters. This pose is our starting point, and it can be modified to assume any pose that we want to apply to the model. The basic female character is fairly similar to the Victoria 4 model, the previous version of female characters made by DAZ. You can notice that it comes with no genitalia and no nipples. This is a feature of the skin—the texture—applied to the figure and something that can be changed easily, if the need for such features arises.

Adding smart content

The **Smart Content** tab of DAZ Studio is context-sensitive to the context in which we are. This means that it changes to display different items depending on what object is selected in the scene. When the scene is empty or when there is nothing selected, the **Smart Content** tab shows the list of categories available, and it presents items that can be added to the scene. If we click on the **Basic Female** figure to select it, the **Smart Content** tab will change to show us what we can do with it; for example, it will show us materials or poses that we can apply to the figure. This feature will become more obvious as we progress with more complex scenes.

Adding clothing

Click on the disclosure triangle next to the **Wardrobe** category. Then, click on the **Outerwear** subcategory; you will see two items: **Jacket** and **Leggings**.

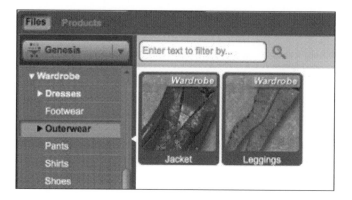

While you make sure that the figure in the Viewport is selected, double-click on the **Jacket** icon. This operation adds the jacket to the scene and then binds it to the character so that the two will move together.

This is called **conforming the clothing to the character**. Without conforming the two objects, the figure and the jacket would be simply two independent items in the scene.

Now click on the **Pants** subcategory in the **Smart Content** tab. In there you will find two other items: **JS Pants** and **Shorts**. Make sure that the female figure is selected and then double-click on the **JS Pants** icon. That will add and conform the pants to the figure.

Now, click on the **Shoes** subcategory and add **JS Boots** to the figure as we did for the other items.

Adding hair

Studio can give you access to hundreds of hairdos that you can customize with colors and styles. The default installation of Studio has a few hair models available. Let's pick one and work with it. In the **Smart Content** pane, click on the **Hair** category. You will see four models of hair; let's add the one called **Aldora**. The procedure is the same as we saw before, but now that the figure is fully clothed, it's not easy to click on a part of the body to select it.

> The fact is you can select the figure by double-clicking on any part of the body, for example, the head. I suggested to use the pelvis because sometimes small movements of the mouse, while double-clicking, can actually move the body part by mistake. I find the center of the body just less sensitive to small mistakes. Call it a good habit.

So, now we can double-click on the head to select the whole figure, and then add the hair by double-clicking on the **Aldora** icon.

Treat yourself

It's now time to take a break and enjoy the fruit of this work. Studio is a 3D environment, so let's start taking advantage of this fact and see how we can take a look at our figure from a different point of view. Look at the top-right of the 3D Viewport, you should see a cube with faces painted in green, red, and blue. That cube controls the position of your camera.

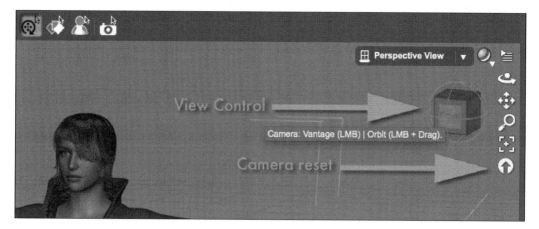

Click-and-drag on that cube to change your camera's point of view. You can now see that we are actually using 3D objects, and that we can place our camera in any place of the scene to take a snapshot in any way we want.

Restore the position of the camera to the default by clicking on the camera reset button.

Strike the pose

To change the pose from the uninspiring "T" default, let's apply a predefined pose. This is one of the strengths of Studio, the ability to save and apply poses to our characters. Luckily for us, Studio comes with a set of predefined poses so we can change our scene with a point-and-click approach.

In the **Smart Content** pane, click on the disclosure triangle next to the **Presets** category. This will reveal three subcategories: **Animations**, **Materials**, and **Poses**. Click on the **Poses** subcategory. This last operation will show you a list of icons representing several poses for our character. While making sure that the **Basic Female** character in the 3D Viewport is selected, double-click on the pose labeled **Female Running 01**.

If everything went well, you should have the same result that you can see in the following image. As we can see, all the garments are following the pose of the main figure. The sleeves bend, the boots adapt to the position of the feet, and everything works perfectly. This is no small feat, as conforming and fitting clothes to a 3D figure is a very complex operation, as we will see in the chapter dedicated to creating clothing. Studio makes this operation very simple, and this is one of the advantages of using this application.

Fixing nonconforming clothing

If you see something different with your scene, like clothing out of place or not following the main figure, it could be that you didn't conform the garment to the figure when the garment was added to the scene. To fix this there is an easy procedure that can be followed, but it uses a part of the UI that we haven't explored yet.

On the right-hand side of the Studio screen, there is a pane that collapsed when we arranged the tabs to be shown horizontally. You can now reveal that pane by clicking on the disclosure triangle for it. Refer to the following screenshot to see where the disclosure triangle is:

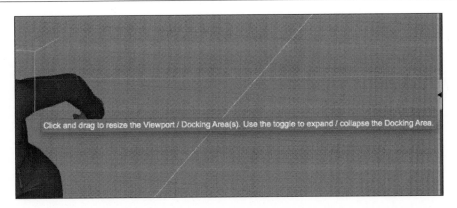

Once you do that, you will see a series of additional tabs: **Scene**, **Parameters**, **Content Library**, and **Tool Settings**. Let's not worry about those for now and just click on the **Parameters** tab. Let's assume that **Jacket** is the item that didn't conform to the figure. So, to correct the problem, follow these easy steps:

1. Click on the drop-down list just below the **Parameters** tab and select **Jacket**.
2. Click on the **General** category.
3. From the right-hand side of the pane, find the **Fit to** drop-down list and click on it.
4. Select **Genesis**.

That's all there is to it. The jacket should now fit the character perfectly.

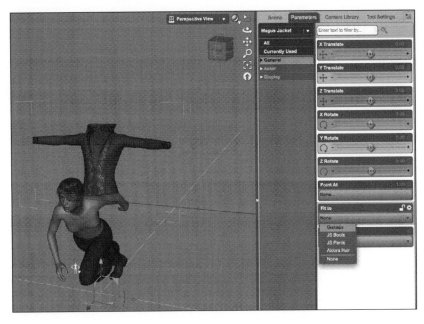

Once you are done with the fix, you can click on the disclosure triangle to hide the pane again and have more screen surface available for the 3D Viewport.

Saving your scene

With so many actions performed at this point, it would be a pity if something happened to our scene. Better save it so that we don't risk losing data. From the Studio menu click on the **File** menu and then select **Save....** As it usually happens for this operation, you will be asked to select a folder where to save the file and a name for the file. Let's select Chapter_01_01 to indicate that this is the scene for chapter 1 and this is the first version of the file. You can use, of course, any filename of your choice. Just be sure to remember what name you used and in which folder you stored the file because Studio, strangely enough, doesn't provide an **Open Recent** menu option. Studio will save the scene into a file named with the name that you selected and with the extension .duf, which is the default used by the application. **DUF** stands for **DSON User File** and it's the normal format for Studio scenes since Studio 4.5.

Adding an environment

As nice as our character is, she is standing in the middle of nothing and that is not right. We need to add an environment. To do so follow these easy steps:

1. Click away from the figure in an empty area of the scene to clear your selection.

2. With no active selection, the **Smart Content** pane now shows all the items installed in Studio.

3. Click on the **Sets** category.

4. Double-click on the **!Preload** icon to add that environment to the scene. Refer to the following screenshot to verify your steps:

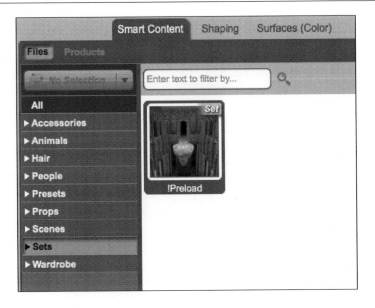

5. The environment is much larger than what we can see with our camera. Use the mouse wheel to zoom out and see more of the scene. You will need to roll the wheel toward the screen to zoom out. Rolling the wheel in the opposite direction zooms in. *Chapter 7, Navigating the Studio Environment*, explains in detail how to move the camera in the scene.

The environment has been added to the scene with a position that places the floor at a point that is much higher than where our figure stands. We need to move the figure so that it looks like she is touching the floor. For this, follow these steps:

1. Select Genesis by right-clicking on the face and then choosing **Select Genesis – Dbl Click** from the menu.

2. You should see the indicator of the Universal tool at the base of the figure. The Universal tool has the ability to move, rotate, and scale any object in the scene. If the Universal Tool is not enabled, use the switch in the toolbar to enable it.

3. Move your mouse to the top of the green arrow, which is pointing up. This arrow allows us to move the selected object up or down. When the arrow is highlighted, click-and-drag up to move the figure until the upper half of it is beyond the camera's frame. The following image shows how the Universal tool appears in the Viewport:

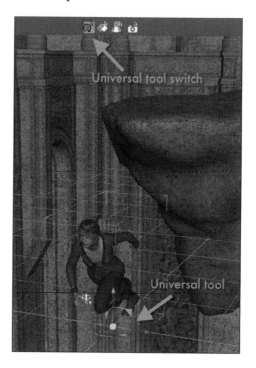

4. Click on the Frame Object camera tool to reframe Genesis. Refer to the following screenshot to see how to find the Frame Object tool:

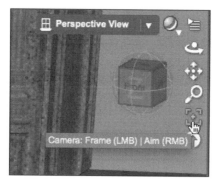

5. Now hover above the tip of the blue arrow of the Universal Tool. This part of the tool allows you to move the selected object in the depth direction. Click-and-drag until you see Genesis standing above the floor. Use the following image for reference:

6. Now use the green axis again to move the figure toward the floor. Keep an eye on the sole of the right boot. When you see that the boot sinks inside the floor, move the figure back up. We want to have our character rest on the floor. There should be just a bit of contact with the floor. For now don't worry too much about it. Just use your best judgment; later on, we will learn how to make precise adjustments.

7. Using the camera cube, adjust the camera angle to make the image a bit more dramatic. A low camera angle, with the camera below the subject's waist, looking slightly up, gives a bit more tension to the scene.

8. If you want to explore some rules of image composition, you can look in your public library for a good, introductory book about photography. There is also a nice article available online at the Digital Camera World website, http://www.digitalcameraworld.com/2012/04/12/10-rules-of-photo-composition-and-why-they-work/.

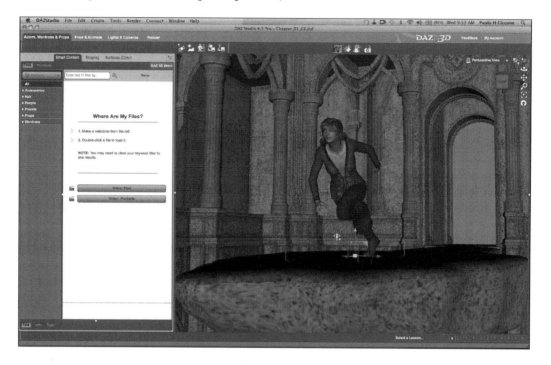

Rendering an image

All that we have done up to now is great, but the target of this activity is to be able to produce an image that we can show independently from Studio; for example, this could be a frame of a graphic novel. Ideally, we would like to obtain a PNG or JPG file that we can show other people. This can be achieved through a process called **rendering**.

When Studio renders, it converts all the 3D elements to a 2D image and in the process, it computes the final versions of the materials. Keep in mind that when we move around the 3D scene, we can only see an approximation of the quality of the scene. This is because it takes a very long time, computer-wise, to compute the final version of all the objects in the scene and their materials. That time would prevent the smooth movement of the camera or the ability to edit the scene in real time.

When we ask Studio to render an image, the software computes all the elements in the scene and it generates an image that is the faithful representation of those elements, including all the details of the materials and lights. We haven't looked at the lights yet, but those are also computed at render time.

To render an image use these steps:

1. From the Studio menu, navigate to **Render | Render**.

2. A window will pop up and in it you will be able to see the gradual development of the image.

   Note that the indicator for the Universal tool and the other icons visible in the 3D Viewport are not visible in the rendered image.

3. If you want to save the image to disk, enter a name in the designated field and select a file format. I suggest .png to avoid the data loss inherent in the JPEG format. The following screenshot shows the render window:

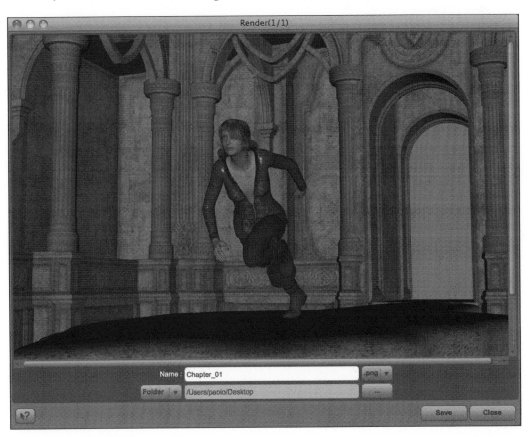

4. Click on the drop-down menu that says **Library** and select **Folder**. Click on the button with three dots to select the destination folder. Select your Desktop for now.

5. Click on the **Save** button to save your rendered image.

6. Using your file manager (Finder on the Mac, Windows Explorer on Windows) go to your Desktop, and you will be able to see an icon with the name that you have selected.

7. Double-click to open the image in your default image viewer.

Congratulations, you have created an image from a 3D scene that includes a human figure, conforming clothing, conforming hair, and a fully featured environment. As a last step, use the Studio menu and navigate to **File | Save as...** to save your scene as Chapter_01_02.

Summary

In this chapter you have learned the following topics:

- Customizing the Studio environment
- Using the **Smart Content** pane to locate 3D assets
- Adding figures, clothing, and hair
- Fitting a garment to a figure via the Parameters tab
- Adding an environment to the scene
- Using the Universal tool to move objects in the scene
- Rendering an image from the 3D scene

As we complete this quick tour of the essential elements of a Studio scene, we have gained considerable familiarity with the program. Take a few minutes to re-examine the work done so far. You should feel good about the progress. Think how complex and time consuming it would be to draw a scene like this using pencil and colors.

Now that you are more familiar with Studio, we can have a look at some of the interesting ways in which we can customize the program to be even more flexible and easier to use. This is the focus of the next chapter.

2
Customizing Studio

Studio is designed to be fully customizable and to adapt to the user's preferences. While this is a very good thing, this aspect of the program can be a "time-sucking" device. It's easy to get lost in all the customization options only to find out later that a couple of hours have passed since we started poking around. In this chapter we will see a few essential customizations designed to make our work with Studio easier, faster, and more fun. Specifically, we will see the following topics:

- Selecting a style that maximizes screen real estate
- Simplifying the UI and getting rid of redundant panels
- Using keyboard shortcuts to access Studio features quickly
- Changing the background color

 All the tips in this chapter are meant to give you a better, easier way of working with Studio. Strictly speaking, they are not required in order to use the lessons in this book, but they are of great help in speeding up the creative process. If you prefer to skip this chapter now, it is perfectly fine. You can apply the customizations described in this chapter at any point in your workflow.

Getting more screen space

Studio makes extensive use of tabs. This is because the Studio UI is quite rich and it provides different sections that are dedicated to specific tasks. For example, in the previous chapter we used the **Smart Content** tab to add 3D assets to the scene. The **Smart Content** pane is activated by clicking on the tab labeled with the same name.

While the tab metaphor makes it easy to locate useful areas of the program, the default size and placement of those tabs can take a lot of screen space. The way Studio tries to solve this issue is, by default, to rotate the tabs 90 degrees to display them vertically. Screens are usually wider rather than taller, so this arrangement seems to make sense, at least on paper. In reality, reading tabs sideways is quite impractical. If the text was shown vertically, like the typical Hotel sign that we can see on the side of buildings, it would be OK, but with letters rotated 90 degrees this solution leaves a lot to be desired.

In the previous chapter we saw how to change the orientation of the tabs so that they return to the usual horizontal configuration. Here we will go one step further and select a UI layout that maximizes screen use and removes some redundant elements that are easily accessible in other ways.

Customizing the layout

A Studio layout is a way of organizing the Studio UI elements on the screen. A layout does not change the functionalities of Studio, and it does not affect your scenes either. It simply re-arranges all the tabs, panes, and buttons of Studio in a given way.

Studio comes with a few predefined layouts, arranged to make the UI simpler for newcomers or richer and fully featured for expert users. Unfortunately, the default layout seems to be quite wasteful and full of redundant parts. We are going to configure our own layout that is efficient, clean, and fully featured.

When you start Studio for the first time, the program configures the **Hollywood Blvd** layout to be active by default. With this layout the Studio workspace is configured to be divided into sections, namely **Actors, Wardrobe & Props**, **Pose & Animate**, **Lights & Cameras**, and **Render**. Refer to the following screenshot for this:

What is interesting to note is that we don't need any of those top tabs to work with Studio. In fact, in the previous chapter we rendered an image without switching to the **Render** tab. Not only we don't need those tabs, but clicking on any one of them adds a noticeable delay and does nothing else other than re-arranging some other tabs and buttons on the screen. The result of all this rearrangement is that we have to relearn where things are, and we need to switch back and forth to regain access to certain tools. All this flickering and switching is actually quite hard on the eyes and it breaks the creative flow. It's much better to use a single configuration where we can rely on things being in the right spot all the time. By using such configuration we can use "muscle memory" to control Studio. This results in spending less time fumbling with the UI and more time performing fun, creative activities.

To achieve this task, we need to switch layout, a task that is easily done by navigating to **Window | Workspace | Select Layout ....**

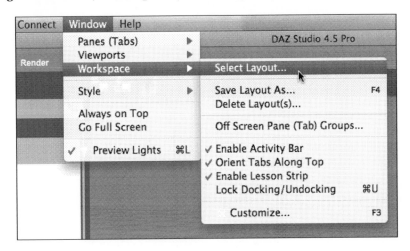

Downloading the color images of this book

We also provide you a PDF file that has color images of the screenshots/ diagrams used in this book. The color images will help you better understand the changes in the output. You can download this file from http://www.packtpub.com/sites/default/files/ downloads/4087OT_Graphics.pdf.

This action calls the layout manager window. The **Hollywood Blvd** layout should be selected by default.

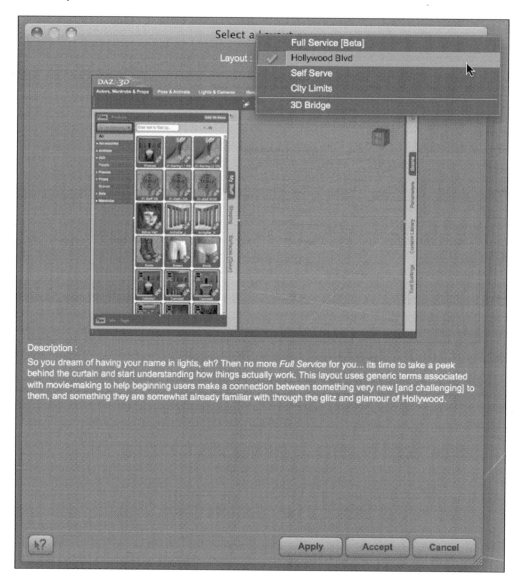

You can click on the other layout names to see an example of their look and a short description of their features. We are going to select the **City Limits** layout. This layout removes the top-level tabs that we mentioned before; it also adds a series of buttons to the toolbar at the top of the screen, and also a couple of sidebars. We can see that when we select the layout, it reverts the tabs to be displayed vertically.

No problem, now we know how to fix this problem by navigating to **Window | Workspace | Orient Tabs Along Top** again. As we do this, the tabs disappear, as the panes that hold them are collapsed by default. Let's click on the toggle triangle on the left.

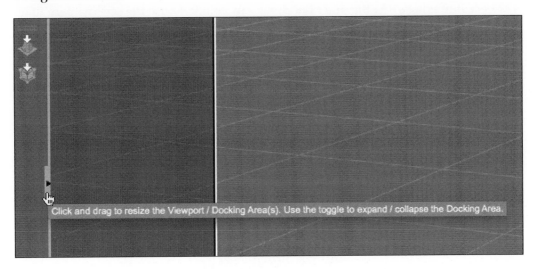

This action reveals the pane containing **Content Library**, the **Smart Content** tab, and other tabs that we will examine later.

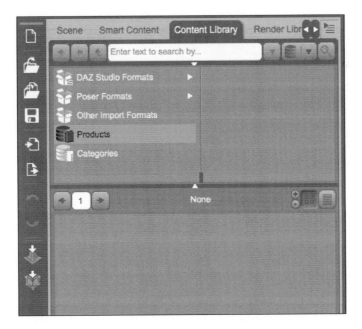

If we look at the left-hand side of the Studio window, we can see a column of gray-scale icons representing document pages and folders. These icons provide shortcuts for actions such as saving and opening scenes. All these actions are easily accessible either via the standard **File** menu, or via key combinations. So this sidebar is of very limited use. On the other hand, we can definitely use the screen space that it occupies, so let's remove this sidebar.

Right-click on an area of the sidebar that has no icons. A pop-up menu should show up.

From this menu, click on **Input Output** to remove the sidebar. Voilà, we gained a few more precious pixels for our 3D Viewport.

If you use a Macintosh, you might not have a three-button mouse. In that case, whenever I mention right-click, you should use the *Ctrl* + click combination to obtain the equivalent result. If you use the Apple Magic Trackpad or an Apple laptop computer, use the two-finger tap. In either case, it's my advice to purchase a three-button mouse. Logitech offers some excellent models that are Macintosh-compatible. Any serious work with 3D applications requires, at a minimum, a three-button mouse.

Removing screen clutter

When we opened the pane on the left, we saw a few tabs preloaded there. Among them is one titled **Render Library**. You can probably also see a couple of horizontal arrows used to scroll the tabs when there is not enough space in the panel to show them all. While working in Studio, we spend a lot of time adding objects to the scene and moving them around. In proportion, we spend much less time rendering and managing the rendered images. It makes much more sense to dedicate screen space to often-used tools than to panes that are rarely, if ever, utilized.

While rendering the images, the filesystem of the computer is what we want to use to manage the files; after all, that is the reason for having a filesystem. The **Render Library** pane is an attempt to manage the rendered images inside Studio, but in reality, it doesn't do much and it gets in the way of proper file management. Therefore, the **Render Library** tab is of very limited use, and we can instead use that space for something more useful.

Fortunately for us, all the tabs in Studio are completely adjustable, so we can configure the program to our liking. Use the following steps to remove **Render Library**:

1. Click on the **Render Library** tab to activate it.
2. Right-click on the tab to call the contextual menu.
3. From the menu select **Close Pane**.

Now the remaining tabs are shown centered on top of the pane. There is a lot of advantage in having a clean UI that is easy to read. It reduces eyestrain and provides a more relaxing environment that is conducive to creativity.

Now, let's do something similar for the right-hand side pane. Click on the disclosure triangle to open the pane.

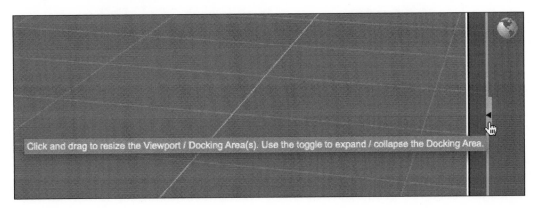

Once the pane opens up, look for the **Lights** and **Cameras** tabs and close them as we did with the **Render Library** pane.

1. Click on the **Lights** tab.
2. Right-click on the same tab.
3. Select **Close Pane** from the context menu. This is the last option in the list.
4. Click on the **Cameras** tab.
5. Right-click on the same tab.
6. Select **Close Pane** from the context menu.

Lights and cameras are more easily managed and changed from the Parameters tabs, so the two tabs that we have just closed were completely redundant. Once again we have gained some screen space and the UI looks less crowded, which has subtle but perceptible benefits. In case you want to explore those tabs, they can be re-enabled via the **Window | Panes (Tabs)** menu.

Saving the new layout

Obviously, we don't want to have to repeat the steps that we just performed over and over again. While Studio saves the current layout automatically, there are situations that could cause the setup to be erased, like for example, if you switch to another layout by mistake or just for testing purposes.

Let's save our layout that we have configured so far, so that it will be easy to recall if the need arises.

From the Studio menu, navigate to **Window | Workspace | Save Layout As...**.

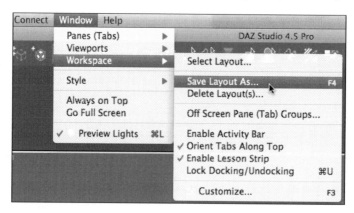

A window comes up in which we can enter a name of our choice for the new layout. I entered `Streamlined`, but you can use any name that you prefer.

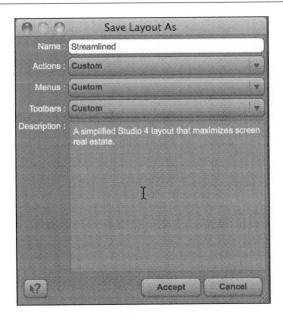

In addition to the name, we can also enter a description for the layout. When you're done with this step, you can simply click on **Accept** and the layout will be saved. It will then be available from the layout selection window.

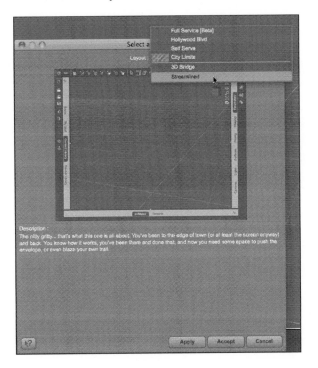

Simpler, faster keyboard shortcuts

The most efficient, fast, and fun way of using Studio is to use a few keyboard shortcuts in combination with the mouse. This workflow avoids interruptions in the creative process caused by searching for specific tools in the UI. For example, it's much faster and less distracting to press *Cmd + S* (on Mac)/ *Ctrl + S* (on Windows) to save a scene, instead of taking your eyes away from the scene, looking up for the **File** menu, and then searching for the **Save** option.

As Studio works on both Mac OS and Windows, it's necessary to find a notation to refer to keyboard combinations that work for both OSs. Macintosh uses the *Cmd* key to trigger special key combinations. Windows uses the *Ctrl* key. So, when you see something like **Cmd/Ctrl + S**, it means that you need to press a key combination that on Mac OS is *Cmd + S* and on Windows is *Ctrl + S*. Similarly, **Opt/Alt + S** indicates *Opt + S* for Mac OS and *Alt + S* for Windows.

If we look at the toolbar that has been created when we switched to the **City Limits** layout, we see that it now has a lot more buttons than when we first launched Studio. That is a good thing. Those buttons represent a lot of tools that we constantly need during the creation of our scenes.

Looking at the toolbar from left to right, we see a couple of buttons that can be used to access the help system. Then, we see a button that can be used to add a camera to the scene, followed by other buttons used to add different types of lights.

We will focus, for now, on the tools in the middle, starting with the one looking like a big mouse cursor to the left of the one highlighted in orange. These tools are listed in the following table:

Icon	Name	Function
	The Node selection tool	This is used to select objects or portions of objects, called **nodes**. For example, the forearm of a human figure is a node.
	The Universal tool	This is used to move, resize, and rotate objects.

Icon	Name	Function
	The Rotate tool	This is used to rotate objects.
	The Translate tool	This is used to move objects around.
	The Scale tool	This is used to enlarge or shrink objects.
	The Active pose tool	This is used to change the pose of a character.
	The aniMate2 tool	This is used to create animations.
	The Surface Selection tool	This is used to select nodes based on a material.

For now we stop at these tools, we will look at the other ones later on. What we want to do is to gain access to any of the tools described in the preceding table with just the pressure of a key. If we move the mouse over one of the buttons, the Universal tool for example, we can see that a little help bubble, also known as a tool tip, shows up telling us that we can activate the Universal tool using the keyboard shortcut **Opt/Alt-Shift-U**. That is one heck of a shortcut. You actually need to engage three fingers in order to get there. It pretty much defeats the purpose of having a keyboard shortcut. That is too bad because having a real shortcut would save us so much time and wrist strain by not having to rely so heavily on the mouse.

The funny thing is that there is no reason to make things this complicated. Those kinds of keyboard shortcuts are necessary when a program processes regular keys, as in the case of a word processor. This is not the case with Studio, which doesn't process regular keys except when we enter specific values, like when we entered the name for the layout that we saved. While using the 3D Viewport though, we don't enter normal text, so it doesn't make any difference if the keyboard shortcut is *Opt + Shift + U/ Alt + Shift + U* or simply *U*. It does change a whole lot for us though; it makes our life a lot simpler, and we are all for simplicity, aren't we?

So, let's change all those pesky keyboard shortcuts to real shortcuts. It's done in just a few easy steps:

1. From the Studio menu navigate to **Window | Workspace | Customize...**, or if you want to be in the spirit of this modification, just press *F3*.

   The **Customize DAZ Studio** window appears.

2. In the left pane titled **Actions**, scroll down until you find a group called **Viewport Tools**.

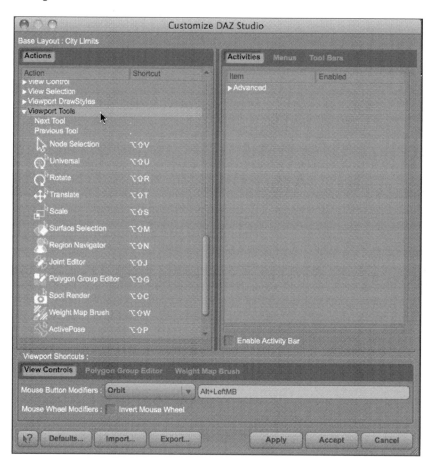

3. Click on the disclosure triangle on the left to reveal what the group contains. As we can see, there is a list of some tools that we saw in the toolbar. In the **Shortcut** column, we can see the keystroke that has been designated to activate each tool. The ⌥ character is the Macintosh symbol for the *Opt* key. On a Windows machine, that key is called *Alt*. The ⇧ symbol represents the *Shift* key.

4. Right-click on the node selection item to show the associated context menu.

5. From the menu, select **Change Keyboard Shortcut**.

6. When you see the text **Please Press a Key** on the screen, press the letter *V*. Now you can activate the selection tool by simply pressing one key.

7. Right-click on the **Universal** entry and repeat the operation. This time use the letter *U*.

8. Continue with the Rotate, Translate, and Scale tools and assign the keys *R*, *T*, and *S*, respectively.

9. Lastly, assign the keystroke *M* to the Surface Selection tool.

10. Confirm your changes by clicking on the **Accept** button.

Now that we have some handy shortcuts, it's a good idea to try them!

1. Let's click on the **Smart Content** tab and then click on the **People** category.

2. Double-click on the **Basic Female** icon to add the figure to the scene.

3. Now, let's press *V* to enable the selection tool. Using the lowercase letter is just fine; I use the uppercase letter in the text for clarity. With the selection tool we can select individual parts of the figure.

4. Let's click on the head. The head appears selected inside a box traced by the four corners. That is called the **bounding box**. When we select a node, the parameters for that node show up in the **Parameters** tab. This tab allows us to precisely alter the characteristics of the selected object/node. We will see more about these later on.

5. Now let's press the letter *U* to select the Universal tool. As the head node was selected previously, the Universal tool is set to act on that node. The Universal tool includes the Translate, Rotate, and Scale tools in one convenient **gizmo** on screen. The curved lines in red, green, and blue are used to rotate the selected node along one axis.

6. Let's hover the mouse over the blue curve and rest it there for a few seconds. A tool tip shows up explaining that that part of the Universal tool modifies the **Side-Side** value. In this case, it tilts the head side-to-side.

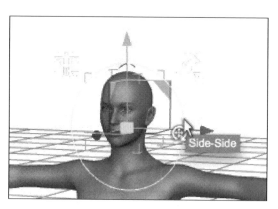

Click on that blue curve, hold the mouse, and then move it up or down. If you hover the mouse over each one of the curves in the tool, you will see a tool tip that explains the function of each part of the Universal tool. We need to use the **Side-Side** curve. Drag on that curve and you will see the head tilt as a result of your action. This is the first step in posing your characters!

Now click on the Pelvis node and use the right red arrow tip to translate (move) the character to the left or right. As we did before, we need to click, hold, and drag the mouse. This time we move left or right. You should see the whole figure move in the 3D Viewport.

Whether you prefer to use the Universal tool or the individual Translate, Rotate, and Scale tools is a matter of personal preference. What is important is that now you have a simple and effective way of selecting each tool with a simple keystroke.

Changing the background color

Studio's background color is set by default to be a light shade of blue. We can change that to any color of our liking. The background color will not affect the rendered image, but it can help our work by presenting the objects against a background that provides good contrast. This makes it easier to find objects and spot possible issues.

Changing the background color is easy. Click on the **Viewport Options** button at the top-right of the 3D Viewport.

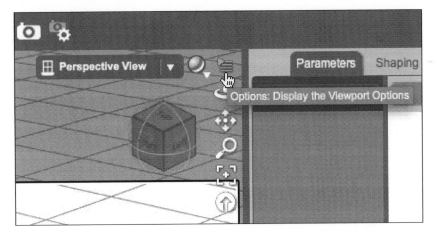

A menu shows up. Select the **Change Background color...** option. The standard Color Picker window shows up and from there we can select a color of our choice. Once confirmed, the scene background assumes the new color.

Summary

In this chapter we have seen how to adapt Studio to our needs. The customizations that can be applied to the program don't stop here. We will see more customizations as we learn more about Studio.

In this chapter you have learned the following topics:

- Switching to a different layout
- Removing unnecessary tabs
- Hiding redundant sidebars
- Saving a layout
- Customizing keyboard shortcuts
- Changing the background color

Controlling the tools offered by DAZ Studio is one of the crucial aspects of making art with this program. Now that we have a simpler and faster way of accessing those tools we can focus on the artistic exploration instead of having to break the creative flow. This will have a deep, positive impact in our artistic work.

In the next chapter, we will use our newly acquired knowledge and start putting together a scene in which we will pose a character from start to finish. It's time to get our hands dirty and it will be fun!

3
Posing Figures

As we saw in *Chapter 1*, *Quick Start – Our First 3D Scene*, figures added to a scene are presented in the standard T pose. When we create an illustration with Studio, we want to change that basic pose and set the figures in the position and situation that fit the scene. In this chapter we will see how we can achieve that. Studio provides a good set of tools to change the poses of our figures, but creating good poses is an art that takes a bit of practice. It's important to have a good strategy in order to get the results that we want.

In this chapter you will learn the following topics:

- Using premade poses
- Creating an original pose
- Sound strategies on approaching a new pose
- Avoiding common pitfalls

The main blocks of a pose

While posing a figure, we can break the process into three main areas:

- The torso and the limbs
- Hands and fingers
- Face

It's important to remember these areas because each presents a different set of challenges. The torso and limbs are the easiest to set up. Fingers are quite delicate to pose in a convincing manner, and setting a good expression on the face is the toughest task. We are going to tackle all these challenges with effective strategies that will make the task at hand easier.

Using premade poses

The figures that we can use in Studio, such as Victoria 4 or Genesis, are completely articulated and they can be posed like a person. They are not only made to look like humans, but they also react to the poses in subtle ways that make the final result convincing. For example, while moving the eyes, the eyelids bulge and deform in ways to conform to the shape of the underlying eye orb. Once we pose a figure, we can save that pose into a file. This allows us to recall that pose without spending all the time that was initially needed to pose the figure. To apply a presaved pose, all that is needed is to load the base figure, and then apply the saved pose to it. Files that store poses are called **Pose Presets**, and Studio comes with a few of these presets already installed with the program.

Let's first explore this approach.

We start by adding a female Genesis figure to the scene. We have seen the steps before, but here they are again:

1. Click on the **Smart Content** tab.
2. Click on the **People** category.
3. Double-click on the **Basic Female** icon.

The figure should appear in the scene in the standard T pose. Now that we have a figure and it's selected, the **Smart Content** tab will adapt and show the items that are relevant to our selection. Let's click on the disclosure triangle of the **Presets** category. Once all the subcategories are shown, we can click on the **Poses** subcategory. This action causes the **Smart Content** tab to show us all the poses that fit Genesis.

 Because Genesis is highly compatible with the previous generation of DAZ figures (also known as Gen4), such as Victoria 4, all the poses for the Gen4 figures can also be applied to any Genesis figure.

You can refine the filter of poses shown by opening the **Genesis** subcategory. This will show the **Basic Child**, **Basic Female**, and **Basic Male** groups. The names of these groups are more of suggestions than restrictions. The fact that a pose is under the **Basic Male** group doesn't prevent us from using it for a female character.

To use a pose preset, once the figure is selected, just double-click on it.

You can verify which object in the scene is selected by finding which object is highlighted by its bounding box, which is the series of four corners enclosing an object. Here is an example:

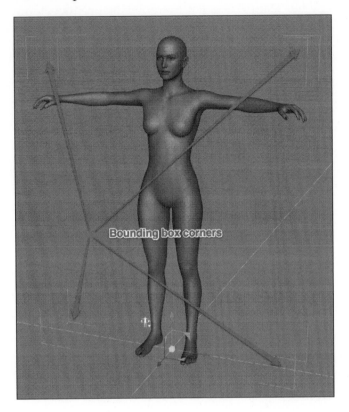

Try applying the **Kid Leaping 01** pose from the **Basic Child** category. As we can see, it works on an adult as well.

A full-body pose changes the whole body, but there are several packages of poses available that only affect a portion of the body, such as the arms or legs. Using those packages of partial poses is a great way of creating complex poses by applying a building block approach. For example, the product Handy for Genesis, sold at www.daz3d.com, has a full set of useful hand poses that don't change any other part of the body. Here is a sample of the poses available in that set:

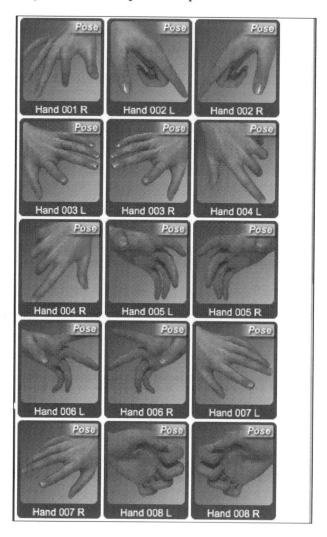

Using that set, we can quickly add some variety to our character's hand and do it in a second. Hands are very laborious to pose, so it saves a lot of time and effort if you have a good library of hand poses. We will see in a later chapter how to find additional products for Studio, including pose sets.

Purchasing the right poses

The ease of applying premade poses to a character can easily lead to filling up your hard disk with tons of pose packages. My experience is that it is rarely a good move. What I found is that, over the years, I rarely use the pose set that I bought. At first it might seem useful to buy a set that contains complex poses that are difficult to recreate. In reality, a very complex pose has very few applications. In the end, I keep revolving around the same few poses that I use as starting points. My advice is to look at some good hand pose sets and some basic, everyday body pose packages, and avoid buying dozens of pose packages. A few sets are OK; let's say between four and five. If you add more than that, you will spend a long time staring at your tiny thumbnails trying to decide if a given pose will fit the scene that you have in mind. This time can be actually used to pose the character and create something unique.

Creating a new pose

If you ever marveled at the drawings of comic book artists, this section of the book will definitely interest you because we are going to pose a full body in action. With Genesis we have a fully posable figure in Studio. All that we need is an idea for a scene. Let's try to make an illustration of a female surfer riding the waves.

Surfing is a very dynamic sport, and the need to keep the balance on the board requires assuming all kinds of poses that are visually very interesting. Because I'm not a surfer, I cannot count on my ability to recreate the right pose from my memory. In cases like this, a good approach is to find a photo or illustration that shows the person in the right pose, and use that image as a reference. With the Web available at our fingertips, there is plenty of material available that can be found with just a few clicks. I searched several sources, including commercial stock photo archives, and I found a very nice photo at deviantART (`http://deviantart.com`), one of the largest art communities on the Web.

Dennis Glover's page at deviantART is full of striking images, but one caught my attention because of the dynamic movement that it conveys, coupled with the fact that the subject is prominently in the frame.

Dennis' page is at `http://thorvold.deviantart.com` and the link for the image that I used is `http://fav.me/d42eisz`.

The image that I used is the one at the bottom-right of the page, titled **Surfer Girl**. I suggest that you download the image and keep it handy throughout this lesson.

In the following image, you can see the result of recreating the pose in the photo. This is what we are going to reproduce in the following pages.

Planning your shot

It's useful to spend a few minutes examining a reference photo, just to identify the major elements and prepare a plan of action. The hands in this image are fairly simple, so we don't need to worry much about them. The torso has a good amount of twist and it's bent forward. The arms are fairly straight. The legs are the biggest challenge so we know where we are going to spend most of our time.

Setting up the scene

For this exercise, we are not going to have waves or a wetsuit. In fact, we are not even going to bother with the surfboard, but we do need something that works in its place in order to get the right angle for the figure and the feet. This situation gives us the opportunity to learn a little bit about a very useful feature of Studio: **geometry primitives**.

Geometry primitives are simple objects that can be created with some variable parameters. The primitives are as follows:

- Cube
- Cylinder
- Sphere
- Plane
- Torus
- Cone

These are basic shapes that can come in handy several times. A sphere can work as a beach ball, a crystal ball or, if deformed, as a lens. A torus is a doughnut shape and can become useful to make bracelets, lifesavers or ...doughnuts! It's useful to get familiar with these primitives because they can provide a lot of flexibility without requiring us to use a specialized 3D modeling program such as modo or ZBrush just to create some useful shapes in Studio.

To access the primitives, you can simply click on the dedicated button in the Studio's toolbar.

The same action is available from the **Create | New Primitive...** menu. Regardless of what method you use, the result will always be to show a small window from where we can select to create one of the primitives that we want.

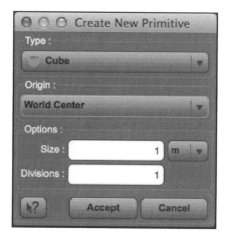

From this window, you can do several interesting things. For example, you can create a cylinder and make it have just six sides. That will create a hexagonal pillar. We will see all the options about the primitive shapes later; for now, let's concentrate on the cube primitive. We need to have some sort of surfboard to pose our character. All that we need is some shape that resembles the surfboard. For this task a cube primitive, correctly sized, will do the trick.

First, let's add a cube to a brand new scene.

1. Click on the new primitive button in the toolbox.

2. From the drop-down menu at the top of the window, select **Cube**.

3. Make sure that the **Size** parameter is set to **1** meter (abbreviated as m) and the **Divisions** parameter is set to **1**.

4. Click on the **Accept** button, and a cube should appear in the center of the scene.

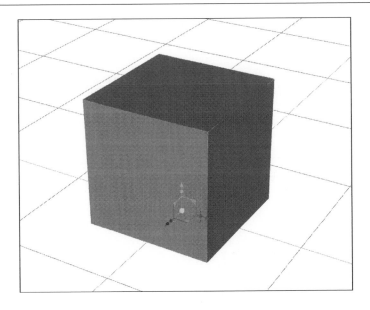

5. Switch to the Universal tool by pressing the *U* key and make sure that the cube is selected.

6. Now, hover your mouse over the little green cube under the green arrow of the Universal tool. A tool tip should appear saying **Scale in Y**. This means that if you click-and-drag on that cube, we will be scaling the cube along the Y (vertical) axis.

7. Click on the Y scale control and drag it toward the floor to make the cube flatter.

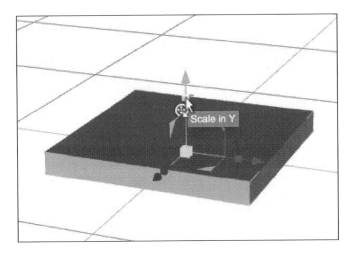

At this point, it's necessary to introduce a new tool. On several occasions, we might need to make precise adjustments to the object in the scene. For example, we might need to rotate an object exactly 90 degrees along the X axis. These kinds of operations are hard to do with drag-and-drop techniques; it's much easier and faster to enter the desired value. To do this, we need to enable the **Parameters** tab of Studio. On the right-hand side of the Studio window, you should see the **Parameters** tab. If the cube is selected, the parameters for its transformations should be visible.

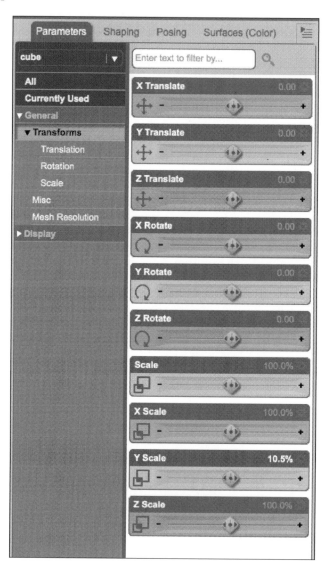

As we can see, the **Y Scale** parameter's slider value is set at **10.5**. Your value is most likely different, but it should be around that range. We want to set the vertical size to be exactly 6 percent. To do so we need to perform the following steps:

1. Click on the number that shows the value of **Y Scale**, in my case, the **10.5**% text.

2. The value is now editable and we can simply enter the number via the keyboard.

3. Enter the value 6 and press *Enter* (on Windows) or *return* (on Mac).

4. Now, we need to adjust the size of the rest of the cube to have roughly the proportions of a surfboard.

5. Click on the value for **Z Scale**, enter 200, and press the *Enter* (on Windows) or *return* (on Mac) key. From now, it's implicit that we need to follow every value entered with the *Enter* (on Windows) or *return* (on Mac) key so that we avoid repeating it.

6. Click on the value for **X Scale** and enter 60.

Now we have our surfboard. Let's go to the **Smart Content** tab and add the **Basic Female** figure to the scene. This is what we should have so far:

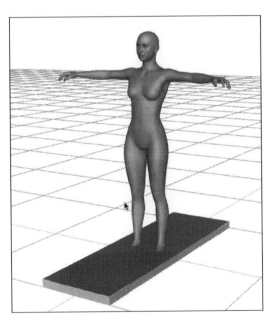

This is an excellent time to save the scene obtained so far. Navigate to **File** | **Save** and use an appropriate name. Let's save it as `surfer_01.duf`.

Looking at the image, the surfboard does seem a bit too thick; so let's lower the **Y Scale** to **4%**.

Using a reference image as a backdrop

Now that we have the objects in place, it's time to work on the pose. A good way to keep the reference photo in sight while working is to set it to be the background image. From the Studio menu, navigate to **Edit** | **Backdrop ....**. This operation allows us to select an image, and that image will then be painted as a backdrop for our scene, no matter how we move the camera. When we select that menu option, a window shows up from where we can select the image for the backdrop and a few transformations to apply to it.

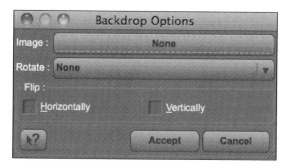

The various options are pretty self-explanatory. For our surfer, we don't need any transformation. To select an image, we need to click on the **Image:** drop-down list and from there select **Browse...**; the standard **Open** window will open allowing us to select an image file. Once the file is selected, it appears immediately in the Viewport. For this to work properly, it's important that the size of the rendered image matches the aspect ratio of the backdrop image.

Selecting an image size

When we watch a show on TV or a movie at the theater, we experience images at a very specific aspect ratio. The size of an image is something that is selected carefully by many artists before they create their work. For example, Laurence of Arabia was shot at a ratio of 2.20:1 (the width is 2.2 times the height) because that ratio conveys the spaciousness of the wide vistas featured in the movie. The decision of using that ratio was taken by the director with the help of the cinematographer, long before the first frame was shot. It was an artistic choice.

The Standard Definition TV that dominated the field for about 60 years was set at a 4:3 ratio. High Definition (HD) TV is set at a ratio of 16:9 regardless of the two resolutions available: 1280 x 720 or 1920 x 1080. Let's verify that. 1920/16 = 120. 120 x 9 = 1080. 1280:16 = 80.80 x 9 = 720.

This little exercise illustrates that aspect ratio, and not resolution, determines the proportions of an image.

The proportions of an image determine how that image is perceived by the viewer. For example, take this photo that I shot using my DSLR:

It's a nice panorama but it has a lot of "dead space" around the main subject, the city of San Francisco. Now take a look at exactly the same photo but cropped:

While the width has not changed a single bit, the cropping has the effect of making the photo look wider. This is why Laurence of Arabia has been shot at 2.20:1 instead of the more conventional 1.78:1 ratio used for most movies.

All this talk about the aspect ratio leads to a fairly simple point. When we render an image in a program like Studio, we will have to decide, at some point, what aspect ratio your image will have. This decision is better taken at the beginning of the process because it influences how we are going to frame the shot. In the case of setting a backdrop, it is also necessary to match the Studio camera frame to the aspect ratio of the image used for the backdrop, otherwise we will get stretching or compressing of the image. There are plenty of videos on YouTube that show people squeezed or stretched. This is caused by the mismatch of the aspect ratio of the original video.

If we look at the dimensions of the image that we want to use as a reference, we can see that it has a resolution of 759 by 497 pixels. 759 divided by 497 gives us a ratio of 1.52, which is not a standard ratio, but this is not an issue. As we want to avoid distortions of the image, we need to check the render settings of Studio and possibly adjust them. If we navigate to **Render | Render Settings...**, we obtain the window that controls all the aspects of rendering an image. From the following screenshot, we can see that the render resolution has been set by Studio to 800 x 600:

Those numbers give us a ratio of 1.33 (800 divided by 600), which is more square-like than what we have with our photo reference. The solution is simple; just enter, for now, the same dimensions used by the photo. While you do that, make sure to uncheck the **Constraint Proportions** checkbox before making the change. After this operation is done, we can close the window by clicking on the close button (X) at the top-right corner.

Setting the position of the surfboard

We have created our surrogate surfboard to obtain a level of believability in setting our character. The board gives us a place to rest the feet of the figure, so it's important to set that object in place before we begin posing Genesis. Before we do that though, it's crucial that we reset the camera by clicking on the designated button in the 3D Viewport.

The reason to do so is to have a stable reference point. At any time during the setting of the pose, we might need to change the position of the camera, which will break the correspondence of the image with the scene in the backdrop. If that happens, we can simply re-click on the **Camera: Reset (LMB | RMB)** button to find our starting point.

Once that is done, let's click on the surfboard and press the *U* key to activate the Universal tool. Our goal is to match the rotation of the surfboard in the reference image. We want to come pretty close to the original, but we don't need to spend too much time on this. Some of the adjustments can be done by hovering with the mouse over the rotate portion of the Universal tool. Once one of the rotate portions is highlighted, click-and-drag to rotate the object along that axis. Another way of applying rotations is by clicking on the + or – symbols in the **X Rotate**, **Y Rotate**, or **Z Rotate** parameters in the **Parameters** tab.

After a few adjustments, you should see something like this:

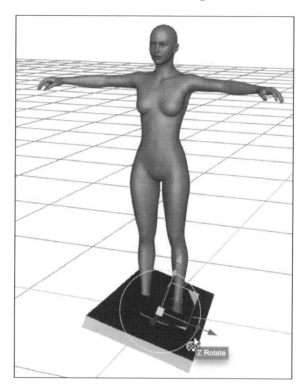

Setting the surfer pose

Now that the surfboard is set, we can work on the figure. First, let's rotate the whole body at an angle similar to the surfer in the reference image. To do this operation, we need to operate on the whole body. If we click on the hips, for example, and try to rotate that part, only that component will rotate. This is a great feature, but not what we need at this time. To operate on the whole body, we need to double-click on a body part. Once we do that, we will see the Universal tool gadget appear at the bottom of the figure. Let's click-and-drag on the green rotate tool, **Y Rotate**, until Genesis follows the reference.

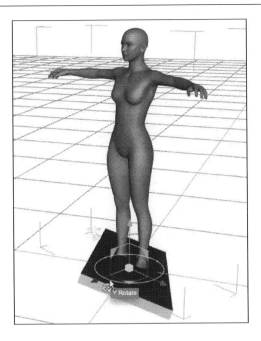

With the body at the right rotation, we need now to apply the right torsion to the abdomen and chest. Let's select the abdomen and slightly rotate it to the right.

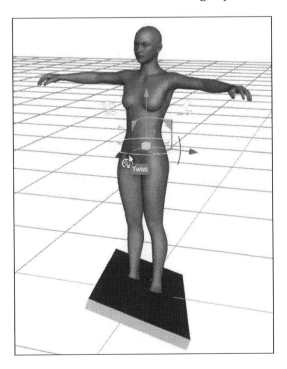

We also want to act on the **Bend** parameter, the one identified by the curve shown in the following image. We can think of it as "rotate the body part on the X axis."

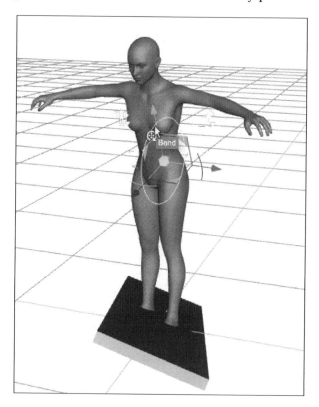

Now let's do the same for the abdomen2 and chest part. We need to apply all kinds of small rotations on different axes to get to the desired pose. This is a perfect time to experiment on your own and become familiar with the tools. It's perfectly OK to take some "artistic license" and create a pose that is slightly different from the reference.

Bodies without limits

You might find that while trying to rotate some body parts, the movement doesn't continue after a given point. The reason is that Studio applies some limits to the movement of the body parts. To be more precise, the figure has been configured to limit the movement of the body parts beyond a point that is considered natural. I think that the basic Genesis has limits that are too low, but this is not an issue as we can easily bypass the limits for any body part by clicking on the gear icon for the parameter involved. For example, if we want to twist the chest part beyond its set limits, we need to perform the following steps:

1. Select the chest part by single-clicking on it in the 3D Viewport.

2. In the **Parameters** tab, locate the **Twist** parameter.

3. Click on the gear icon for the parameter, and a pop-up menu appears.

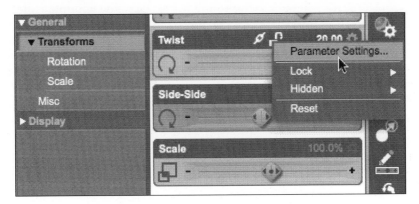

4. From the pop-up menu, select **Parameter Settings...**. A window appears.

5. From this window, uncheck the **Use Limits** checkbox and click on **Accept**.

Now we can move the chest part as much as we want, but watch out for unnatural torsion and weird folds in the skin.

To finish, position the torso and keep in mind that we have several parts that we can work with. Starting with the hip and moving up we have the abdomen, abdomen2, the chest, and the left and right collars. All these parts are movable on the three axes.

To help me assess the original pose, I usually move the figure on the side so that it doesn't obscure the reference image. At any time we can reset the camera as we saw before. To obtain the best results, remember to work on the rotation parameters instead of trying to move the body parts. If the Universal tool is too "rich", you can also try to use the Rotate tool instead. I like the Universal tool because it provides all the operations in a useful widget without the need to switch continuously between the Translate, Rotate, and Scale tools. This is just my personal preference, there are no rules. Use whatever is most convenient for you.

Avoiding common mistakes

Creating a convincing pose is a matter of caring for small details. It is a painstaking job of making subtle adjustments. One way of identifying those adjustments is to use a human reference and study each element of the body accurately. Taking photos of ourselves with a camera phone can be a great way of obtaining references for natural poses.

Keep a level head

There are some common pitfalls that can make our pose to look unnatural. The position of the head is one of those. If we take a look at photos of people involved in activities such as surfing, we can see that we humans try to level our head as much as possible. The head just doesn't stick out from the shoulders in a perpendicular fashion. To illustrate this point, let me show you an image of the model with the chest positioned almost at the right angle, but with the head unchanged from the default position.

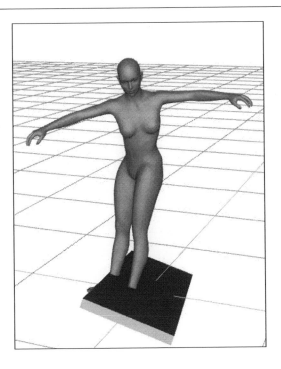

There is an unnatural stiffness to that head. Just a little bit of rotation and side-to-side bend makes the pose look much more natural. Here is the difference:

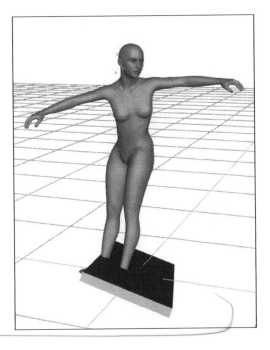

This looks much more natural even with the "dead gaze" typical of the default configuration.

The **Head** and **Neck** parameters are often very useful, and it can be easier just to work directly with those instead of trying to move the body part directly. Here is a screenshot of the parameters used to position the head in the preceding image:

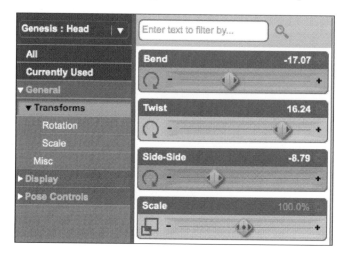

Bend moves the chin up and down, **Twist** rotates the head along the vertical axis, and **Side-Side** moves the head toward one shoulder or the other.

The neck has similar adjustments. Keep in mind that it's important to distribute the movement of the head between the neck and the head body parts in order to make the movement look natural.

Posing the lower part of the body

Once the torso is positioned correctly, it's time to tackle the toughest part of the task: the lower limbs.

Positioning the legs

To start with, we need to bend the thighs quite a bit. Let's start with the left thigh. We select it directly in the 3D Viewport, and then rotate it by acting on the **Bend** parameter. Next, we need to click on the Left Shin part and act on the **Bend** parameter as well. We repeat the operation for the right leg. At this point, it's best to not spend too much time trying to match the original pose perfectly; we just need to get an approximation of the pose. Let's check where we are at this point.

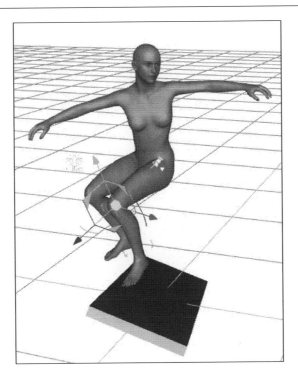

We are getting closer, but the surfboard is now in the wrong position. Let's click on it and use the Universal tool to move it under the figure's feet. Moving the camera around can help to verify that the position is correct.

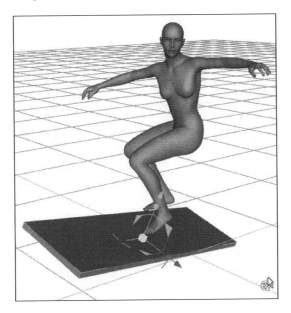

Positioning the legs with Inverse Kinematics

The reason why we didn't spend too much time in positioning the legs is because there's a very effective way of doing that, and it's called **Inverse Kinematics (IK)**.

IK is a technique that moves a series of joints based on the movement of the element at the end of the limb. For example, if we move the foot while IK is activated, the shin and thigh will automatically move to follow the position of the foot. IK is generally active when we load Genesis, but it can be turned off for those situations where it could potentially interfere with fine adjustments of the feet. We can verify that IK is turned on by navigating to **Edit | Figure | Inverse Kinematics**.

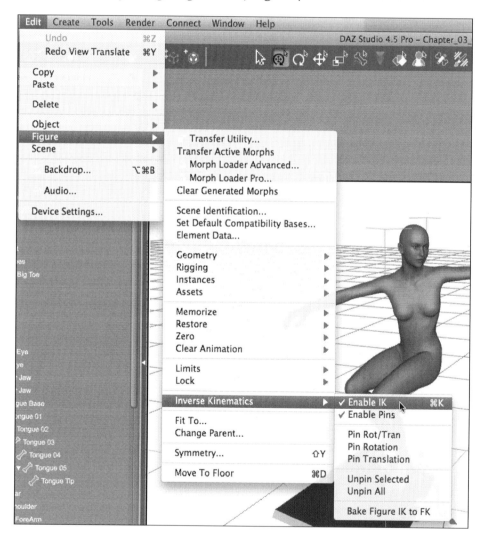

With IK enabled, we can now drag the left foot into position so that it touches the surfboard. The leg will follow. To do this, it's best to click on the left foot and then use the **Camera: Frame** tool. This action will zoom the camera close to the foot, a bit too close for what we need to do, so we need to use the mouse wheel (or trackpad) to zoom out a little bit, just enough that the leg is visible. Now we need to click on the foot, hold the click, and then drag the foot to get in the right position, in contact with the surfboard. The leg will automatically follow and adapt to have a very natural pose. The Bend angle of the foot might need to be adjusted a bit. For that operation, the easiest approach is to use the **Parameters** tab.

Once the left leg is done, we can proceed to the right one noting that the foot needs to be positioned further down, toward the tail of the board. The procedure is the same though and the adjustment should be done in a few minutes. Using the board as an alignment plane, we can position the feet at the right height and incline it, so that they seem to touch and rest on the board. If we try to move a foot further below the surface of the board, we can see that there is no problem in penetrating the object. Unlike objects in real life, 3D objects have no law of physics that prevents them from intersecting each other. For this reason, it's important that we work very carefully and make the feet rest on the surface of the board, but not much below. As we work with bare feet, in this case, we need to convey the illusion of them being slightly flattened by the weight of the figure. To do this operation, we need to push the feet just barely below the surface of the board. Not enough to suggest the intersection, but also careful that the figure doesn't seem to be hovering above the surface of the board.

Finishing touches

It's now time to focus on the small details that define a natural-looking pose. We are going to look at both posing and expression.

Arms and fingers

Looking at the arms of the base image we can see that the left one is pushed back quite a bit, as a way of creating counter balance. These are important clues that help in delivering a believable pose. To achieve that position, we need to select the body part called **Left Collar** and adjust the **Front-Back** parameter until the arm is in position. As it happened before, the limits applied to this joint are too low to express a realistic range, so we need to disable them before we can turn the left collar to the desired point.

The hands are bent slightly up and the left fingers are very straight. Those adjustments are all easy to do by using the Universal tool with its rotate widgets.

The final result should be something like this:

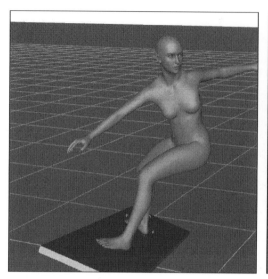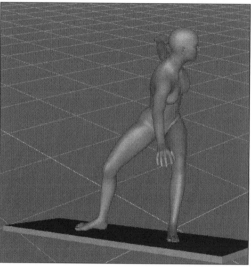

Removing the "gaze of death"

All the 3D figures that we add to a scene come with that dead stare that screams "fake" at the viewer of our image. Here is a clear example:

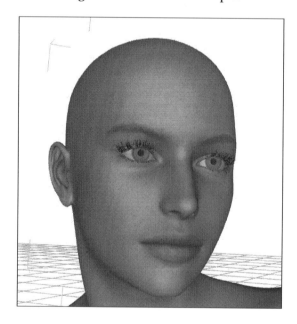

The reason why that stare looks so artificial is that the eyes are oriented to be perfectly parallel. If we were able to extend the pupils forward, they would draw two perfectly parallel beams. Human eyes always converge a bit, even when we stare at something. It takes very little to improve any Studio figure, even if we don't create a full facial expression. Follow these easy steps to inject a bit of life into Genesis:

1. Click on the head.
2. Use the **Camera: Frame** tool to zoom in close to the head, so that the eyes are clearly visible.
3. Click on the left eye and press *V* to activate the Node Selection tool. This tool is almost invisible on screen, so it allows us to have a clear view of the eyes.
4. To orient the eye, we are going to use a new approach and introduce the Pose tool, which is that globe we can find at the top-left of the 3D Viewport.

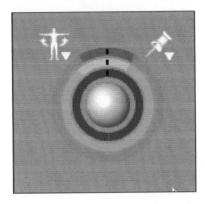

5. The sphere at the center of the tool acts like a trackball. Whatever rotation you apply to it is reflected on the selected object or body part.
6. Rotate the eye a little bit to the right-hand side of the screen.
7. Click on the right eye.
8. Rotate the eye a little bit to the right-hand side. Check the resulting look and make slight adjustments, until the eyes appear like they are both observing the same object at a distance.

Let's see the difference:

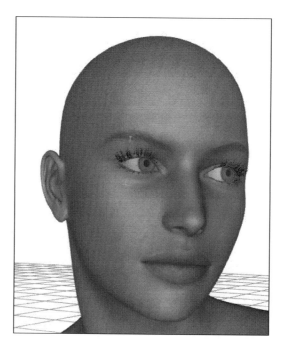

It takes a little more work to create a believable expression, but at least now we have removed that lifeless stare and it took just a few seconds.

Saving the pose

After all this hard work, it would be great if we can save this pose so that we can re-use it in the future. We might even start thinking about making poses for commercial use, so saving them into files is definitely something that we want to be able to do.

This is very easy, so you can immediately relax. All that we need to do is select the Genesis figure and then navigate to **File | Save As... | Pose Preset**.

When we do that, the standard **Save** window shows up. In there, we need to enter the name of the file that we want to use for our pose. I selected `Chapter3_SurferPose.duf`. Once that operation is done, Studio shows us the window where we can select some other options for the way we want to save the pose.

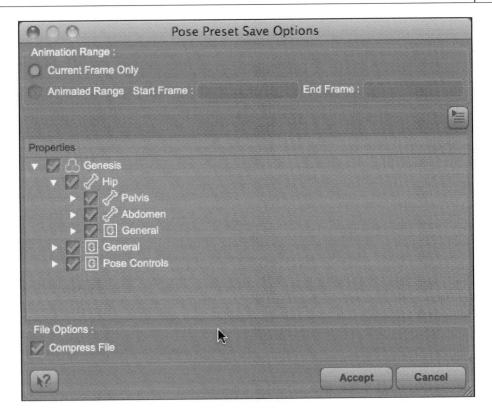

For now we can simply click on the **Accept** button.

To test the pose file, let's create a new empty scene and add the Basic Female figure to it. To use a custom pose file that is not part of the content manager, we need to navigate to **File | Merge** and select the file that is saved with our pose, in my case, it's Chapter3_SurferPose.duf. Immediately, Genesis should appear in the surfboard-riding pose that we have crafted so carefully.

Summary

In this chapter we have seen valuable methods for creating believable poses. By using photo references, we removed the guesswork and the stress caused by trying to imagine the right pose for a scene. After we use this approach a few times, we can gain great practice that, in time, will make the task of posing a figure enjoyable and effective.

In the next chapter, we are going to explore the power of morphs for creating not just variations of a character, but complete new figures.

4
Creating New Characters with Morphs

A **morph** is a modification of a geometric model that alters its original shape. Using morphs, we can change any character into something completely different. Studio makes this operation as simple as moving sliders on the screen.

In this chapter we will have a look at the following topics:

- Applying morphs
- Mixing morphs to create new characters
- Saving morph presets for future use

Understanding morphs

The word *morph* comes from *metamorphosis*, which means *a change of the form or nature of a thing or person into a completely different one*. Good old Franz Kafka had a field day with metamorphosis when he imagined poor Gregor Samsa waking up and finding himself changed into a giant cockroach.

This concept applies to 3D modeling very well. As we are dealing with polygons, which are defined by groups of vertices, it's very easy to morph one shape into something different. All that we need to do is to move those vertices around, and the polygons will stretch and squeeze accordingly.

To get a better visualization about this process, let's bring the Basic Female figure to the scene and show it with the wireframe turned on. To do so, after you have added the Basic Female figure, click on the **DrawStyle** widget on the top-right portion of the 3D Viewport.

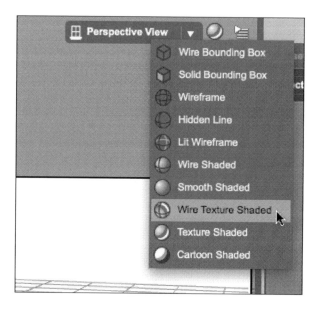

From that menu, select **Wire Texture Shaded**. This operation changes how Studio draws the objects in the scene during preview. It doesn't change anything else about the scene. In fact, if you try to render the image at this point, the wireframe will not show up in the render. The wireframe is a great help in working with objects because it gives us a visual representation of the structure of a model. The type of wireframe that I selected in this case is superimposed to the normal texture used with the figure. This is not the only visualization mode available. Feel free to experiment with all the options in the **DrawStyle** menu, most of them have their use. The most useful, in my opinion, are the **Hidden Line**, **Lit Wireframe**, **Wire Shaded**, and **Wire Texture Shaded** options. Try the **Wire Shaded** option as well. It shows the wireframe with a solid gray color. This is, again, just for display purposes. It doesn't remove the texture from the figure. In fact, you can switch back to **Texture Shaded** to see Genesis fully textured.

Switching the view to use the simple wireframe or the shaded wireframe is a great way of speeding up your workflow. When Studio doesn't have to render the textures, the Viewport becomes more responsive and all operations take less time. If you have a slow computer, using the wireframe mode is a good way of getting a faster response time.

Here are the **Wire Texture Shaded** and **Wire Shaded** styles side by side:

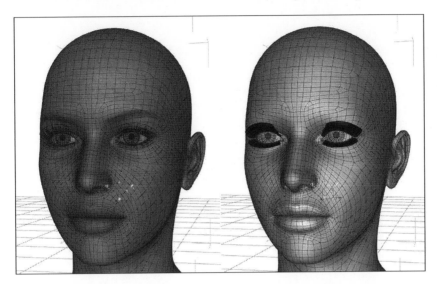

Now that we have the wireframe visible, the concept of morphing should be simpler to understand. If we pick any vertex in the geometry and we move it somewhere, the geometry is still the same, same number of polygons and same number of vertices, but the shape has shifted. Here is a practical example that shows Genesis loaded in Blender.

Blender is a free, fully featured, 3D modeling program. It has extremely advanced features that compete with commercial programs sold for thousands of dollars per license. You can find more information about Blender at http://www.blender.org. Be aware that Blender is a very advanced program with a rather difficult UI.

In this image, I have selected a single polygon and pulled it away from the face:

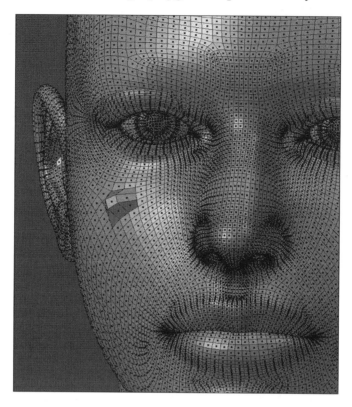

In a similar way we can use programs such as modo or ZBrush to modify the basic geometry and come up with all kinds of different shapes. For example, there are people who are specialized in reproducing the faces of celebrities as morph for DAZ V4 or Genesis.

What is important to understand about morphs is that they cannot add or remove any portion of the geometry. A morph only moves things around, sometimes to extreme degrees.

Morphs for Genesis or Gen4 figures can be purchased from several websites specialized in selling content for Poser and DAZ Studio. In particular, Genesis makes it very easy to apply morphs and even to mix them together.

Combining premade morphs to create new faces

The standard installation of Genesis provides some interesting ways of changing its shape. Let's start a new Studio scene and add our old friend, the Basic Female figure.

Once Genesis is in the scene, double-click on it to select it. Now let's take a look at a new tool, the **Shaping** tab. It should be visible in the right-hand side pane. Click on the **Shaping** tab; it should show a list of shapes available. The list should be something like this:

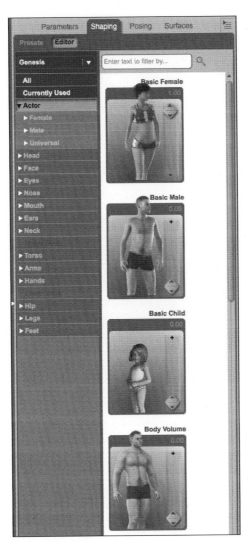

As we can see, the **Basic Female** shape is unsurprisingly dialed all the way to the top. The value of each slider goes from zero, no influence, to one, full influence of the morph. Morphs are not exclusive so, for example, you can add a bit of **Body Builder** (scroll the list to the bottom if you don't see it) to be used in conjunction with the Basic Female morph. This will give us a muscular woman. This exercise is also giving us an insight about the Basic Female figure that we have used up to this time. The figure is basically the raw Genesis figure with the Basic Female morph applied as a preset.

If we continue exploring the **Shaping Editor**, we can see that the various shapes are grouped by major body section. We have morphs for the shape of the head, the components of the face, the nose, eyes, mouth, and so on.

Let's click on the head of Genesis and use the **Camera: Frame** tool to frame the head in the view. Move the camera a bit so that the face is visible frontally. We will apply a few morphs to the head to see how it can be transformed. Here is the starting point:

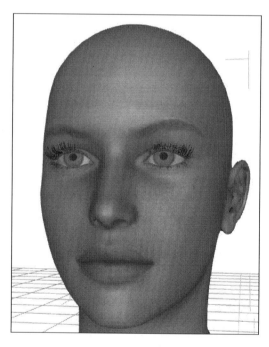

Now let's click on the **Head** category in the **Shaping** tab. In there we can see a slider labeled **Alien Humanoid**. Move the slider until it gets to **0.83**.

The difference is dramatic.

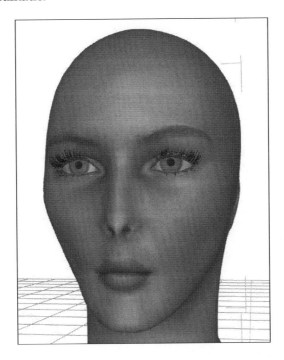

Now let's click on the **Eyes** category. In there we find two values: **Eyes Height** and **Eyes Width**. To create an out-of-this-world creature, we need to break the rules of proportions a little bit, and that means to remove the limits for a couple of parameters. As described in *Chapter 3, Posing Figures*, click on the gear button for the **Eyes Height** parameter and uncheck the **Use Limits** checkbox. Confirm by clicking on the **Accept** button. Once this is done, dial a value of **1.78** for the eyes height. The eyes should move dramatically up, toward the eyebrow.

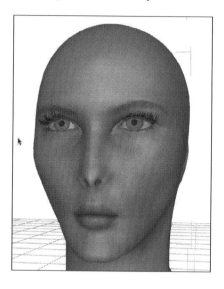

Lastly, let's change the neck; it's much too thick for an alien. Also, in this case, we will need to disable the use of limits. Click on the **Neck** category and disable the limits for the **Neck Size** parameter. Once that is done, set the neck size to -1.74. Here is the result, side by side, of the transformation.

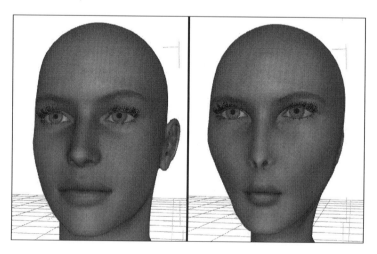

This is quite a dramatic change for something that is done with just dials, without using a 3D modeling program. It gets even better, as we will see shortly.

Saving your morphs

If you want to save a morph to re-use it later, you can navigate to **File | Save As | Shaping Preset...**. To re-use a saved morph, simply select the target figure and navigate to **File | Merge...** to load the previously saved preset/morph.

> Why is Studio using the rather confusing term **Merge** for loading its own files? Nobody knows for sure; it's one of those weird decisions that DAZ's developers made long ago and never changed. You can merge two different Studio scenes, but it is rather confusing to think of loading a morph or a pose preset as a scene merge. Try to mentally replace **File | Merge** with **File | Load**. This is the meaning of that menu option.

Character creation with morphs

Hard to believe that the "cutie" shown in the following image is our old friend the Basic Female, but it really is the same figure. I created that lovely character using an additional product called **Genesis Creature Creator Heads**, which is sold at `http://www.daz3d.com/shop/genesis-creature-creator-heads`.

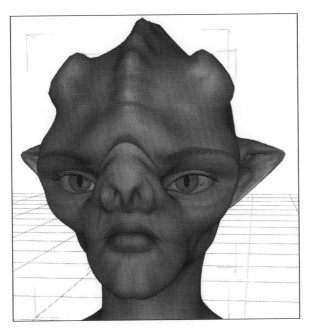

Once that product is installed, Studio will provide a plethora of head morphs that can be dialed to create a vast set of unique characters. In the following steps, I will show you how easy it is to obtain the preceding figure.

Inside the monster factory

As usual, let's start with a new scene (**File | New**) and add the Basic Female figure. Click on the head to select it, and then click on the **Camera: Frame** tool to frame the head fully inside the frame. If you have the Genesis Creature Creator Heads product installed, you will then be able to see a series of interesting morphs in the **Shaping** tab. Look in the **Editor** subtab and inside the **Head** category.

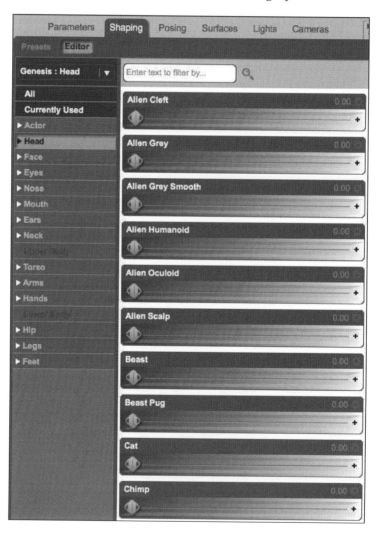

The list goes on and on. All those variations can be mixed together. Remember that you can click on the value of a slider to enter its value directly via keyboard. This is one of those times where this feature is much more useful than trying to move a slider with the mouse.

1. While in the **Head** category, dial **Alien Grey** to **0.12**.

2. Set the slider of **Alien Oculoid** at **0.33**.

    This is already shaping the head in a radical way.

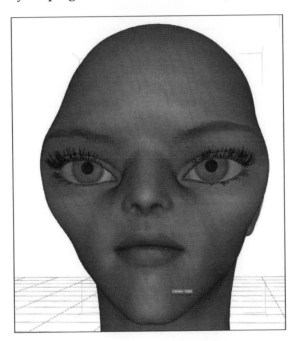

3. To regain some volume for the cranium, set the slider of **Alien Scalp** at **0.22**.

4. Set the slider of **Beast** at **0.36**.

5. Set the slider of **Beast Pug** at **0.20**.

6. Set the slider of **Demon** at **0.69**.

7. Set the slider of **Frankenstein** at **0.24**.

8. Remove the limits for **Horns Front High** and set the slider value at **2.15**.

Here is how the morph dials should look at this stage:

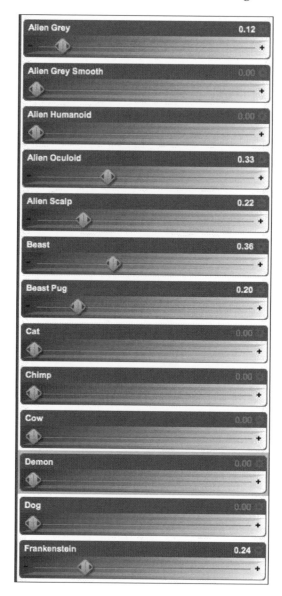

9. Set **Scalp Crest** to **0.96**.

10. If you rotate the camera to look at the figure, you see that the nose looks quite flat. Click on the **Nose** category and look for the parameter called **Nose Size**. Disable the limits for it and set the value to **2.69**.

11. Monsters don't have long eyelashes, so we need to fix that. Click on the **Eyes** category and look for the eyelashes values. If you look at the top of the list of values, there is an input field labeled **Enter text to filter by...**. This field can be used to restrict the list of values shown. Enter the text lashes to show only the values that have that string in their name.

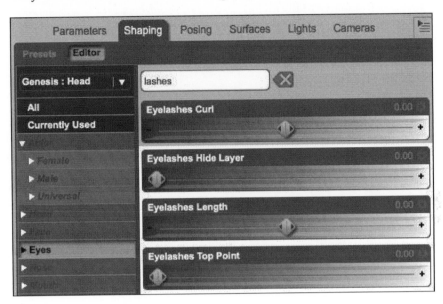

12. Set the slider of **Eyelashes Curl** at **-1**.

13. Set the slider of **Eyelashes Hide Layer** at **1**.

14. Set the slider of **Eyelashes Length** at **-1**.

15. In the filter field, remove the lashes string and enter pupil to show all the values with that word in their name.

16. Find the **Pupil Slit** value, disable the limits for it, and set it to **1.73** to give the character a cat eye.

17. Change the filter to show the **Iris** values and set the **Iris Size** to **-0.5**.

18. Clear the filter by clicking on the red arrow with the X in the middle.

19. Click on the **Mouth** category.

20. Find the **Mouth Height** parameter and set it to **-0.6**.

Admire your creation; it should be the same as the one shown at the beginning of this section. The only issue is the vaguely unsettling effect of seeing lipstick on a monster. This is the result of using the original texture for the Basic Female figure. Let's not worry about this problem just yet. We will need to get familiar with materials and the **Surfaces** tab to change the lip material to something more suitable. We will see how to master materials in *Chapter 8, Building a Full Scene*. This chapter is all about modifying shapes, and we have seen how far you can go by simply entering some values in the appropriate fields.

Summary

What can be done with good morphs is quite astounding. We can take an everyday figure and turn it into something really different. Using the same workflow, we can create human characters that are different from the basic figures provided by Studio. By purchasing special morphs, we can also create a large variety of characters with one single basic figure. For example, there are ethnic morphs available that cover a lot of different races, which can be wonderful for adding variety to your scenes.

What we have seen in this chapter is all about the substance of the scene, its content. In the next chapter, we will see how to obtain a finished image from our scene, so that we can create illustrations that can be freely distributed to other people. That is the role of **rendering**.

5
Rendering

When we work with a 3D program, any 3D program, we can see and manipulate the geometry in real time. In other words, we can move, rotate, scale and do a lot of other operations on the geometric objects right on the screen, and the software responds to our actions immediately. What we see on the screen though is an approximation of the final image. This is because it would take too long to draw all the objects in the scenes and to calculate the effects of lights and materials. In fact, creating a faithful representation of the final image can take several minutes or even a few hours, depending on the complexity of the scene and the hardware available.

The creation of an accurate image that takes into account all the geometric transformations, all the lights, and all the materials is called **rendering the scene**.

In this chapter you will learn the following topics:

- Rendering an image to a file on disk
- Selecting a graphic format for your image
- Adjusting the rendering settings
- Creating multiple cameras
- Lighting up a scene
- The fundamentals of framing

Gearing up for rendering

If we consider DAZ Studio to be a virtual photographer's studio, rendering is equivalent to taking a photograph with a camera. All the placing of the objects in the scene, the addition of props, wardrobe, hair, and so on is the equivalent of posing the models in the studio, having make-up artists, and fashion stylists prepare human models for the photo-shoot. Rendering, in other words, is the culmination of our work in Studio. The rendered image is what we aimed to obtain when we started working on our scene.

Framing the scene

There are several factors that affect the final image; it's not just a matter of pressing a button and obtaining a JPEG file. One of the most important factors that we need to pay attention to is the frame. Framing affects the mood of the scene. When we put a frame around a scene, we exclude everything that is outside the frame. Framing is the first form of editing of the photographer and visual artist. For example, here are three frames of a sample scene that I prepared for this chapter. You can find the scene in the file `Scene_01.duf` in the `Chapter_05` folder of the projects files.

The first frame shows the scene slightly from above. The subject looks small and the environment has a predominant effect. Please don't pay attention to the flat, boring lighting; it is intentional as we are focusing on framing. I didn't want to influence the image with elements that could distract from the subject at hand, which is framing the shot.

The second image emphasizes the idea even more by using a wide angle lens, this time with a low angle. The cavernous nature of the space is definitely imposing, which gives an idea of danger, even without dramatic lighting.

The last image is a close-up. The mood is completely different. This time the emphasis is on the "heroine", the scene is more human, and the slight low angle of the camera suggests dynamic tension (say it like Dr. Frank-N-Furter). We can anticipate the figure jumping out of that position in a blink of an eye. The frame cuts out most of the environment, so the viewer cannot see what happens around the figure or what she is looking at.

These are three completely different images from exactly the same scene. Nothing has been moved, rotated, or changed in any way. The only thing that is different between those images is the position of the camera and the focal length of the lens.

Choosing the camera

Before we can work on setting the frame, we need to select a camera and a type of lens. Studio provides, by default, a view on the scene called **Perspective View**. This view is not a camera. While you can technically render an image from **Perspective View**, this action should be avoided. This is because **Perspective View** is not a real camera; therefore, it cannot set the resolution of the image to be rendered and it doesn't provide any control on the lens used in the view. You can see what camera is used at any time by checking the top-right of the 3D Viewport.

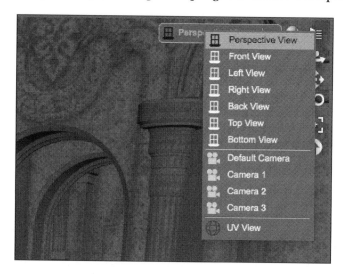

Often people start positioning the frame assuming that they are using a real camera, just to discover later that they were using **Perspective View**; so, all that work needs to be redone with a proper camera.

The easiest way to avoid this situation is to enable the creation of a default camera whenever a new scene is created. To do so, call Studio **Preferences** (the *F2* key), and from there, click on the **Scene** tab. From that tab, enable the **Create a "Default Camera"** option.

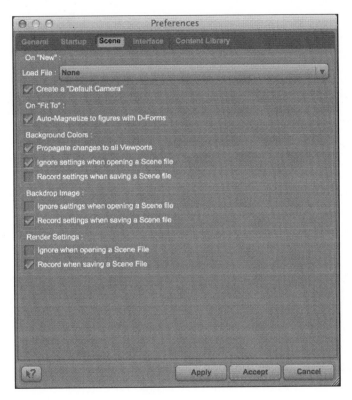

Another way of creating a camera is to navigate to **Create | New camera** or its shortcut in the toolbar.

 You can have as many cameras as you want in a scene and use them to switch to any point of view at any time. Each camera remembers its own position until you change it.

Once you have a real camera to frame the shot, select it as the active camera. Also, make sure that the **Show Aspect Frame** option is active in the Viewport options. Refer to the following screenshot for reference:

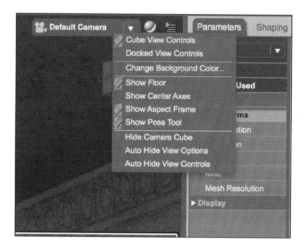

The Render Settings menu

Studio can render an image in several formats and at any resolution that you need. To determine those choices, we need to access the **Rendering Settings** panel. This is done by navigating to **Render | Render Settings**. We can also use the *Cmd + Shift + R* (Mac) or *Ctrl + Shift + R* (Windows) keyboard shortcut. Either way, the result will be presented with the **Render Settings** panel, which looks like this:

Your settings will very likely be different. Let's see what all those values mean.

The first slider at the top-left controls the quality of the final image, from 1 (worst) to 4 (best). Why would we like to degrade the quality of our image? As higher quality rendering takes more time, we can save some seconds by using the lower quality settings. This is in theory. In practice, the lower quality settings are so horrible to be useless. Stay at the highest quality; even in that way we need to work quite a bit to make the images look good.

Next is the **Shader:** field value under **Render Style:**. This comes with two choices: realistic or cartoon rendering.

The section titled **Dimensions** is one of the most important as it determines the resolution and aspect ratio of the frame.

The resolution of an image, expressed as the number of pixels in the width and height direction, determines four things:

- The size of the image file
- The size of the image on screen or print
- The level of detail of the image
- The aspect ratio of the image

Of all these, the aspect ratio is often overlooked and it's quite important. There are several situations in which you need to be mindful of the aspect ratio or your image will not fit with others. For example, High Definition TV has a ratio of 16:9 (pronounced sixteen by nine). If you need to create an image that needs to be intercut in a HD video, you must create that image at one of the two 16:9 resolutions supported by HDTV: either 1280 x 720 or 1920 x 1080. If you want to create a banner for web advertisement, you need to know the dimensions upfront or your banner will not fit the page. Typical banner dimensions are 728 x 90.

For all our images, we will typically use the lower resolution HD dimension of 1280 x 720. This is a good cinematic frame and the resolution is not too high, so the rendering times will be quite short.

Make sure that the **Constrain Proportions** checkbox is unchecked before you start typing the new dimensions. Enter 1280 for the width and 720 for height.

As soon as we enter the dimensions of the frame, Studio updates the Viewport. The frame border shows us exactly the limits of what the camera sees, which allows us to frame the shot exactly. From this point, we can enable the **Constrain Proportions** checkbox, so that we can increase or decrease one dimension and Studio will automatically calculate the other dimensions, resulting in a new frame with the exactly same aspect ratio. In the following screenshot, we can see the camera frame border, or mask, being highlighted by Studio. Notice that everything outside the frame is darkened to show the portion of the scene that will not be included in the rendered image. Notice also that the drop-down menu that lists all the frame size presets turns to **Custom**. If we want, we can save this preset by clicking on the button labeled **Save Preset...**. When we press that, Studio asks us for a name for the preset. We can use HD 720. In HD TV the dimensions are expressed based on the vertical resolution.

Selecting the image format

When we render an image, we can select a file format for it. After all, there are several graphics formats available, so which one should we select for the storage of our image? Studio supports four file formats: PNG, JPEG, TIFF, and BMP. BMP should never be used. It's a legacy format that is mostly supported only on Windows. It is not a web standard and its files can be larger than other, more modern, formats. TIFF is nice, but its features are wasted for the task of rendering, unless we need to target a post-processing app that prefers TIFF. TIFF supports a lot of features, such as multiple resolution images, but most of the time we don't need those features and the resulting images tend to be a lot larger than JPEG or PNG. TIFF is an open standard, but it's not a web standard so it cannot be displayed in a web browser. So, we are basically left with JPEG and PNG. JPEG uses a lossy data compression and doesn't support the alpha channel. The compression issue means that every time you save a JPEG file, you lose a bit of color definition. In other words, this means that when you save an image using JPEG, it has already lost some color information.

If we edit the image in a graphic editor, such as Photoshop, every time we edit and save a JPEG file we lose some definition; it degrades more and more. JPEG has the advantage of requiring less disk space for its images, but it should be used only as a final delivery format and not for something that needs editing.

The alpha channel is the support for transparency. As JPEG doesn't have an alpha channel, we cannot render our images without background and then replace the background in Photoshop. So, it comes down to PNG. PNG (pronounced ping) is an open standard, a web standard, it's multiplatform, well supported by a myriad of applications. It compresses well without losing information, and it supports 256 levels of transparency. PNG files can be, sometimes, slightly larger than JPEGs, but storage is very cheap nowadays and all the other factors weight more than this little issue. If we really need to deliver the final work in a smaller file, we can always convert the final PNG file, after all the edits, to JPEG.

So, from now on we will set all the renders to the PNG format.

The bottom of the render setting panel is dedicated to the selection of the file format, and to what is done by Studio when the render command is executed.

First, we can decide if we want to generate a single image, a series of images, or a movie. The series of images is generally the option used when creating an animation. Contrary to the common belief, animators don't create video clips for animations. Instead, they generate a single file for each frame. There are 24 frames per second in a standard movie, so, for example, if we create a five-minute sequence, we end up with 7200 single files. While this might seem like a file management nightmare, it is how animations are done normally and is much simpler to manage than it first seems. We will see later why selecting a movie is almost always a bad choice for rendering animations; for now, we stay with the **Still Image (Current Frame)** choice.

The next choice is a represented by two radio buttons (mutually exclusive choices) that select if the render will appear in a new window or if it will be directly saved to disk. It's always nice to see what happens with our renders, so the **New Window** choice is what I suggest to use. From the window that shows the render, you always have the opportunity to save the image to disk, so it's a win-win solution.

The final fields are about selecting a name for the image and a location. The name is whatever you prefer. Note that to the right of the name there is a drop-down menu that selects the format for the file. Of course, we set that to PNG. So, if we set the name of the file to be `MyFile`, Studio will save the render to a file named `MyFile.png`.

Lastly, we have the destination for the render. Studio provides two choices here. One is Library and the other is a folder of our choice. The Library option is basically a way for Studio to save the renders into a predetermined folder. For example, on Mac OS, it's `/Users/<user name>/Documents/DAZ 3D/Studio/Render Library`. I find it much simpler and more flexible to set up my own location, so let's click on that drop-down menu and select **Folder** instead. Once this option is selected, a button with three dots is shown to the right of the folder path. We can click on that button to select the destination folder where our renders will be saved.

That's all that there is to set **Render Settings**. There are many more options available in the **Advanced** tab, but those are rather esoteric and not necessary for every day use of the render functionality.

We can now close the render panel by clicking on the small x at the top-right of the window. Our choices will be remembered and will affect every render that we will start from this point on.

Rendering

I have prepared a sample scene to show how to render images in Studio. From the project files, you can load the file named `Scene_03.duf` in the `Chapter_05` folder.

In that scene we have a real camera that we can use to frame our scene, so let's make sure that it is selected. In the top-right of the 3D Viewport, you can see the name of the active camera. If **Perspective View** is selected, click on that drop-down list and select **Default Camera**.

The camera switches to its own frame, which should be like this:

Let's render this by pressing *Cmd* + *R* (Mac) or *Ctrl* + *R* (Windows). A new window will pop up and the render will start appearing gradually. The result should be something like this:

This is a terrible render! Everything is lit evenly, everything is visible at the same time, and there are no shadows. This is just horrible, flat, uninspiring... and totally expected. Do you remember the old movie cliché: "Lights, Camera, Action!"? Well, we got the camera, but we didn't add any lights. Without light there is no image. For this reason Studio "floods" the scene with even light whenever we render without lights in the scene. You can see from the highlights in the sleeves where the light is positioned, just above the camera.

So it's time to start playing with lights. If you haven't done any lighting work with photo cameras before, this task might look pretty intimidating. It is. Lighting is the foundation of artistic photography. The great Italian cinematographer Antonio Storaro is fond of saying that he "paints with light". That phrase represents well what we need to do. Lighting is not about illuminating a scene, it is about expressing our own artistic sensibility.

I cannot teach you everything about lighting in this book, the subject can easily fill a book or two on its own. What we can see is a series of simple techniques to help make some scenes a bit more interesting.

The art of lighting

The role of light in art is not to make objects visible. It might seem like it is, but it is a mistake to think so. The role of light is to create shadows. Shadows are so important that in some expressionist movies of the 1920s, the director had the set lit with flat, diffuse light that didn't create shadows, and then had the shadows painted by hand. Look at movies like the old horror classics, Frankenstein (with Boris Karloff), Dracula (with Bela Lugosi), and others. The images, the mood of those movies are defined by their long, sharp shadows.

The first light that you place in the scene should be defined by what shadow it will make. Ask yourself, "Where do I want the shadows to go?", and then place the light in a way that will create the shadows that you want. This light is called the "key light". To help you understand light positioning, you can use a flashlight and objects in the room or even just your hands.

Let's start by adding a spotlight to project shadows on the face and on the wall to the left of the character. Click on the toolbar icon that represents a spotlight.

Alternatively, you can navigate to **Create | New Spotlight...**. Regardless of the method used to create the light, Studio will show a window in which we can set the name of the new light. Let's call it **Key**. Studio will add a new light in the scene at position 0, 0, 0. From there we need to position it in a way that makes sense for our scene. We could use the Universal tool to do so, but I find that one of the easiest ways of positioning a light is to use it as a camera and aim it in that way. This is one of the greatest features of Studio. You can look at the scene not only through a real camera, but also through any of the lights. The view can look a bit skewed, but that is because a light acts very differently from a camera. Nevertheless, this is a great technique. From the camera selection drop-down list, select **Key**; the image will change immediately to show the **point of view (POV)** of light.

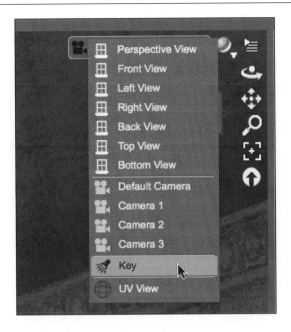

Using the standard camera controls, position the light so that this is what you can see through it:

Notice the outline of the spotlight and use that as a reference. Don't worry if your frame is not exactly the same; just make it as close as possible.

Now switch back to **Default Camera** and press *Cmd + R* (Mac) or *Ctrl + R* (Windows) to render the image.

This is a bit better, but where is the shadow that we wanted? There is a bit of shading on the right-hand side of the face, but it's not very realistic and there is no shadow on the wall. This is because unlike what happens in real life, lights in Studio can turn off the projection of shadows. This is completely artificial and not something to use willy-nilly, but it has its reason to be in the fact that calculating shadows is a slow process and so, Studio gives us the chance to disable it. Don't get used to this. Lights in real-life projects shadows, always. If we don't want to see a shadow, we better reposition the light, reframe the shot, or work on other strategies to make the light work.

So, let's turn on the shadows. In the **Parameters** tab, click on the drop-down menu at the top and select the light named **Key**. Click on the **Shadow** category and from the panel select **Deep Shadow Map**. Then set the slider of **Shadow Softness** at **22.0%**.

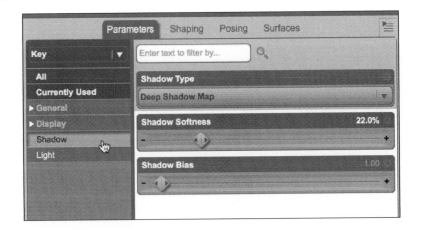

As we can see, there are two types of shadows that Studio can trace. One is Deep Shadow Map and the other is Raytraced. The Raytraced option draws shadows that are perfectly sharp. Their edges are as if they were drawn in black ink. This type of shadow can be useful, but most of the time, even with candles or small other light sources, the shadow has a certain level of softness. For this scene, I want the lights to feel like they were cast by candles or torches. So they have a bit of a soft edge. Not much, but just a bit blurry. That's why we dialed a 22 percent softness. Let's re-render and see the difference:

That's more like it! See the shadow projected by the arm to the inner right thigh? And that great, powerful shadow projected on the wall? That is what gives a sense of depth to a bidimensional image. It's still too stark, and half of the frame is lost in total darkness, but we are definitely getting somewhere.

Faking ambient light

If you look around, you will see that light bounces off objects and gets scattered around in the environment. That is the effect of **indirect light** or **ambient light**. The spotlight that we have in the scene has a very narrow field of action. There is no light bouncing off the wall and reaching the darker parts of the scene. This is because lights in Studio are not based on a realistic, physical model, but that's how most renderers behave.

> Studio renders its scenes through a software called 3Delight. DAZ licenses 3Delight from a company called DNA Research. 3Delight is integrated in Studio, but it is effectively a separate component. This introduces the concept of multiple renderers, where the same scene can be rendered through different renderers to achieve different looks. We will see how this works in *Chapter 10, Hyper-realism – the Reality Plugin*, when we will be talking about the Reality plugin and rendering through the physically-accurate LuxRender.

For this reason we need to fake the effect of ambient light. This is done with a distant light. Distant lights simulate lights with rays that are parallel, as if they are coming from the sun. Distant lights are not physically accurate, but they provide an easy way of having some global illumination in the scene. It's best to dial the intensity of the distant lights low so that they are not overpowering. For our scene, we need to get some of the details from the environment back, so that they don't disappear in complete darkness.

Let's add a new distant light by either navigating to **Create | New Distant Light…** or the toolbar shortcut. Hover the mouse over each light icon to find the one that we need. When Studio asks for the name of the light, enter Fill.

Once the light is in the scene, switch the camera to use that light and position it as shown in the following image:

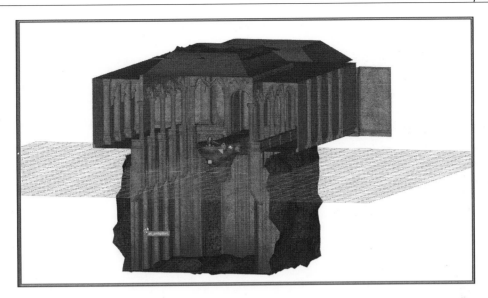

Again, don't worry too much about getting the position exactly as in the image; just do your best to approximate the position.

In the **Parameters** tab select **Fill light**, click on the **Light** category, and set the intensity to 18 percent. This gives us the feeling that there is some light bouncing around, but it doesn't create a visible source of light that can be distracting and unrealistic.

Switch back to **Default Camera** and do another render; it should look a bit like this:

Notice how a few parts of the image fall in to complete darkness, but we can still see part of the corridor walls. This is nice, but it lacks a bit of life and the left leg is almost completely in the dark. That is not good because the pose loses power by having the stretched leg invisible. Let's add a new spot to create an outline for that leg and make it stand out.

Add a spot to the scene and call it **BackLight**. In the **Parameters** tab select the **Light** and, in the **Light** category, set the spread angle to 30.10. A spotlight has a cone shape light. The spread angle determines how wide the cone is. When we want to focus the light in a narrow way, we can use the spread angle to restrict the spread of the light. Switch the camera to look through it, and position the spotlight to look at the scene in this way:

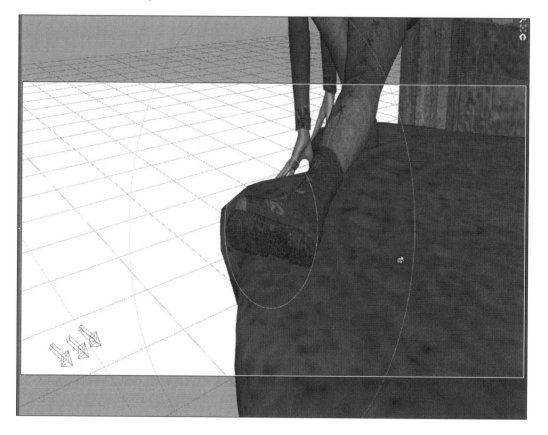

Enable the **Deep Shadow** shadows for this light and set **Shadow Softness** to **36%**.

Let's verify the effect of this by doing another render.

Now the boot is visible and we have a nice drop shadow projected to the platform. The image is getting better, but it lacks a bit of vitality. We can add a bit of sparkle by introducing a final spotlight, called a **kicker**. The kicker is a light used to create highlights or accentuate the silhouette of a figure. In this case, we are going to add a spotlight to the left of the frame, shining a bit on the figure.

Let's start by adding a new spot to the scene and naming it `Kicker`. Set the spread angle (in **Parameters** tab's **Light** category) to `23.61`, and position the light as shown in the following image:

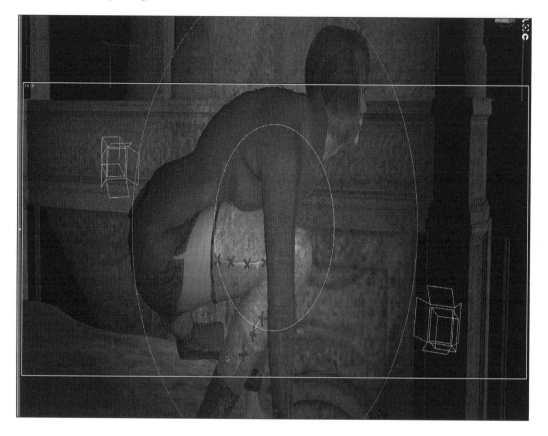

Switch back to **Default Camera** and render.

Now the image pops out more than before. The highlights on the right sleeve are great and the tip of the left boot is brighter, making it stand out more. You can save this image to the disk by clicking on the **Save** button in the render window. Make sure that you select a destination directory and a name for the file before you do so.

Replacing the background

From time to time, it might be useful to render a part of a scene in Studio and replace the background using an application such as Photoshop. This is similar to what VFX companies do for movies when they employ Green Screen (Chromakey) techniques. The advantage that we have in Studio is that we don't need to use any green color. Because we save out images using PNG, which has built-in support for the alpha channel, the background is automatically transparent. If we don't have any object in a portion of the scene, that part of the scene will be rendered transparent. That's all there is to it. You can then load the image in Photoshop and place any background image in another layer, and you're done. The important thing is to save the images to PNG. If you use JPEG, this technique will not work because JPEG doesn't have support for the alpha channel. Another reason to use PNG as our default image format is that you can always export to JPEG *after* you have replaced the background in Photoshop.

Summary

This chapter showed an important concept about lighting: interesting lighting is defined by the contrast of shadow and light. There are situations where it makes sense to flood the scene with lots of light but there is a difference between "lots of light" and "flat light". Light needs to match the mood of the story. In fact light can define the mood of the story for the viewer, but the mood is created first in the mind of the artist. The mood of the story is a combination of elements. The frame is one of them. Lighting is another.

While we talked about framing and lighting, we didn't address the strange, absurd quality of the materials in the scene presented. We don't quite know what type of fabric is used for the jacket. Why is it so shiny? It doesn't matter for now, what is important is that we now know how to set up lights and how to obtain a PNG file.

Compare the first image that we have rendered, the one with one single spotlight, with the last one and you'll see how much fun it is to "paint with light".

Following the guidelines in this chapter, you will be able to create your own lighting.

In the next chapter we will see how to expand our content library with products that are available from the leading content sellers in the market.

6

Finding and Installing New Content

While Studio comes bundled with some great figures, there is a vast market of available products that can be added to it. From science fiction sets to medieval castles, you can create the world of your dreams with inexpensive content available on the Web.

In this chapter we will see how to find additional products for Studio from the major websites that specialize in ready-to-use content.

Once a product has been purchased, you will need to install it and make it available to Studio. By the end of this chapter, you will be able to do the following:

- Finding great 3D models on the Web
- Installing content from all the major 3D sources
- Configuring Studio to use such content

Places to find more content

If you do a search for figures for DAZ Studio, you don't find a whole lot from Google. There is a simple reason for this, but we need to learn a bit of history. In 1995, Larry Weinberg created the first version of a program designed to pose human-like figures. That program was, of course, Poser. While of modest aspirations, Poser caught the attention of many aspiring artists who saw in the program a way of overcoming the difficulties of drawing human figures by hand.

Poser came with a set of built-in models, but the set was limited and soon the need for more models and more options started manifesting. In the years that followed, Poser became more and more sophisticated and a market of independent content providers was born. A large crowd of 3D artists started creating all kinds of additional content that could be used in Poser, such as clothing, objects, hair props, vehicles, buildings, and all the elements that somebody would likely employ in the creation of a new artwork.

Then people started experimenting with creating morphs of the Poser characters. During the expansion of the Poser market, a new company called **Digital Art Zone**, abbreviated as **DAZ**, spun off from Zygote, a company specialized in medical 3D models. Zygote had provided some human figures to be included in Poser. DAZ expanded that business and specialized in the production of what, at that time, were called the "Millennium figures". These figures were female and male human models ready to be used in Poser. They were given the names Victoria and Michael and a version number.

Victoria 1, released in 1999, was the first model that provided a vast array of customization options. She is rather primitive by today's standard, but the model represented a milestone. In 2001, DAZ released an improved Victoria, version 2, with more geometric detail and more facial expressions. She was highly compatible with Victoria 1 (V1) and she could use the same conforming clothing. In 2003 DAZ released another female figure, Victoria 3. V3 increased the number of polygons drastically and sported a much improved "rigging" (joint definition and behavior), which created more natural-looking results.

All these figures were strictly made for Poser since DAZ Studio did not exist at that time. Meanwhile, the Poser market was in full swing and many different 3D artists produced hundreds of products for it. All those people needed a way of selling their products and reach the pool of Poser users. DAZ jumped at the opportunity and provided "brokering" services for independent artists. This model is the same used today by the Apple App Store. DAZ provides third-party products on their site, and it brokers the whole transaction from payment to delivery. In exchange they retain a percentage of the sale, which is usually 50 percent.

This brokerage model has been adopted by several other companies, which are very active in the Poser/Studio content market. Two of the biggest players, together with DAZ, are Renderosity (www.renderosity.com) and RuntimeDNA (www.runtimedna.com), which we will examine shortly. They both offer a very wide catalog of products that can be used in DAZ Studio.

In 2006 DAZ released Victoria 4, the most successful 3D human figure to date. V4 has taken the market by storm; its high-detail mesh and morphing capabilities have captured the attention of thousands of users and vendors alike. Today there is simply no other 3D figure that can advertise the amount of body shapes, clothing, accessories, and skin texture that Victoria 4 has. V4 is still today a very popular product and it's used daily to create excellent artwork. V4 was soon joined by Michael 4, Aiko 4, and others. All these figures are based on the same mesh, which is then morphed to create all the different variations. Collectively these figures are called **Generation 4**, generally abbreviated as **Gen4**.

The original Victoria 4 is available at www.daz3d.com.

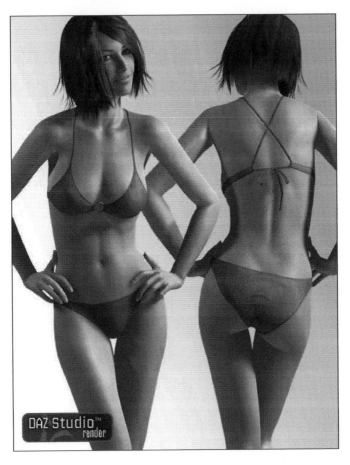

The beginning of the DAZ Studio era

After years of targeting the Poser market with original products, and by brokering third-party creations, DAZ decided to enter the field of software development with a product that would provide an alternative to Poser.

In the fall of 2005 DAZ released version 1.0 of such a product, called DAZ Studio. Studio 1.0 lacked several features of Poser, but over the years DAZ continued to update it and improve it, and today with version 4.6, they have a complete 3D application that can pose and render premade content with ease and power.

Since day one though, Studio provided seamless integration for Poser figures and DAZ continued to develop new products, such as Michael, Stephanie, The Girl, Aiko, and others, which were all based on Poser technologies. DAZ Studio read and handled those Poser files seamlessly. Some of these products come with materials designed to take advantage of Studio's own rendering system, but the integration in both Studio and Poser has been always complete, letting people use the 3D products regardless of what 3D application they preferred. This was an ideal scenario.

Genesis and the market

Although we have worked with Genesis since the beginning of this book, the Genesis figure is a new development and it doesn't have yet the wide support of the market. It is handy because it comes bundled with Studio, and so it doesn't cost a penny to start working with it. The problem with Genesis, though, is that it was designed without compatibility with Poser in mind. This was a first for DAZ and the move has been highly criticized by the market. Officially, their decision was caused by the alleged lack of certain technologies in Poser, but that is quite debatable. By excluding the largest portion of the market to access Genesis, DAZ has caused a split in the market. Developers of add-ons for figures need to target the market that makes more sense for them. Trying to make content that works for both the Gen4 and Genesis is difficult and time consuming. In addition, content that targets Genesis will not sell in the Poser market, causing a large lack in revenue. This is why Genesis has quite an uphill battle to conquer the market.

The biggest improvement of Genesis, compared to the Generation 4 figures is the use of weight mapping for the definition of the joints. Weight mapping is a technique used by high-end 3D applications such as modo and Maya; it provides a more natural way of bending the geometric mesh when limbs bend and twist.

Weight mapping was added to Poser 9, which was released just after the release of Genesis. Smith Micro, the developer of Poser, had been in talks with DAZ during the time Genesis was developed so, the imminent support for weight mapping was a well-known fact at the time. Runtime DNA has released a version of V4 that uses weight mapping in Poser, which gives users the best of both worlds: compatibility with the past and modern technology. Hopefully, DAZ will introduce this capability in Studio as well.

With the advent of Genesis DAZ has shifted its strategy and released the subsequent updates to Victoria and Michael, versions 5 and 6, as morphs for Genesis. The same happened for Stephanie, Aiko, and The Freak. This strategy caused the lack of success in the adoption of V5 and V6, as they cannot be loaded as Poser native figures. DAZ has tried to provide a solution via the DSON plugin for Poser, but the program never quite worked well, resulting in very slow reaction times.

Sources of content

Given the facts illustrated earlier, the best source of additional content is the Gen4 figure set. For example, there are thousands of products available for V4, from all ranges of period pieces to situations. You can find sci-fi outfits, armors, shoes, guns, hats, jewelry, poses, skins, and pretty much everything else. Many of these products are very inexpensive. Several products for V4 will apply to Genesis as well. For example, any skin texture that works for V4 will work for Genesis as well. The important thing here is to look for V4 textures and not Genesis textures or you will find just a handful of products. The same is true for clothing, although V4 clothing requires a little bit of work to be used with Genesis. As Gen4 figures were designed to integrate with Studio, we can use those figures with Studio 4 and retain many of the advantages.

Buying from DAZ

DAZ has its marketplace at www.daz3d.com. The front page changes often, but the basics of the shopping experience remain fairly stable. You need to establish an account with DAZ in order to order any product. This is something that you probably have already, since it is a requirement to have an account to download Studio; but just in case you obtained the program from a magazine, it is mentioned here. The DAZ site doesn't remember the login information, so you need to make sure that you have logged in before you start browsing for new products, or prices will be different and the shopping cart will be acting in a peculiar way.

The DAZ website is the best resource for finding Genesis-related products. In there you can shop for morphs, textures, and other add-ons.

The best way to find what you need is to use the catalog filter feature. From the main page, hover the mouse over the **Shop** menu and a large pop-up window will be shown.

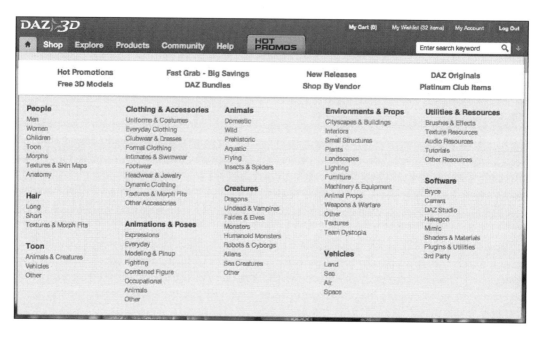

Let's navigate to **People | Women** in the top-left area of this window to show all female characters available in the market.

Once the first result shows up on the page, let's search in the left column for **Compatible 3D Figures**. If we click on one of the names in that list, the page will be updated to show only the products that are compatible with the selected base figure.

Let's click on **Victoria 4**; the list will only show character morphs based on V4. Keep in mind that this list changes often, so your result will most likely be different.

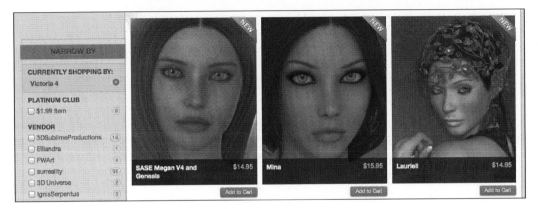

You can see in the **Narrow By** box the search filter that is active at this time. We can combine multiple filters together to narrow your search to the most likely candidates.

For example, we can combine the **Victoria 4** filter by navigating to the **Genre | Sci-fi** filter. Please note that some of the boxes in the left column scroll to reveal more choices. This is not always evident by looking at the page. You need to place the mouse cursor in the box and scroll with either the mouse wheel or the trackpad.

If you don't have it already, I strongly suggest getting Victoria 4. It usually costs about $20.00 and it's well worth the price for all the options that it provides. The link for the base product is `http://www.daz3d.com/victoria-4-2-base`.

There is also a **Starter Bundle** that offers the great Morphs++ package, basic skin textures, a hair prop, and the excellent **Basic Wear**, a conforming bikini with several useful textures. The Starter Bundle is very nicely priced and is definitely of a high quality; you can find it at `http://www.daz3d.com/victoria-4-2-complete`.

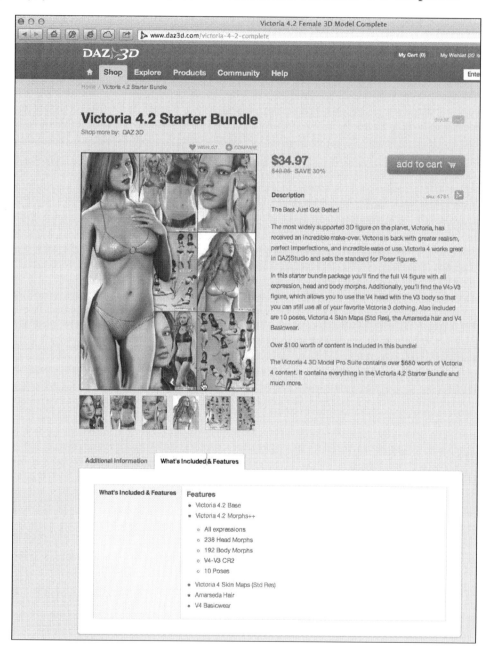

The rest of the process is fairly standard. One word of caution about the credit card information, the DAZ site allows you to save your credit card number for convenience of shopping. As a general rule, it's best to avoid storing your credit card in someone else's database. There are some exceptions such as PayPal, Amazon, and Google checkout, but those companies employ security experts and they have the infrastructure to keep data safe. In addition, in light of many problems that www.daz3d.com has had in recent past, I strongly suggest entering the credit card number with every purchase.

The DAZ products come with installers for both Mac OS and Windows. Often, a product is available for both Poser and Studio. The name of the installer can help in determining which one is which. Look at the following excerpt from the available downloads in my account:

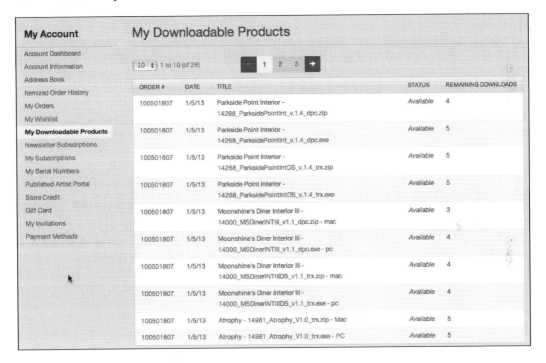

The files with the extension `.zip` are generally for Mac OS. The files with the extension `.exe` are the installers for Windows. Obviously, we need to download only the files that are targeting our OS. If we look at the name of the very first file, it ends in `dpc`. This indicates a Poser product. Poser archives might need to be installed even while using Studio. This is because the author of the product is targeting both Poser and Studio. Because Studio has support for Poser format, this is a very valid strategy. In addition to the Poser files, there is often an additional, smaller archive that includes Studio-specific materials and data. To do a complete installation, we then need to download both the Poser and Studio installers. In my case, as I use Macintosh, I need to download the first and the third archive in order to install the **Parkside Point Interior -** product.

The third archive ends in `DS_v1.4_trx`. Here, `DS` stands for DAZ Studio and it indicates Studio-specific data.

We will see later on how to organize your library of content (called a **Runtime**). For now, we are going to explore how to use the main sites providing content.

Purchasing from Renderosity

Renderosity provides a huge amount of content made by independent artists. The site is mainly dedicated to the brokerage of 3D content, with a little bit of software available, notably my own Reality plugin for Studio and Poser. Renderosity also includes numerous forums and one of the best image galleries on the Web. In fact, the site is so vast that it can be intimidating. Like other sites, Renderosity requires a free membership to make purchases from it. In my experience, Renderosity is very careful with its members' information. You can subscribe and unsubscribe to the notifications that you want to receive; it's up to you. In years that I have been a member of the Renderosity, I have never received spam from them.

The Renderosity community has about 750,000 users (at the time of writing this book), and their weekly newsletter reaches about 130,000 people (at the time of writing this book), which is great news if you plan on becoming an author of content for Studio.

From the main page, you navigate to **MarketPlace | MarketPlace** to enter the store.

Renderosity works with a progressive filtering system based on the Departments (**Dept**) page widget.

Similar to what we have done at the DAZ site, we click on the **Characters** link to search for morphs and skin textures that can add diversity to our characters.

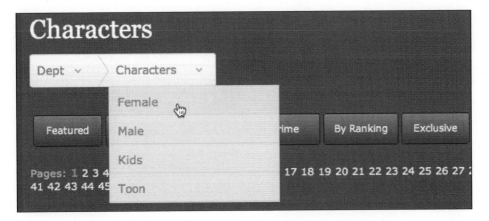

The **Characters** department reveals the **Female** option, which we can click on to reveal the choice to find models based on V4-A4-G4-S4. These abbreviations stand for Victoria 4, Aiko 4, Girl 4, and Stephanie 4. Aiko is a Japanese and Anime character based on the same mesh of V4. The Girl is a cartoonish character with exaggerated features. Stephanie 4 is a human female character with a face and proportions different from V4. When we look at the amount of characters based on the Gen4 figure, we find that at Renderosity alone there are 56 pages of products (at the time of writing this book), each page containing 30 products. This is a total of 1,680 products. Searching for Genesis returns a listing of 90 products.

Clicking on a thumbnail shows a page with detailed information on the product. This is another strong point of Renderosity. The size and detail of the promotional images is phenomenal, and the layout of the page is easy to read while it contains all the necessary details.

Pricing is shown clearly, and if a product is on sale, the end date for the sale is also visible. One valuable option is to add the product to a wishlist. This list is saved in your account and kept for reference until you change it. It is a very easy way to keep track of products that you want to purchase at some point, if not today. The page also allows to give the products as a gift for somebody else.

 While the features and behavior of a wishlist change from site to site, all major brokers of content provide the wishlist.

Renderosity does not provide installers for its products. Instead, the delivery system of choice is a ZIP file. While this system is a bit more manual than having an automated installer, it offers three advantages:

- The ZIP file is platform independent and so it works on both Mac OS and Windows
- The user retains the maximum control on where the product is installed without wondering if the installer will target the right folder
- The ZIP file is guaranteed to work in the future

The last point is quite important. DAZ's installers for the Mac from a few years ago were made to run on the PPC Mac. As we moved to the Intel architecture, those installers don't work anymore on modern Mac OSs, and it's becoming a big issue for Mac users. ZIP files don't have that problem and can be easily opened to look at the content of the archive. Even if we can run an installer, we still have to accept the result **Site Unseen** because we can't expand an installer and see what files it contains. So, the ZIP file might be a little more work but it has clear pros.

Renderosity is heavily geared toward Poser, with just a few products specific to Studio, but that is not a problem because we know that Studio works with Poser files without problems.

In the top menu of the page, we can find a **Free Stuff** option. Renderosity has a pretty large catalog of free items.

The amount of free items at Renderosity is quite stunning and a lot of them are unremarkable, but there are several gems that make browsing through all those pages worth our time.

Purchasing from RuntimeDNA

The Poser format organizes each model into a series of folders inside a top folder named `Runtime`. Both in Poser and Studio parlance, it's common to refer to models that we have in **our Runtime**. In 2002, RuntimeDNA was started as an online community and 3D content broker. The concept is that the site provides DNA for enriching your Runtime. RuntimeDNA's website is strong on design, with an emphasis on fantasy and sci-fi themes that gives them a very powerful visual impact.

Their catalog is not as vast as Renderosity's, but it is carefully curated. RuntimeDNA is a smaller company of the group, but it has established itself solidly in the community and now they are a very strong player. If DAZ and Renderosity were MGM and Universal Studios, RuntimeDNA would be Miramax.

The store is clearly accessible from the menu in the front page. When we click on the link, some of the new products and best sellers are displayed.

To find new characters based on the V4 figure, we can click on the **Figures** link in the left column. This presents a summary of the major figure categories available. As before, we can see that the lion's share is given to the Gen4 products, identified here as **DAZ Females**. It is nice to see a more "human" way of categorizing their offering.

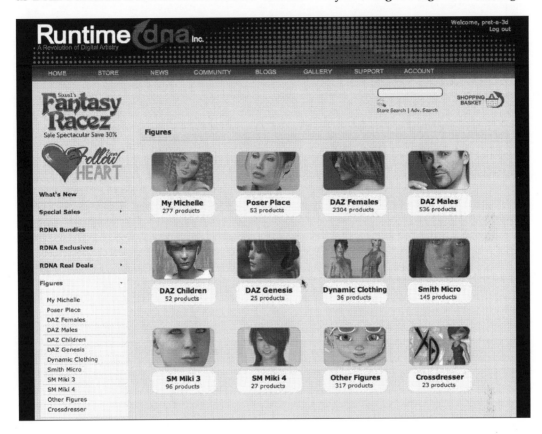

The product pages are very detailed and elegantly designed. This is an example based on their renowned **Vanilla Sky** product, a hyper-realistic texture package and character morph for V4.

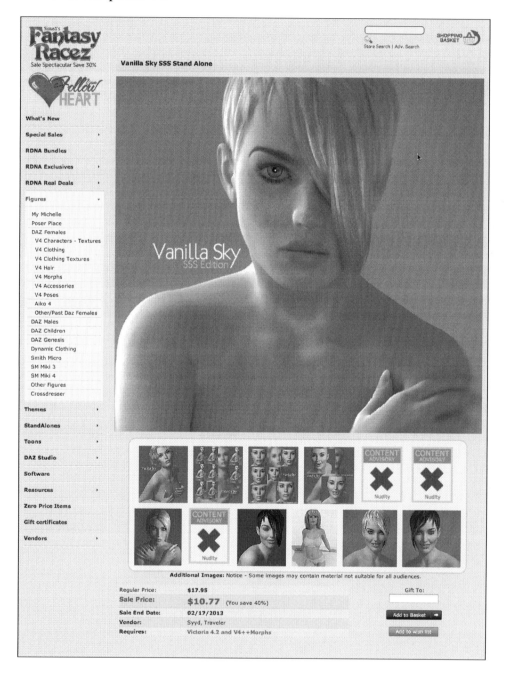

RuntimeDNA also distributes its products as ZIP files, which are clearly labeled in the download page. In fact, if we look at the download manager of RuntimeDNA, we can see that each download link has a clear description, which doesn't leave us wondering what is getting downloaded.

	#	Status	Products	Downloads	DLs	Date	Total
		Processed	Sweetheart Slayer	[Download]	2	Jan 2, 2013	$4.49
			Sweetheart Dress for V4	[Download]	1		
		Processed	Young Soul: Lemonade	[Download]	1	Jan 1, 2013	$10.47
		Processed	The Qabbalah accessories	[Download]	2	Dec 31, 2012	$18.92
			AMP - C-Suit	[Download]	1		
			Desir Hair	[Download]	1		
		Processed	Developer Trade Secrets	[Download]	1	Oct 27, 2012	$30.00
		Processed	Angeloi - the Outfit	[Download]	1	Sep 23, 2012	$34.91
			Angeloi - the Accessories	[Download]	1		
			The Malaik wings	[Download]	1		

Search results

Search again

Check all / Uncheck all

This level of attention to details is a nice touch and one that has created a very vital community in the RuntimeDNA forums. DNA's image gallery is also very well designed and full of stunning images that showcases their products. It is worth mentioning that RuntimeDNA is the home of high-profile vendors AlphaSeed and Sixus1, among many others.

RuntimeDNA has also a section with free products, some of them actually pretty nice. In the left navigation column, look for **Zero Price Items**. One major item in that category is a fully posable figure named **SAMEDI**.

Downloading free models

In addition to the free sections of Renderosity and and RuntimeDNA, there are a few places on the Web where you can download free models from. One such place is ShareCG (www.sharecg.com), a website dedicated to people legally sharing models and assets for computer graphics. To download anything from the site you need, as usual, you need to create a free account with ShareCG. There is a vast number of models available at ShareCG, so we need to be smart about our search criteria or we will be swamped with results.

To start our search, we need to click on the **3D Models** link at the top of the page. This action opens the search controls that we can see in the following screenshot:

We want to enable the DAZ Studio and Poser checkboxes to filter the compatible formats. In the preceding screenshot, I have also enabled the **Architecture** checkbox to obtain a list of buildings. The top one in the list is a detailed reproduction of England's Buckingham Palace, which is a very useful model that could command a good price on a commercial site.

Like many sites of this kind, the quality of models offered varies greatly, but ShareCG is definitely a good place to browse from time to time.

Installing content in Studio

There are many strategies that can work while installing Studio content. While considering the organization of our Runtime, we need to keep a few points in mind:

- The system must be able to scale. It's one thing to have half a dozen models and it's a completely different deal when we handle hundreds of products. We need to think about the long-term scenario.

- The organization must work with content from different sources. For example, while DAZ products come with an installer and an uninstaller, the vast majority of other sites distribute models via ZIP files. We cannot rely on uninstallers to clean up the mess if the situation arises.

- We must be able to locate the files belonging to a given model with a minimum amount of navigation of the filesystem.

It is important to be very comfortable with the filesystem of your computer. If you are not familiar with the handling of directories and subdirectories, it's better to find a good text and become very comfortable with the intricacies of storing files on your hard disk. Assuming that you are a filesystem wizard, we can continue examining a possible strategy for the storage of hundreds of 3D models.

Selecting the location

The first order of business is to group all the files that are handled by Studio in a single place. I usually create a directory called DSContent in my home directory. The home directory, or home folder, on the Mac is the one named after your username and represented by a little house in the Finder. Similarly, in Windows the home folder has your username account and is listed in the Start menu of Windows (Windows 7 and previous versions).

So we start by making a folder called `DSContent`. In there, we want to group items by major categories so that there is a distinction between the files that are used by different kinds of models, such as garments, buildings, hair, and characters. So, under `DSContent` we create the following folders:

- `Hair`
- `Wardrobe`
- `Environment`
- `Character`
- `Prop`
- `Pose`

This division allows us to find the files belonging to a certain product based on what it is. If it's a building, we know that we have to look for it under the `Environment` folder. If we need to check a texture used by a custom character, we start scanning the `Character` folder and we don't have to sift through the files used for hair, poses, or other elements of our Runtime. At the same time this grouping doesn't have finer granularity, which can slow down Studio operations considerably.

So, when we launch the installer from DAZ, we just have to select the **Customize Installation** option and point the installer to the right folder.

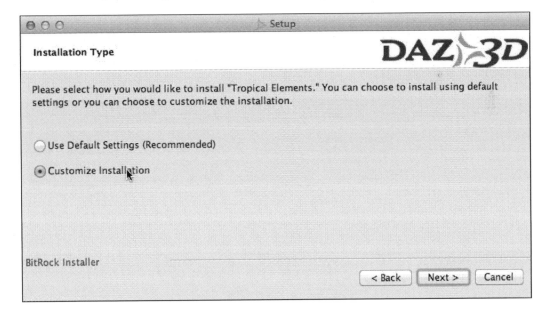

Next, choose **Installation Path:**.

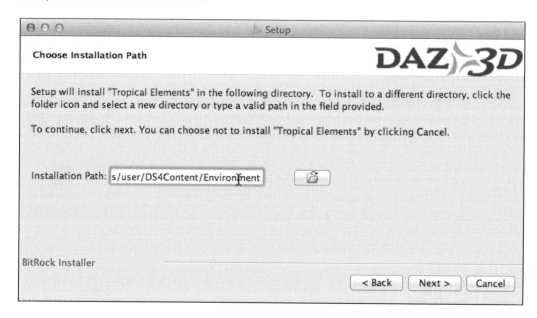

If we are using ZIP files, we can then unzip the files in the correct location and we are all set. ZIP files distributed by brokerage sites are already organized internally with the right subdirectories. All we need to do is to unzip the archives and move the content of the ZIP files in the right location. Here is an example of my DSContent directory with some ZIP files ready to be installed:

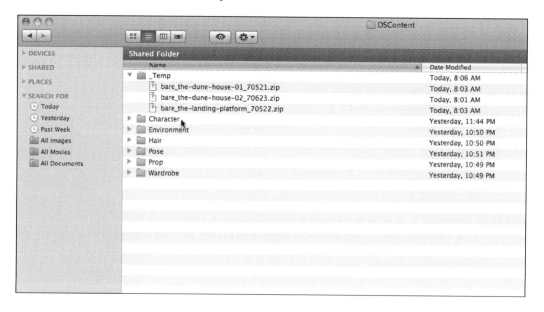

Those three archives are from the Renderosity `Free Stuff` archive, and they are three small sci-fi structures that we want to add to the **Environment** folder. You can download them using the following direct links:

- `http://www.renderosity.com/mod/freestuff/download_item.php?item_id=70521`

- `http://www.renderosity.com/mod/freestuff/download_item.php?item_id=70522`

- `http://www.renderosity.com/mod/freestuff/download_item.php?item_id=70623`

I added a directory called `_Temp` where I park the ZIP files to be expanded. The starting underscore helps keeping the directory at the top of the list, which makes it easier to find.

The idea is to start the expansion from this location and target the destination directory. If you use Windows, this is pretty simple if you have WinZip installed and configured to automatically handle your ZIP files. In that case, you simply double-click on the archive, and from the WinZip window, select the destination directory, for example, `Environment`. Make sure that the **Use Folder Names** option is selected so that the content of the archive is merged with pre-existing content on disk.

On a Mac, the Finder has built-in support for expanding ZIP files, but it does not merge the content of the archive with the existing folders. This means that we need to do some work ourselves, but it's pretty simple. This is where the `_Temp` directory comes in handy.

 Even if you use Windows, please read the following paragraphs because they contain information about the organization of ZIP files that can be very useful for you too.

Before we get to the cool way of doing things, we need to see what happens if we simply double-click on each archive to unzip them.

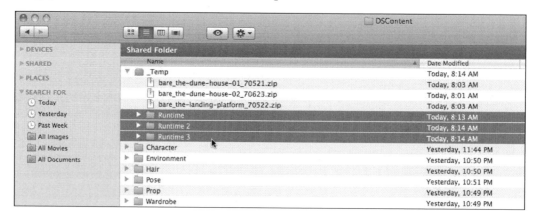

Each ZIP file has a single subdirectory inside called `Runtime`. The second archive expands into a directory called `Runtime 2` and the third to a directory called `Runtime 3`. This is because the Finder renames the new directories to avoid conflict with the first one. Here, we get confirmation that Finder cannot handle merging two directories together. The presence of the `Runtime` subfolder is consistent with what I was explaining about how Poser organizes its content.

If we expand those Runtime folders, we can see this:

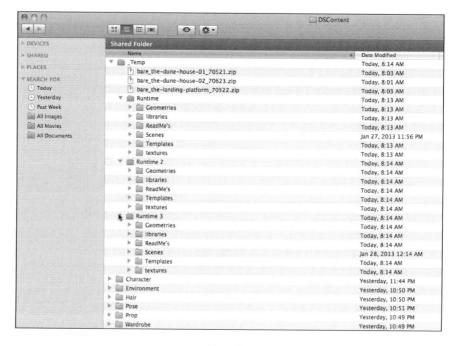

The `Geometries` folder contains the OBJ files that define the raw geometry. The `libraries` folder contain the Poser files that define the model in terms of combination of the geometry files, materials, and so on. The `textures` folder contains the image files that are used for texturing the models. There are more folders, but these three are the essential ones to keep in mind.

 OBJ is a file format for the exchange of 3D models. It was defined years ago by a company called Waveform, and it's commonly used by many 3D applications. It is the lingua franca of 3D assets.

Instead of going through the painstaking process of merging all the folders manually, we can use a tool built-in inside Mac OS. This tool is called **ditto** and it is a command-line program. Now, let's not panic about this. If you have never used the command line, this is finally the time to get familiar with one of the most powerful tools in the computing arsenal.

First of all, we don't need those directories that we have expanded from the ZIP files. Select them and move them to the trash.

Next, we need to open the Terminal because that is the program that allows us to use the command line.

You can find the Terminal by navigating with the Finder to the `Applications/Utilities` folder.

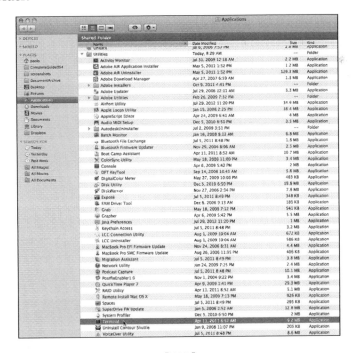

Double-click on it to launch the application. This is what it should look like:

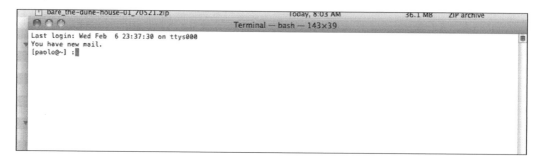

The command line, also known as the shell, works in a very simple way. We give commands by writing them on the command line, and we execute those commands by pressing the *return* key. Think of the command as a verb and the act of writing the command as writing a phrase. The verb starts the phrase and it can be followed by other words, each one separated by a space, which direct the verb to act in a certain way. Try this: type the word ls and press the *return* key.

The ls command lists the files in the current directory. Whenever you use the shell, you are positioned inside a directory. Commands are not executed in the void. The name of the current directory is listed to the left of the cursor, after your username. In the preceding screenshot, we can see that my username is paolo and that I'm at the (@) home folder, which is abbreviated to ~. At any time, we can change the current directory by using the cd command followed by the name of the directory. Try this:

```
cd Documents Return
```

In the preceding command line the Return word means to press the *return* key, not to type the word Return.

Please make sure that you type the command *exactly* as described in the command line. The command line is case sensitive. Your prompt, the text to the left of the cursor, should have changed to show the new current directory.

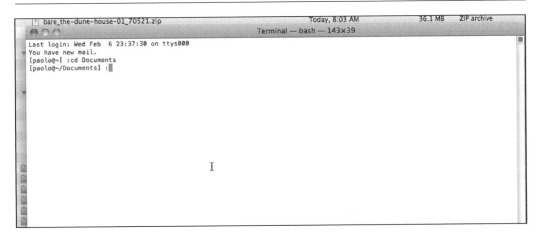

Now type the following command:

`cd .. Return`

The `..` text (two periods) indicates the directory above the current one, which brings us back to the home directory.

OK, so now we need to position ourselves inside the `_Temp` directory, which is inside the `DSContent` directory, which in turn is inside the home directory. From now on, I will omit the word `Return` at the end of the command; it is implicit. If you don't press *return*, the shell doesn't know that you have finished typing the command and that it's time to execute it. Type the following commands:

`cd DSContent`
`cd _Temp`

Verify from the prompt that you have the right directory.

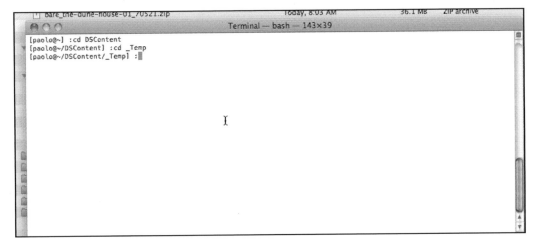

Now what we need to say is "dear ditto command, please take those three ZIP files, expand them, and merge the content of all of them in the Environment directory just above where we are now". It turns out that we can do that with just a few words typed on the command line. So, while being sure that we are in the _Temp directory, this is what we need to type:

```
ditto -xk bare*.zip ../Environment
```

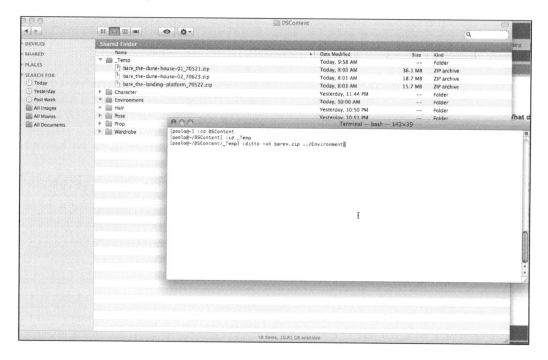

Please note that there is a space between ditto and -xk, one space between -xk and bare*.zip, and one final space before ../Environment.

This is what the command means: the first word is calling the ditto command. ditto has the ability to merge a source archive or directory into a target directory. The source directory or archive is listed first, the target directory second. For example, have a look at the following command:

```
ditto source_dir target_dir
```

This command takes all the files and directories of source_dir and copies them into target_dir. The original files in source_dir are not moved or affected at all; they are copied. If a directory exists in both source_dir and target_dir, the files are merged. Please note that whole files are copied. If a file with the exact same directory and name exists in both source and target locations, the source file will overwrite the target file.

The `-xk` portion that we used in our command instructs ditto to extract (`x`) a ZIP file (`k`). Without the `-xk` modifier, the whole ZIP file would be copied into `Environment`. The k letter is used to identify the ZIP file in honor of Phil Katz, the late author of the ZIP file format. When it was released, it was called the PKZIP file format. Lastly, we used the `bare*.zip` notation to act on all three archives in one single command. The `*` works as a wildcard, expanding in its place the matching names from the current directory. This is equivalent to using the following commands:

```
ditto -xk bare_the-dune-house-01_70521.zip ../Environment
ditto -xk bare_the-dune-house-02_70623.zip ../Environment
ditto -xk bare_the-landing-platform_70522.zip ../Environment
```

Since all the archives start with `bare`, it's much easier to use this abbreviated form and let the shell expand the names for us. After all, that's what computers are good at. Lastly, we used the notation `../Environment` because the `Environment` directory is not a subdirectory of `_Temp`, but it is above the current directory. Yes, there is a lot of power in the command line.

Now, let's expand the `Environment` directory for a few levels and see what happens.

It seems indeed that the ditto command has done its job admirably. By the way, if you still find the command line intimidating, you can get an inexpensive program called **DittoGUI**, which is a graphic frontend to the ditto command. It's point-and-click simple and costs about $2. But the command line is more fun!

Configuring Studio for the new content

Now that we have installed the new content, it's time to tell Studio where it is so that we can use the new models in the program. This is very straightforward. Let's switch to Studio and call **Preferences** by pressing *F2*. Click on the **Content Library** tab and then on the **Content Directory Manager…** button.

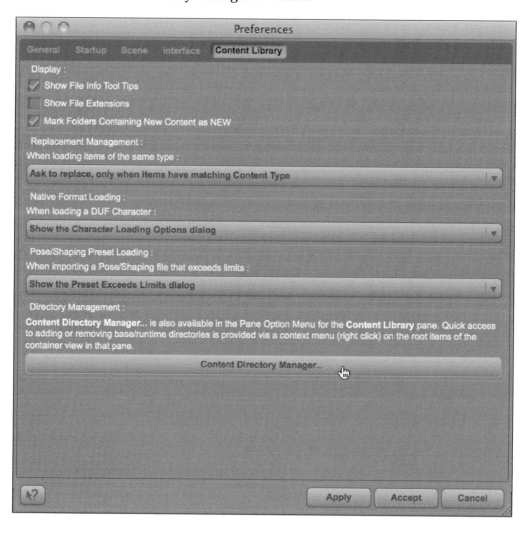

In the window that opens, expand the **Poser Formats** section, as the models that we have installed were distributed as Poser files. Then click on the **Add...** button to add the DSContent/Environment directory to your home folder.

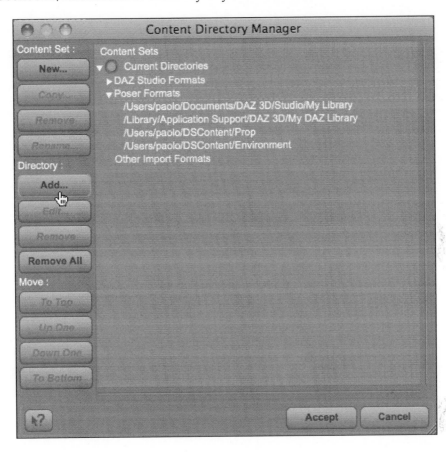

After that, click on the **Accept** button. To find the new models, we need to click on the **Content Library** tab and navigate to **Poser Formats | Environment | Props**. A **Logan** folder will show up with the three models that we have installed.

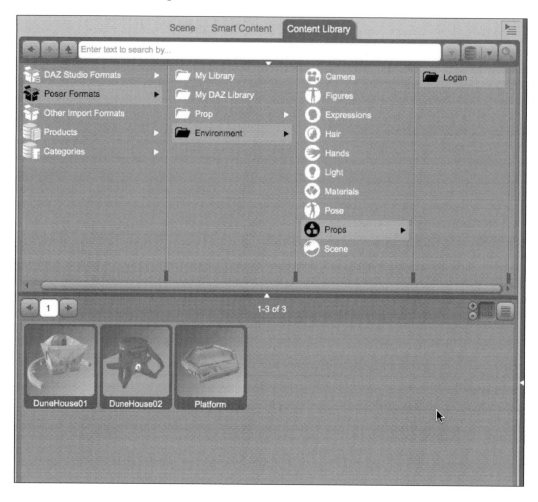

If we install models using the DAZ installers, we just need to point the installer to the right subdirectory inside the DSContent directory. The latest DAZ installers automatically add the path to the **DAZ Studio Formats** section. Older installers, such as the ones released during the DS3 era, don't have that capability; so we need to add the path manually as we just did, but this time in the DAZ Studio Formats section. The easiest option is to add the six subdirectories, Character, Environment, Hair, Pose, Prop, and Wardrobe to both the Studio and Poser sections. Once we do that, all the products installed there will be automatically found, and we will not need to change the Studio configuration anymore.

Summary

In this chapter, we have seen that we can find content for Studio from several websites and that we can create a large library of premade content by purchasing from these e-stores. We have become more familiar with the different file formats and the delivery systems used by each store.

Lastly, we have created a system for keeping 3D models organized in our disk in a way that is expandable with hundreds of new products.

With all these elements, we are now able to use DAZ Studio for production of complex illustrations based on many different 3D models.

In the next chapter, we are going to delve deeper into the Studio environment, and learn more about how to organize and use the content that can be acquired through the sources that we have discussed here. We will learn more about how to use cameras and lights to our advantage. It's going to be fun.

7

Navigating the Studio Environment

Up to this point, we have seen Studio in action by performing specific tasks. It is now time to expand our knowledge of Studio by delving into the details of some of the tools offered by the program.

The secret to using a 3D program successfully is to be able to move around the 3D space and control every element with ease.

In this chapter we explore how to do the following:

- Understanding the building block of geometric models
- Changing our point of view and the camera perspective
- Setting the frame for our render
- Selecting objects, parts of objects, and materials
- Adding and changing lights
- Organizing our content with categories
- Importing 3D assets from other programs

Polygons – the building blocks of our scenes

Up to this point, we focused on using figures such as Genesis for creating scenes. Every 3D asset is built upon elementary elements called **polygons**. A polygon is basically a facet of an object, a plane that is formed by at least three points called vertices, but more often based on four vertices. Each vertex is a point in space, which is represented by three coordinates: x, y, and z.

In Studio the x axis runs horizontally, the y axis runs vertically, and the z axis runs in the depth dimension. Other programs use different conventions. For example, in Blender the z axis runs vertically, while the y axis defines the depth.

In the following screenshot, we can see the Genesis figure showing its polygons. The polygons are curved so that they create a smooth surface.

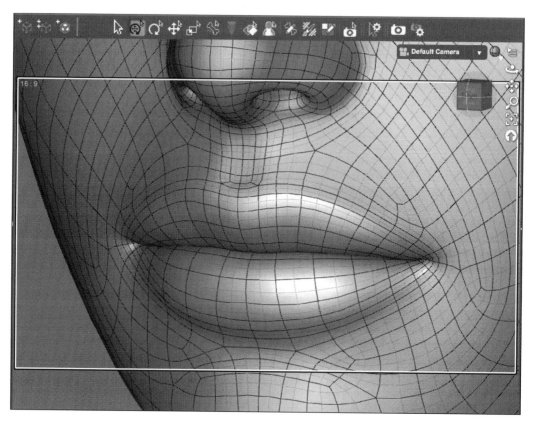

To switch to this type of view, click on the Drawstyle icon in the top-right corner of the 3D Viewport and select **Wire Shaded**.

The Wire Shaded view is excellent for faster workflow and for visualizing the geometry that forms a 3D object.

While we don't manipulate the polygons directly in Studio, there are many situations in which it's important to be able to see the topology of a model. The term topology refers to the distribution and layout of polygons that form a 3D object, such as the Genesis figure.

It is useful to be mindful of the amount of polygons that we have in a scene. The larger the amount of polygons, the larger the amount of RAM needs to be installed in a computer to handle such geometry. A high number of polygons also dictates longer render times.

Finding the number of polygons in the scene

Studio provides a handy panel that provides statistics about the working scene. In the **Window | Panes (Tabs)** menu, click on **Scene Info** option and a new panel will be displayed. In the following screenshot, we can see some interesting data:

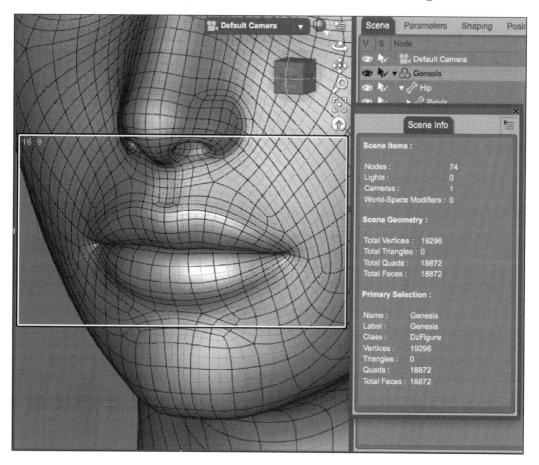

The **Scene Geometry** section gives us the total amount of polygons and vertices in the scene. This is a total that includes every object present. In our case, we have only one figure, Genesis.

The **Primary Selection** section reports the same type of data, but only for the currently selected object. Since I have selected Genesis, the two sections are identical. We can see that a single Genesis figure includes a total of 18,872 polygons (**Total Faces**) and that those faces are also all quads. In 3D there are two main types of polygons: triangles and quads. The word **quad** is a common abbreviation for **quadrilateral**, a polygon with four sides. From that report, we can see that Genesis is completely made out of quads, with no triangles. Many 3D objects are made of a mixture of triangles and quads, and sometimes they are made all of triangles.

Quads are generally preferable for human anatomy because they can be easily subdivided.

Subdivision

You might have noticed that the wireframe representation of Genesis has some lines that are thinner than others. The thinner lines indicate the subdivision of the geometry. Subdividing is the operation of dividing each polygon along the edges. In the case of Genesis, since the figure is made out of quads, each polygon is subdivided into four smaller polygons. This operation allows the program to obtain a finer geometry from a coarser one. There are advantages in calculating subdivided geometry from a base mesh instead of loading an already detailed geometry.

 In 3D parlance, a group of polygons is often called a **mesh** or **geometric mesh**. This term can be used to refer to subparts of a model as well.

For example, a figure that is distant from the camera can be set to use the base, coarse geometry, saving considerable RAM and render time, while a figure that is closer to the camera can use one or two levels of subdivision to provide a smoother result. If the figure has been defined already with a very detailed mesh, we would not have this kind of flexibility.

Keep in mind that each level of subdivision quadruples the number of polygons, so it's best to use the lowest level of subdivision necessary to obtain the right result.

We can set the level of subdivision using the **Parameters** tab. First, we need to select Genesis. Then, we will see the **Mesh Resolution** property available.

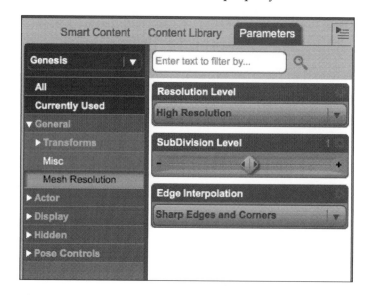

The default value is **1**, which quadruples the mesh resolution from the base 18,872 to 75,488. Another level of subdivision would bring the total polygon count to 301,952. This is for one single naked figure. Even with a very capable machine, we need to be careful about raising this value.

If we have a scene with multiple figures and some of them are away from the camera, it might be helpful to set the level of subdivision for those to zero. The camera will not catch the difference, but the resulting render times will be shorter and Studio will be more responsive.

Moving in the 3D space

The space offered by Studio can be vast and complex. In addition to human figures, we can easily create scenes that contain entire cities or at least a few blocks filled with buildings, cars, and all sorts of objects. Being able to move in that space with comfort is fundamental if we want to be able to find great points of view to create our images. It is a bit like being a photographer scouting for ideal places to snap great photos.

Similar to a photographer, we look at our scene through the lens of a camera. At any given time a camera is active in the scene. There is also a special camera called **Perspective View** that represents an outside point of observation. Unlike real cameras, the Perspective View lacks a lot of adjustable parameters and I suggest avoiding it. By default, Studio doesn't create a default camera unless a setting in the configuration is activated. It's better to have Studio create a default camera at all times. If we don't do that, it will be easy to start framing the shot using the Perspective View only to find out about the mistake later on, forcing us to repeat the work with a real camera.

So, let's open the **Preferences** window and click on the **Scene** tab. In there, we need to make sure that the **Create a "Default Camera"** option is enabled. Once that is done, Studio will create a camera for each scene and it will make that camera the default view.

Benefits of using a real camera

The reason a real camera is necessary to frame our shot is that perspective control and other artistic tools are only available with a real camera. A camera uses a simulation of a lens, which can be set to have any focal length. The focal length of a lens dramatically changes the field of view and perspective of a scene.

In the following images, we can see the effect of changing the focal length while not moving the camera. In the first image we can see the setup of the scene. The camera is about two meters away from the subject and the walls are quite distant, at least 8 or 10 meters behind Genesis.

In the second image we see the result of rendering the scene with the lens set to 200 mm. Long lenses—lenses with a focal length of 70 mm or more—are very good for portraits because they compress the perspective quite a bit. The face is nice and round. The nose is not too prominent. All in all, it's a very flattering effect. If we look at the background, we notice that the walls seem a lot closer than they actually are. This is the effect of perspective compression.

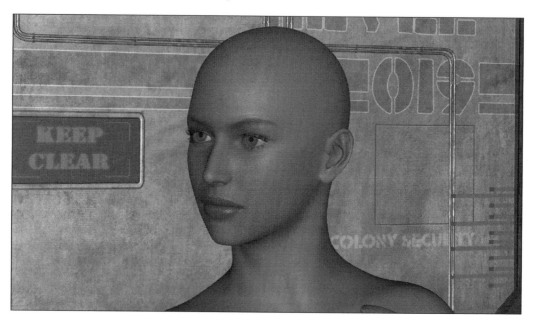

This trick is used often in action movies, for example, when showing somebody chased by a car or truck. Although the distance is much greater than it looks, the perspective compression of long lenses makes it look like the actor is just a few centimeters away from certain death.

Now let's look at the third image. Notice that I did not move the camera. The only change was to set the lens to 25 mm, which makes it a wide-angle lens. This kind of lens exaggerates the perspective. The field of view has expanded considerably, and now we can see the figure almost completely, while before we only framed the head. The room also looks much deeper.

To change the focal length for a camera, select the camera in the **Scene** tab and then switch to the **Parameters** tab. In there we can find a **Camera** group that contains the **Focal Length (mm)** value. By changing that value, we change the field of view and the perspective of the camera.

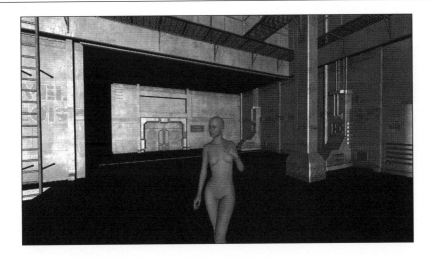

Again, we didn't move the camera, we just zoomed out.

Now let's see what happens if we move the camera closer to the subject while not changing the focal length. What we want to achieve is to frame Genesis in a similar way to the frame obtained with the 200 mm lens, in other words, to frame the figure so that nothing below the shoulder is visible. The result is quite different from what we had with the 200 mm. The nose is very pronounced, the head shape has been elongated considerably, and the eyes are bulging out. The room is also much deeper and the **Keep Clear** sign is in fact not visible in the frame.

This is the result of the perspective change caused by both the shorter focal length and the change of the position of the camera.

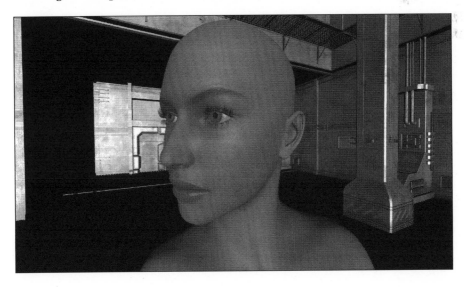

While creating portraits, using a longer focal length—from 80 mm to 200 mm or even more—will bring the most flattering results. While rendering small spaces, a short focal length will give us a way of capturing more of the scene. When we deeply understand how focal length works, we can use it as an artistic tool.

It's important to be familiar with focal length and perspective adjustment. I suggest that you practice recreating the preceding images. Obviously, you don't need the same space station environment, any closed space will do. What is important is to see the difference in focal length *without moving the camera*. Then, you can try the reframing using the 25 mm lens to see the distortion caused by the wide-angle lens. Go ahead, practice for a bit, and then come back to this chapter.

Moving the camera around

When we render a scene, we frame a portion of the 3D world and we cut the rest out of the frame. Setting the frame is a very important part of the overall composition, and so it is vital to be able to move around so that we can "work the shot" easily.

There are several ways of moving the camera in Studio. One way is to use the camera cube in the top-right corner of the 3D Viewport. The cube has a few useful applications. For example, if you double-click on the inner square that says **Front**, the camera will switch to a frontal view. Similarly, if you double-click on the **Top** word in the cube, the camera will switch to a vertical position looking straight down to the center of the frame.

More often, though, I find that using a combination of keyboard and mouse provides a more direct and faster way of moving around.

If we press the *Opt* or *Alt* key while clicking-and-dragging with the left mouse button (LMB), we are able to orbit the camera, as if it was on a trackball. Try it now.

If we press the same key, but we use the right mouse button (RMB), we can pan the camera left and right, as if it was mounted on wheels.

Finally, using the mouse wheel allows us to zoom in and out.

A last way of adjusting the camera position is by manipulating it directly. To do this, it is best that we split the Viewport into two, so that in one pane we see the camera from outside and in the other pane we see the camera frame as we move around. This is where **Perspective View** comes in handy. It's our director's view that we use to look at the stage from a point of view that is outside any other camera.

To split the Viewport, we navigate to **Window | Viewports | Top and Bottom**.

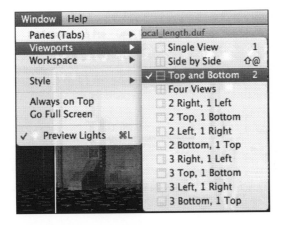

You can see that in my configuration I assigned the keyboard shortcut *2* for this task. Here, *1* is used to restore the single pane Viewport. To assign these shortcuts use the same procedure described in *Chapter 2, Customizing Studio*.

With this configuration we can click on the camera from **Perspective View** and treat it like any other object that we move in the scene. As we click-and-drag it to change its position, the other pane in the Viewport shows us the updated frame of the camera. Once the frame is perfect, we can then switch to a single camera point of view, if that is convenient. This technique can be very effective when we need to move the camera through a large distance, like while using vast landscapes.

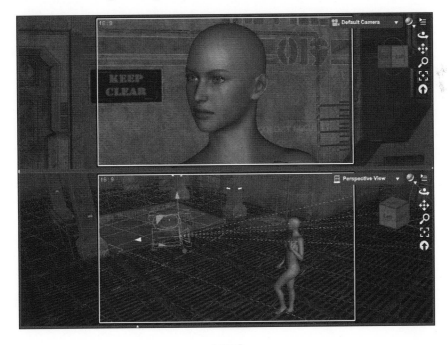

Learning about the Viewport tools

Up to this point, we made extensive use of the Universal tool to manipulate objects in the scene. There are other tools that can be used to manipulate scene objects and now it's time to see what they do. We saw these tools in *Chapter 2, Customizing Studio*; here they are again for reference:

Icon	Name	Function
	The Node selection tool	This is used to select objects or portions of objects, called nodes. For example, the forearm of a human figure is a node.
	The Rotate tool	This is used to rotate objects.
	The Translate tool	This is used top move objects around.
	The Scale tool	This is used to enlarge or shrink objects.

The Node selection tool

In the toolbar where the U.T. is, we can find the Node selection tool. This tool is useful when we need to select an object or a part of a figure, like the eye, but we don't want to see the U.T. gizmo in the view. For example, if we want to adjust the position of the eye with the parameters sliders, the U.T. gizmo would get in the way.

The Scale, Rotate, and Translate tools

These are all subsets of the U.T. They do exactly what we expect them to do. I personally don't use them at all. The U.T. is now "muscle memory" for me and it does all that the other tools do.

The Translate tool moves objects in the Viewport. If we select it and then click-and-drag on a object, we move that object around. If it is applied to a figure's limb, it moves the limb within the limits of what is allowed by the limb's joint.

The Rotate tool rotates an object along any of the three axes, based on the center of the object.

Finally, the Scale tool scales an object along any of the three axes.

Other useful tools

There are several other tools provided by Studio. Some of them are of use for creators of figures or clothing, and are not particularly useful for everyday work by the 3D artist. Others are very handy. One of them is the Surface Selection tool, which we have mapped to the *M* keystroke when we have reassigned the keyboard shortcuts. This tool can be thought of as the Material Selection tool. When we use it, the surface that is under the cursor becomes highlighted, and if we stop moving the mouse for a couple of seconds, the name of the material is shown in a tool tip. If we click, the material becomes selected and active in the **Surfaces** tab, where we can edit it. This is a great timesaver that allows us to find the right material to edit by simply pointing at it.

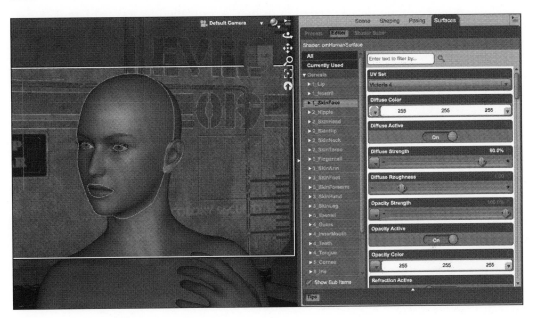

Let there be light

Like in photography, there is no scene without light. Studio provides a default light when you create a scene. This light is the equivalent of a very broad spotlight mounted on the camera. It only has the purpose of allowing you to see something while rendering the scene. The camera light gives us one of the worst possible results, light-wise, and should be avoided at all costs. Once we add a real light to the scene, the camera light is disabled and it stops doing its damage.

Lights are one of the most important parts of creating a scene. Good lighting with mediocre materials will lead to better results than poor lighting with excellent materials. Spending time in understanding lighting is probably one thing that will contribute the most effective results to your work. Forget technology, resolution, polygon density, and texture resolution—lighting is where miracles happen.

So, to understand how to light a scene, it's necessary to know what kind of lights we can use, what they do, and when to use them.

The spotlight

Spots are very versatile. They provide several options to shape the light that they produce. A spotlight defines a cone of light that is controlled by a spread angle. We can decide if the spotlight will be wide or narrow. We can also control the color of the light.

To add a spot, click on the Spotlight icon in the toolbar, or navigate to **Create | New Spotlight**.

When you add a spot, it's very likely that your scene will plunge into darkness, if the spot is the only light that you have. This is because Studio will turn off the camera light. Do not panic, this is a good thing.

If we add a spot and use the default setting, the light will be placed at the origin or $X = 0$, $Y = 0$, $Z = 0$.

We can activate the Universal tool by pressing U and then clicking on the light. As we position and rotate the spot, we can see the cone of light that it projects.

If the darkness of the scene is a problem, we can turn off the simulation of lights, and have a scene that is evenly lit, by navigating to **Window | Preview Light** or by pressing *Cmd + L* (on Mac) or *Ctrl + L* (on Windows).

When a spotlight is selected, there are several parameters available that we can modify. The sections in the **Parameters** tab that are of importance are: **Display**, **Shadow**, and **Light**.

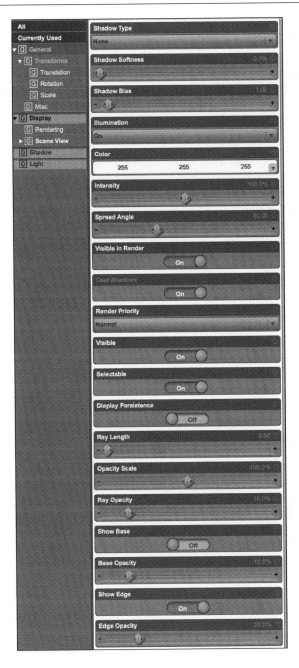

The **Display** section is about how the light shows in the scene. It affects our ability to work with the light, not the quality or behavior of the light while rendering.

The **Light** section controls the color and intensity of the light. It has also an illumination control, but I don't suggest using it, except for turning the light off or on. The **Spread Angle** value controls how wide the cone of the spotlight is. The value is in degrees. A narrow cone can be obtained with values between 5 and 30 degrees. The default is 60, which is pretty wide.

Casting shadows

An important set of values is under the **Shadow** category. This category is common for all lights, and it controls how shadows are created for each light. In real life, you control the sharpness of shadows by changing the size of the light. For example, a large light generates soft shadows. The larger the light is, the softer the shadows. This is a phenomenon controlled by physics. In extreme cases, such as during an overcast day, there are almost no visible shadows. This is caused by spreading the sunlight through the clouds. The area of the clouds is enormous, and so it becomes a very large light source that creates extremely soft, almost invisible, shadows. This is a very important concept to remember; the softness of the light has nothing to do with the brightness of the light and everything to do with the size of the light.

Regardless of how soft or sharp the shadows are, there is a very constant law of nature: a light projects shadows. No way around it, except when using some 3D software. As we can see in the **Shadow** category of Studio, the default for **Shadow Type** is **None**. This means that the selected light generates illumination, but it doesn't project a shadow. This is a highly unrealistic situation and one that should be avoided. If we click on the **Shadow Type** list, we see that there are two different types of shadows available: **Deep Shadow Map** and **Raytraced**.

Deep Shadow Map generates a map showing where shadows will fall. The generation of the map takes quite a long time, even for a single light. During this time there's nothing rendering on the screen. The biggest issue with this setting is that the resulting shadow can be imprecise and low in resolution. Ray tracing is based on more exact tracing of the line of sight. It is usually best to select Raytraced shadows and dial in a bit of shadow softness for realism. If we are talking about spotlight, a softness of 30 percent will be appropriate.

My suggestion for shadows is to turn them on by default. The act of placing a light that doesn't create shadows leads inevitably to unrealistic results. We might not be able to put our finger on what is "off" with the image, but our brain knows it instinctively and it will be yelling "fake!" to us while looking at the image.

A render doesn't have to be photo-realistic. A Rembrandt painting is not photo-realistic, but the light and the shadows work as expected. So, I encourage you to resist the temptation to turn off shadows when some lighting situation creates double or triple shadows in your shot, and instead find a natural solution, the same type of solution that is used by photographers and cinematographers daily. There are, of course, exceptions, but try to resist as much as possible the impulse to turn off the shadows. Your images will benefit from it. If you end up with multiple shadows that you want to remove, you can move the lights higher and to a different angle and move the camera to slightly reframe the shot.

Point lights

While spots project light in one direction, point lights are like a conventional household light bulb. They project light at 360 degrees around the center of the light.

Point lights are the hardest lights to control and should be used only when the exact type of light is needed, for example, when you have to place a light inside a lampshade.

Similar to the spotlight, we can change the color, intensity, and shadow configuration.

Distant lights

Distant lights are a special case. These are completely artificial lights that are generally used to simulate indirect lighting. Light in the real world bounces off objects and gets reflected with different hues, depending on the object that reflected it. Light in 3Delight, the renderer of Studio, doesn't behave like that. If we place a spot inside a room, the spot will generate a cone of light and illuminate the objects that it "sees", but the light will not bounce around. The effect is artificial and it screams of **Computer Generated Image (CGI)** to the viewer.

Distant lights are directional, which means that the light starts from a source and moves in the direction the light is oriented. The rays of light are parallel so as to simulate the sun. If we place a few distant lights in our scene, in strategic positions, we can simulate the effect of indirect lighting and increase the realism of our scenes. To make the illusion correct, we need to turn off the projection of shadows for these lights. This is the exception to the rule mentioned previously. Except for this case, shadows should be present for all lights.

We will see later on, while working with the Reality plugin and LuxRender, how all these tricks can be set aside if we work with a physics-based renderer such as LuxRender.

If you want to learn more about lighting techniques, I suggest reading the excellent *Digital Lighting and Rendering* by Jeremy Birn.

Managing content

We have seen how the Genesis figure is accessible from the **Smart Content** tab. We have seen how to buy and install additional content through websites such as Renderosity and RuntimeDNA. It is now time to examine how to access all that content from Studio.

The Smart Content and Content Library tabs

With Studio 4, DAZ has introduced the **Smart Content** tab. This part of the UI manages the installed content that has metadata, information that describes the product, and how it relates to other products. Metadata provides a way for Studio to know what products are made for a given object or figure.

For example, if we add Genesis to the scene and we select it, the **Smart Content** panel changes to show only the content that applies to the selection.

 Finding the right terms for UI elements is useful, so let's examine the world of tabs for a moment. The tab is the element that sticks out and which when clicked, causes a pane or panel to be shown. So, we click on the tab to make the panel visible. We make our choices inside the panel, not the tab.

So, we will see only morphs, poses, and accessories that have been tagged to work with Genesis. This system is somewhat helpful, but in actuality, it's not something that we can rely on. It's important to understand that the categories that are shown by the **Smart Content** tab are based on the metadata set by the content creator. If we don't find that categorization intuitive, there is nothing that we can do about it.

While the **Smart Content** tab is an interesting concept, the vast majority of the models that are available in the market are Poser models that contain no metadata for Studio. With more than 10 times the available product for Victoria 4 than for Genesis, we have to find a way of accessing the content in Studio in a quick and organized way.

Unfortunately, Studio doesn't provide a unified content manager and instead, it uses the **Content Library** panel for managing content that has no metadata.

At first, it can be confusing to have to click on two different tabs for basically the same function… and it is. Nothing to do about it.

We need to remember that if the content is coming from the DAZ store, it will *likely* be in the **Smart Content** panel, otherwise it will be in the **Content Library** panel. I said likely because there are plenty of products that have no metadata information or that don't fit in the Smart Content philosophy and are sold at the DAZ store.

Content management in Studio is something that needs to be approached with a bit of patience.

Organizing the Content Library tab

We have seen in *Chapter 6, Finding and Installing New Content*, how to add products to the **Content Library** tab. There is an alternative, faster way. We can right-click on the **Poser** or **Studio** category, and then add a new folder directly from there.

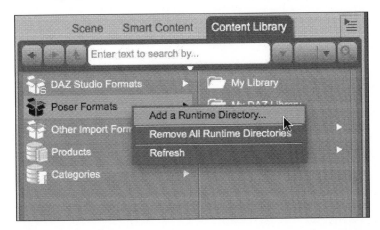

This is a very quick way of adding or removing a runtime to the Studio library, but it doesn't give us a view of the whole configuration. That's why it's important to know where the list is actually managed, as we saw in *Chapter 6, Finding and Installing New Content*, so that if something needs to be adjusted and if something doesn't quite work as expected, we know where to look for the full list of directories handled by the content manager.

As we can see in the **Content Library** tab, Studio divides the content into two major categories: **DAZ Studio Formats** and **Poser Formats**.

That division can make sense, in a way, but it's really not very useful when we work on a scene. After all, we do not care in which format a given 3D asset is kept, we just want to use it. For example, if we want to add some hair to V4, it doesn't matter if it is designed as a Studio-specific product or as Poser product that can be used in Studio. We just want to have a place were, ideally, all the hair props for Victoria are found. This can be achieved if we create our own categories.

The **Categories** entry that we see at the bottom of the **Content Library** can be populated with our own choice of subcategories nested to any level that we want. Let's see how that can be done.

We can create a folder on disk called DSContent. As explained in the previous chapter, we should divide the content into several major groups: environments, hair, vehicles, wardrobe, and so on. Also, we should have a folder named Victoria4, where all the data for V4 is stored.

To start with, we add all the folders to the **Poser Formats** category. Also, we add the Victoria4 folder to the **DAZ Studio Formats** category because that folder contains data that is in both formats. This is rather common for models that are designed to work in both Poser and Studio.

Once this setup is done, we can start creating our own categories. When we click on the **Categories** category, we just see a subcategory called **Default**. We are going to ignore that.

Let's right-click on the space just below the **Default** subcategory; a pop-up menu will appear with the **Create a Sub-Category...** option. Let's click on that.

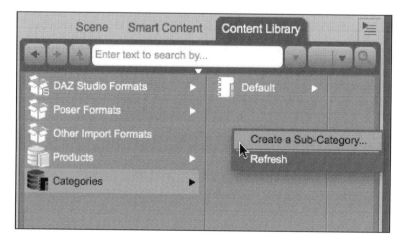

When asked for the name, let's type People. Now let's right-click on the **People** subcategory and from the menu select **Create a Sub-Category**. In the prompt enter V4. The final result should look like this:

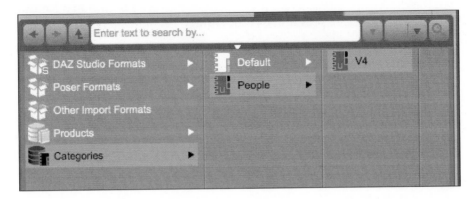

Now we need to repeat the same series of actions to create the following structure under **Categories** as shown in the following screenshot, which is is the final result while showing the **Content Library** tab as a tree instead of the list format used by default:

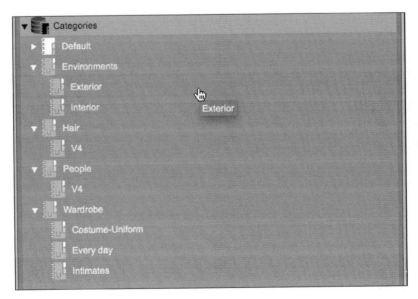

The purpose of this exercise will become clear in a couple of minutes. Now we have a series of categories that we can associate to our content. If we assign a category to a 3D asset, that asset will show every time we click on the category. It's custom tagging for our 3D content.

Here is how we assign a category to an object.

1. Click on the **Poser Formats | Wardrobe** category.

2. In there, we can see the usual list of entities that we can find in a Runtime:
   Camera, Figures, Expressions, Hair, Hands, Light, Materials, Pose,
   and **Props**.

3. Click on **Figures** and the list of all the products that have been installed in
   that Runtime shows up. In my case, I have **DAZ's Victoria 4 Clothing, LM
   ShadowDancer**, and **SteamPunk Ladyblaze**.

4. At this point, we need to click on one of those folders. By clicking on the top
   one, I see the content of the V4 Basic Wear package, which is a collection of
   bikini and sportswear.

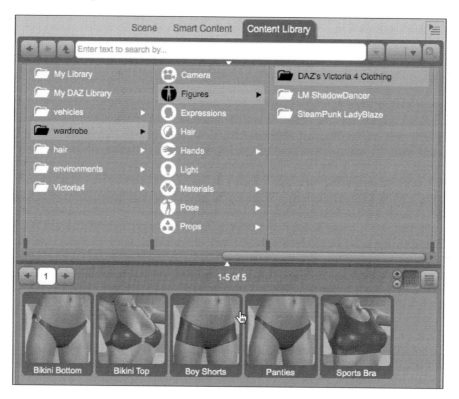

5. We need to select all those thumbnails together, so that we can apply a
   category to them. To do so, we click on a area of that lower pane that doesn't
   have the thumbnails, the area with the gray background. After we do that,
   we use the keyboard shortcut *Cmd + A* (on Mac) or *Ctrl + A* (on Windows)
   to select all the thumbnails.

6. Once the thumbnails are highlighted, we right-click on one of them to show the context menu. From that menu we select **Categorize...**.

7. A window will appear listing all the categories that we have created before. From there, we can assign the desired category to the selected objects.

8. Let's navigate to **Wardrobe | V4 | Intimates** and click on the checkbox on the left of the subcategory to make the assignment.

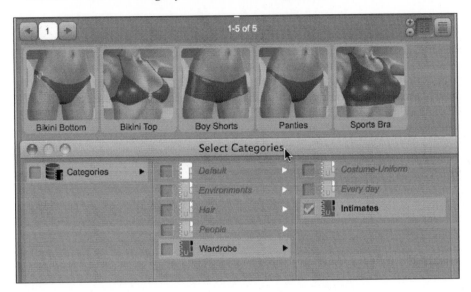

At this point the assignment is done. If we go to our **Categories** group and navigate to **Wardrobe | Intimates**, we will find the same five items. By itself this is a modest change, but when we add more products and more subcategories, we can then create our own way of finding all the items that we need for a certain situation, and we don't have to remember if a certain item was made for Studio or Poser.

Keep also in mind that we are not limited to one category per item. A model can belong to multiple categories, allowing us maximum flexibility.

Importing models from other applications

While Studio has built-in support for Poser files, it can also use models made with other 3D applications. The most common file format used to exchange 3D assets is called **Wavefront OBJ**, commonly abbreviated to **OBJ**.

This file format describes simple 3D assets using a plain text file in which the list of vertices, polygons, UV maps, and other details are listed.

Studio can read OBJ files with ease, which means that we can import models made with programs such as modo, ZBrush, or Blender. All that we need is to have those models exported to OBJ, something that is provided by all 3D programs nowadays.

Scaling issues

While exchanging 3D assets between programs, we need to understand that each program has its own unit of measure and its own axis rotation. For example, Studio uses the centimeter as a unit of measure. This means that if we move an object by one positive unit along the Y axis, we are moving it vertically by one centimeter. Blender, on the other hand, uses meters and the Y axis represents the depth, not the height. So, an increase of one unit on the Y axis moves the object one meter away from the camera.

This is important to remember because the measurements written into an OBJ file are not based on a specific unit. There is nothing inside the OBJ file that describes what unit of measure has been used. As a result, the program that does the import has the responsibility to scale the object based on a selected unit. In other words, it is our responsibility to tell Studio, while importing an OBJ file, how we want it to be scaled. If we don't know what application produced the file, we can open it with a text editor and look at the beginning of the file. Often, there are comments in there that describe the program that generated the file. If such information is not available, we have to just resort to trial and error.

Importing an OBJ file

We are going to learn how to import an OBJ file by using a model available for free at ShareCG. Use `http://www.sharecg.com/v/19515/3d-model/Basic-Hill-1` to download it.

The model is a section of hill with staircases and stone floors.

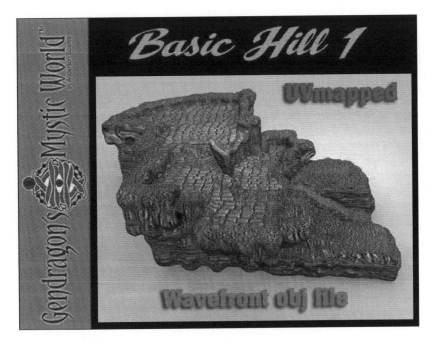

Download the archive and unzip it into a directory of your choice. The `Desktop` one will work fine for now. In a real-world scenario, we will need to create a backup copy so that we can reinstall the model if the need arises.

From the **File** menu we select **Import...**, which will prompt us immediately to select a file to import. Select the `GPTH2C-2.obj` file that has been unzipped from the downloaded archive.

Studio recognizes automatically that the file is of type OBJ, and so it shows a window that provides the parameters to drive the import.

We cannot know what is the scale of the object because there are no details about it. For now, let's just use a 1:1 scale and so we select the **DAZ Studio (1 unit = 1cm)** preset from the drop-down menu at the top.

If the object is too small or too big, we can use Studio's scale parameter to adjust the size. For this operation, we assume that the model is oriented using the same axis orientation of Studio. If our guess is wrong, the model will appear with the wrong orientation.

When we click on the **Accept** button, Studio starts importing the file and it shows a progress bar. After a few seconds the model appears in the scene. Let's place Genesis next to it to show the relative scale.

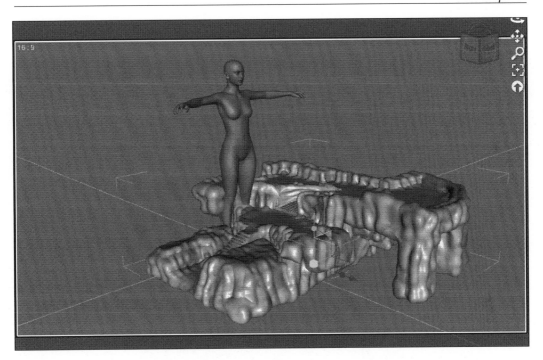

Clearly the model is too small. In fact, it's probably 10 times too small. This is not a problem. We can click on it, delete it, and try again with a different scale. If we look at the list of presets in the import window, we can see that there is one for Silo that assigns 10 centimeters per unit. That sounds like exactly what we needed. Reimporting the model with that scale works perfectly.

At this point we have a new model in Studio that was made with a different program! How cool is that? We have a lot of new possibilities and we can search the Web for models, and be fairly sure that we can use them in Studio.

The only issue is that this model appears completely gray. This is because the OBJ file, in this case, didn't have the right material definition. OBJ files have limited features when it comes to materials, but they can have textures applied.

Now, if we look at the image advertising this model, we see that the author claims that the model is **UV mapped**. UV mapping is a technique of describing how flat, two-dimensional images, can be painted on the surface of a 3D object.

For now this is all that we need to know. Reread the preceding description until it sinks in. What it means, in this case, is that the model is ready to receive an image designed using a specific pattern, and that map will be projected on the surface of the model to make it look like it's made of rocks and tiled floor and so on.

It is finally time that we look at the **Surfaces** tab. This tab contains a panel that allows us to define and edit materials. A given model can be divided in many material zones. For example, Genesis' face is made on one surface that has the face and lips materials. Each material can be defined by a series of properties that we call **channels**.

There is a channel to describe the color of the surface and that is called the **Diffuse** channel. Another channel is used to define the shine of the surface and that is called the **Specular** channel. There are many other channels and they all have a function. Together they define the final result of the material. The set of all these channels is called a **shader**.

All these channels and their definitions are available in the **Surfaces** tab. Let's click on it. The **Surfaces** tab has three subtabs: **Presets**, **Editor**, and **Shader Baker**. We need to click on the **Editor** tab to edit the materials settings for the hill model. The material for that model is called **GPTH2C-2**; make sure that it's selected. Once it has been selected, the series of values appear to the right-hand side of the pane.

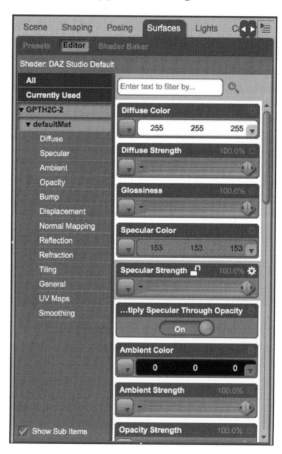

Don't be alarmed by the bewildering set of values and unfamiliar terms. We are going to work on one channel only for now. The very first value, **Diffuse Color**, is what we need to change. Despite the fact that it's called color, that value is actually a combination of an image and a color. Right now it has only the color and no image, that's why the hill model appears gray. The square with an arrow pointing down is the image map selector for this channel. Right now it's empty, but we can edit it. Click on it and a drop-down menu will appear. The first choice is what we need to use now, the one titled **Browse…**.

Click on it and we are presented with the usual file selector. The hill model comes with its own image maps ready to use; they are in the same folder where the OBJ file is. Navigate there and select the file named HILL2.jpg. As soon as we select that file, we see the model in the 3D Viewport change and assume the right look, with rocks and moss painted on the 3D surface.

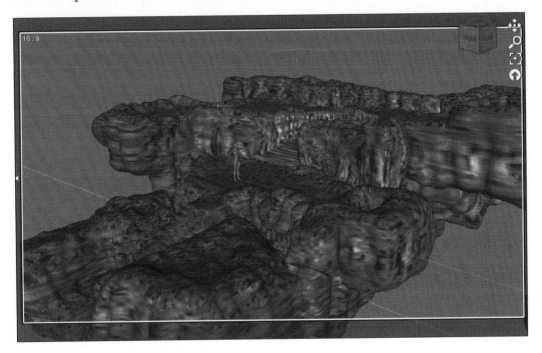

The map fits perfectly, thanks to the UV map that has been defined. A UV map maps every vertex in the 3D model with an appropriate point (pixel) within an image map.

Summary

In this chapter, we have deepened our understanding of how 3D models work by examining the building blocks of every model: vertices and polygons. We saw that we can subdivide polygons to obtain a higher resolution mesh with smoother surfaces.

We also learned how to move around with a camera and why it's important to use a real camera instead of relying on **Perspective View**. The use of focal length and camera position showed us how we can dramatically change the perspective of our scene by either stretching or compressing the depth. The same trick can be used to distort the faces of our characters or to create a flattering portrait.

We saw what kind of lights are available in Studio, when it's appropriate to use them, and how to handle the shadows projected by them. We talked about keeping the shadows on and how that aspect of our scene can contribute to the overall realism of the scene.

The presence of two content managers in Studio can present some challenges, and so we examined how and when to use one or the other. With the **Content Library** tab, we are in control of defining our own categories and assign them to our content as we see fit.

Finally, we saw how to import content made with other 3D applications via the OBJ file format.

All these options provide us with a rather complete toolset for creating our 3D scenes. That is the topic of the next chapter, in which we will see how to create a scene that tells a story via posing and lighting.

8

Building a Full Scene

Now that we know how to move around Studio, it's time to have some fun! Let's build a complete scene with a character in a full environment. This will give us the chance to look at many aspects of 3D composition. At the end of this chapter you will be able to do the following:

- Building a full scene with a figure and an environment
- Conforming clothing to a figure
- Changing the material settings
- Setting the right materials in short time
- Combining colors and images together

Adding an environment

Creating an image is generally about telling a story. In a single frame, like the painters of the past, we can describe a situation, a hero in danger, the triumph of good versus evil, and so on. The element that gives the most immediate sense of where we are is the environment. There are many different models that are available in the marketplace. We can use sci-fi environments, medieval castles, a modern metropolis, or an exotic garden. The possibilities are infinite and in addition to what is available, we can easily mix elements from one set to the other. For example, we could take a medieval tower and place it in the middle of a spaceport. Surely, we can come up with a good reason for that to happen!

The point in this is that we have no limits because unlike physical models, we can move things around with just a few clicks of the mouse. Keep that in mind and let your imagination run wild.

So, the environment is generally the element that determines the mood of the scene, unless we are making a portrait. For this chapter we are going to create a sort of adventurous scene, with a character in a situation of danger. We will get a dynamic pose that will stress the limits of the conforming clothing, which will give us the opportunity to see how to fix the poke-throughs.

A poke-through is the effect of the skin of a character poking through the clothing. This issue is fairly frequent, and it happens for a number of reasons. Poke-throughs are often caused by clothing that is very close to the surface of the character, and with extreme poses doesn't adapt perfectly. Poke-throughs are inevitable and part of the complexity of adapting clothing to a figure that moves. They are not necessarily a symptom of poor quality of the garment. It's part of the work of the 3D artist to deal with them and to resolve the issues.

To create our scene, I decided to use a very fun modular environment made by Eric VanDycke, also known as Traveler, of RuntimeDNA. This environment called Platez provides several walls, door walls, floors, and other elements that can be combined together to create a vast array of environments based on the author's creativity. We are going to take advantage of this flexibility and build this scene:

The image has been rendered with LuxRender via my Reality plugin. Refer to *Chapter 10, Hyper-realism – the Reality Plugin* for more details about the Reality plugin. The image looks a lot better in full color; there is a copy of the file in the project files in the `Chapter_08` folder. Look for the file named `MainScene.png`.

Putting the scene together

You can get the DNA Platez product for free by downloading it from RuntimeDNA. The link for it is `http://www.runtimedna.com/RDNA-Platez-Volume-1.html`.

You will need to add the product to your shopping cart and then perform the checkout procedure. As the product is at zero cost, there will be no request for a credit card. You will receive a link for downloading the product in your e-mail. After you download it, install it using the conventions seen in *Chapter 6, Finding and Installing New Content* in the `Environments` folder of your content.

After installation, DNA Platez will be found in the **Content Library** tab under the **Poser Formats | Environments | Props | DNA_Platez** category, assuming that you followed the installation template that we have discussed previously.

If we look at the following image, we can see that the scene is built in the tradition of Hollywood movies; just build the pieces that will be visible by the camera.

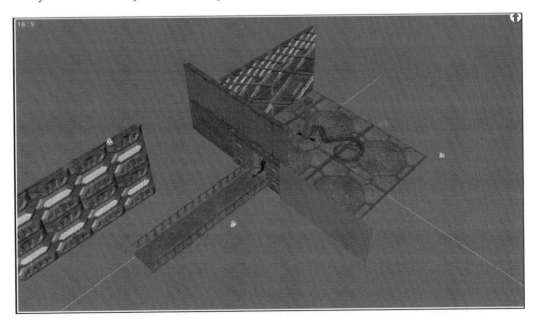

The floor is a series of six **Floor 004** plates aligned side-by-side. To make this job easier, we can simply place the first floor plate, select it, and press *Cmd + C* (on Mac) or *Ctrl + C* (on Windows) to copy its coordinates. Then, place another plate by double-clicking on the **Content Library** tab again and pressing *Cmd + V* (on Mac) or *Ctrl + V* (on Windows) to make it jump to the same coordinates of the first plate. At this point, press *U* to switch to the Universal tool and select one of the arrows to slide it along one axis without altering the other axes. Align it to be side-by-side with the previous plate, making sure that there is no gap between the two. Sometimes, it helps to move the camera to look from below; it makes it easier to spot gaps between the pieces.

Repeat the operation until you have all six plates aligned to form the floor.

The door is a **Door Wall 004** plate. Above the door, there is a **Wall 008** plate. Use the copy and paste trick here to align the two plates.

 The copy and paste trick also works with lights. This makes it very valuable when you have multiple lights to align in the same area.

The wall to the right of the door is a **Wall Plain 002** plate. The wall above it is another **Wall 008** plate.

The walls that are at 90 degrees from the door are two Wall 005 plates. Above them there are a couple of **Wall 007** plates just to add variety.

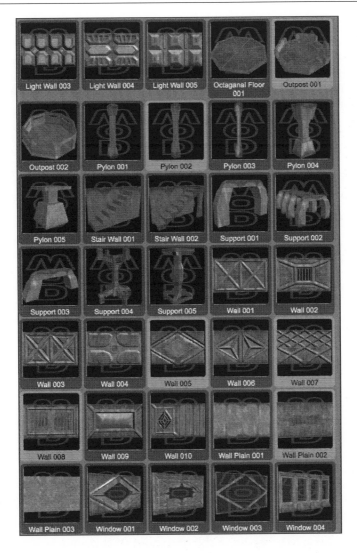

In the middle of the scene, we have **Outpost 001** with **Pylon 002** just to add movement and balance the frame. The outputs have been scaled down considerably so that now it looks like a containment structure. This is a case of changing the purpose of a piece by simply scaling it and placing it out of context. **OutPost 001** has been scaled down to 20.5 percent and rotated slightly, about -2.0 degrees on the y axis. Again, this is just to add something interesting to the frame.

Behind the door there are two instances of **Bridge 001**. Only one section is visible in the frame, but having the second section provides a certain degree of freedom in moving the camera around. To the side of the bridge there are four sections of **Light Wall 004**. As we can see, the sections are floating in mid air and are not connected with anything else. In fact, they are quite separated from the rest of the body of the scene. This is OK, as we are just building what is visible from the camera.

So, now we have built our stage, which gave us some insight into the process of creating a set from scratch. With other premade environments that are already preconfigured, we don't need to place every single element, but this exercise helps us become more familiar with the process of altering the environment to our imagination. We don't have to always use whatever is premade, we can alter it to become something different.

Adding the character

For this scene we will choose to use Victoria 4 instead of Genesis. V4 gives us more selection of clothing and hair, and it's nice to have a bit of variety. If you don't have V4, I strongly suggest to purchase it, as it will give you a lot of options. While there is a figure called V5 available, it is a drastic departure from V4 and it breaks compatibility with its predecessor. Compatibility was never achieved before, but with V4, the market of related products exploded. Literally, tens of thousands of products have been made and continue to be made. People have a large investment in V4. In addition V4 is a very well designed figure that provides good joint design and a high level of realism. For this reason, compatibility with V4 was highly expected and it was disappointing to not see it happen. In any case, you can follow this chapter by using Genesis and the outfit of your choice.

The idea for our scene is to show a character that was running just a second before, and she just came through the door only to face something horribly dangerous that made her stop suddenly.

The first thing to do is to bring V4 in the scene and start posing her with the techniques that we have seen before. This will take some time. For your convenience, I included the pose file in the project files folder, but I encourage you to not use it and instead, try to pose V4 on your own. It doesn't matter if you don't get the pose exactly the same.

Using Inverse Kinematics (IK)

There is a feature that allows us to position the limbs, legs, and arms of a character quickly and realistically by dragging either the feet or the hands to the final position. This feature is called Inverse Kinematics and it's automatically turned on in Studio for figures like Victoria 4 and Genesis.

Instead of moving the thigh, shin, and foot one by one, we can simply use the Translate tool and grab a hand or a foot and drag them around. You will see that the rest of the body will react usually in a logical, expected way.

If this feature doesn't seem to work, navigate to **Edit | Figure | Inverse Kinematics** and make sure that the option **Enable IK** is checked.

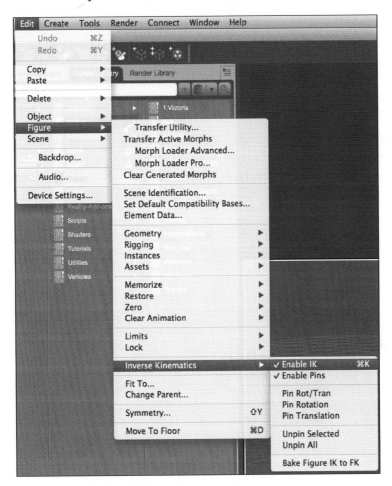

Dressing the character

Once Victoria is in the right pose, we can add the outfit. For this scene, I decided to use a great outfit called Stormchaser by BadKitteh Co sold at Renderosity. You can find it here `http://www.renderosity.com/mod/bcs/ stormchaseroutfitgnd/67510/`.

Stormchaser is a great example of a good outfit that is not limited to the basic shape of V4; it also has morphs for alternative shapes based on the V4 geometry. For example, it fits the Aiko 4 figure, which is a Japanese morph for V4 with strong anime influences. It also fits Alice by AlfaSeeD and The Girl Next Door by Darkehearted, both well-known companies that create high-quality morphs and products for Studio and Poser.

To dress our character, we need to select V4 and then double-click on the garment that we need to add. If the garment doesn't seem to stick to the figure it means that it was not conformed or fitted. This can be easily fixed by selecting the garment and then by navigating to **Edit | Figure | Fit to...**. In the window that comes up select **Victoria 4** and the outfit will conform to V4.

If you have the same outfit, you will see that even when it's configured to fit or conform the body of V4, the outfit itself is not following the shape of the body well. Part of it is sinking inside Victoria.

This is caused by the fact that the morph for the V4 standard body is not enabled. Given that this outfit adapts to many different shapes, there is no automatic way to select which shape should be applied. The creator of Stormchaser didn't set a default, so it's our task to enable the right morph. This is very easy to do. With the Stormchaser outfit selected, let's look in the **Parameters** tab. In there we can find a **Characters** category, in addition to the standard one. Let's click on it. This category groups all the different body morphs that we can apply to the outfit. The values can simply be 0, the morph is disabled, or 1, the morph is active. Let's set the **V4Default** slider to **1** and the bodysuit fits V4 perfectly.

You can expect similar sliders on many types of clothing and even hair props.

After adding the bodysuit, I continue adding the boots to the figure. Once again, if the boots don't snap in position automatically, we need to fit them manually via the menu or by clicking on the **Fit to** drop-down menu in the **Parameters** tab. We need to set the type of figure shape as well and repeat the process for all the other elements of the outfit.

The boots give us the opportunity to see how to handle a couple of different challenges. The first one is generally quite evident. Pointy boots are narrower than the feet that they enclose. Generally, you will find a special pose in the Pose folder connected with the boots that sets the feet and toes of Victoria to be deformed to be inside the boot. This works well if you have open shoes with which you can see the foot. In this case, we have a completely enclosed boot, so it's much easier to simply make the feet invisible. To do so, we need to click on one foot and then look in the **Scene** tab. The node for the foot will be selected. To the left of it there is an icon showing an open human eye. If we click on it, the eyes close. This makes the associated node invisible. It doesn't show in 3D Viewport and doesn't show in the render. We will still be able to select it and pose it, which in turn will move the corresponding area of the boot.

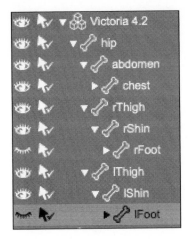

The second issue that we need to address with boots and pants is the overlapping of these two pieces of wardrobe. The outfit could be used with the boots or with other types of shoes. For this reason, the pants are designed to flare out in a natural way. This design presents a problem. When used with the boots, the pants stick out past the boots. This is a simple case of poke-through.

In this case, we are lucky because the author of the outfit has anticipated this situation and created a morph to make the two parts of the outfit work together.

The best way to work with poke-throughs is to switch the view to **Hidden Line**. This view mode is similar to wireframe, but it hides the lines that are not facing the camera.

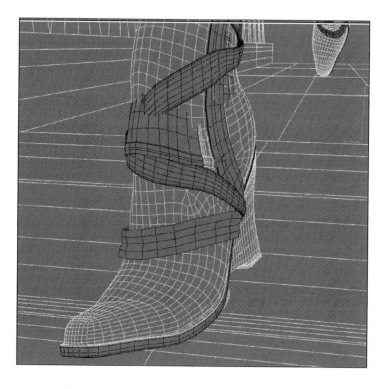

Overlapping pieces of geometry show very well in this mode, as the wireframe patterns cross and break the flow in unnatural way, regardless of what color or texture is used for the surface of the objects.

So, to fix the problem we need to act on two objects: the pants and the boots. For this outfit, the control to adjust the pants is in the main object; so we simply click on the **BodysuitStormchaser** object to select it and open the **Parameters** tab. In there we can find a category called **StylingMorphs**. That category holds all the sliders that control the morphs for this outfit that help in adapting to different circumstances. Here is a small sample of what is available:

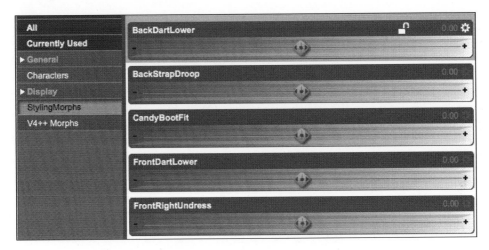

If you are not using the same outfit, don't worry. The same logic is used for hundreds of clothing accessories in the market. Each one is different, but the concept to remember here is that an outfit can be adapted to several situations via premade morphs, and that those morphs are available in the main body or in selected parts of the outfit. Generally, a product lists the morphs that are available so that we can check before the purchase if the outfit will work with the scenes that we want to build.

The morph that we need in this situation is called **ZippyBootFit**. The boots used in this scene are called **ZippyBoots** and if we set the slider to 1.0, the end of the pants will stop flaring out and will stay inside the boots.

While this adjustment fixes the bulk of the problem, we can take care of other, more subtle, poke-throughs via a morph in the boots. Keep this procedure in mind as a general strategy; it applies to other garments, not just the ones in Stormchaser. If we select the ZippyBoots in the scene and open the **Parameters** tab, we can find a **Fit Over Pants** morph in the **Boot Styling** category. Set that slider to **1.00** and the boots will expand to provide more room.

If an outfit doesn't have specific morphs, we can still adapt it by using the scale parameters. By acting on the individual values for scale x, y, and z, we have a lot of flexibility to adapt an object to many situations. Now the boots-bodysuit combination is set, let's move to the next issue.

If we look at the V4 figure closely, we can see that with a pose like this, there are several other poke-throughs in the body of the suit.

These issues are caused by the strong torsion of the abdomen and chest areas, which are pushing this skin-tight outfit to the limit. Stormchaser has several controls to adjust those parts, and we could also just increase the scale of the chest and abdomen areas by a fraction of a point. Instead, we are going to use a function of Studio 4 that is designed to fix these issues automatically.

Let's select the outfit and then navigate to, from the Studio menu, **Edit | Figure | Geometry | Apply Smoothing Modifier**. At first, it might seem like nothing happened, but in a matter of a few seconds those poke-throughs will be gone. The smoothing modifier checks the polygons of a conforming figure and makes them avoid collision with the base figure. This command is very useful when we need to fit very tight garments, like stockings, opera gloves, or wetsuits.

Delving into material poses

We have seen the Stormchaser outfit up to this point decorated in black with white piping. The piping was actually meant to be golden, but the result that we see is caused by the lack of Studio-specific materials. The material files supplied are designed for Poser, and Studio has a limited understanding of those. This apparent issue will actually give us an opportunity to delve into the Studio material manager and fix it by hand, an experience that will come in handy in many situations.

Regardless of this issue, what we need to address is that a single outfit like this can actually assume many different configurations based on the type of material that we apply. So, how do we apply these different materials?

When a product has more than one material configuration, there are several material files that are provided with it. These files can apply different material configuration or alter the way a part of the product works. For example, a shirt can have material files that hide the sleeves or provide a few different configurations: long sleeves, short sleeves, and no sleeves. Material files can provide a lot of flexibility.

To apply a material, we need to have a figure or prop selected and then double-click on the material file in the content library. Old versions of Poser didn't have specialized files for applying materials, and so the MAT files have been traditionally created as pose files that don't pose but apply material settings. It's a bit confusing, but the fact is that most materials will be found in the Pose folder of a product. Those material files can be of two kinds: Studio materials and Poser materials.

If a product has been designed specifically for Studio, you can expect the best result. If a material has been designed for Poser, the result can be unpredictable. Studio has the ability to read the most basic Poser material settings, but it cannot interpret complex Poser procedural materials.

Nevertheless, many authors of content nowadays post clearly in the product description if Studio materials are included. Many products are provided with both Poser and Studio materials in the same package, allowing users to share those products between the programs seamlessly.

The following screenshot shows some of the material files found in the **Pose | GNDStormchaser | MatPoses** folder.

From the icon and the name of the file, we see that each file needs to be applied to a specific part of the outfit. In other words, we need to select the suit body, the boots, or the gloves first, and then double-click on the material icon to apply that material.

Editing materials manually

Let's see now how we can fix the issue with the piping being white instead of gold. The original material was designed for Poser, and something in it didn't agree with Studio.

First of all we need to identify one of the materials involved. Let's switch to **Perspective View** so that we don't change our carefully designed frame, and then move closer to the outfit so that we can easily select the areas of interest with the mouse.

Once we have the outfit maximized in the 3D Viewport, let's press *M* to activate the material selection tool. Now as we hover with the mouse over the outfit, we see the material zones being highlighted. When the material for the piping in the center of the abdomen lights up, let's click on it. When we click on it, the material is selected in the **Surfaces** tab where we can edit it.

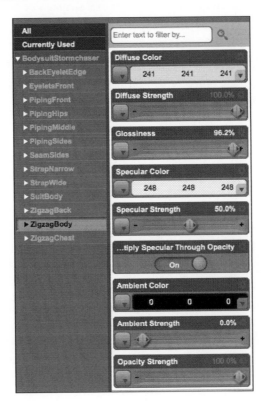

Using channels

A material is divided into areas that describe a certain function of the material. For example, there is an area that determines the amount and shape of the transparency. Another area determines the color of the surface of the material. And another area determines how shiny the material is. All these areas are called **channels**.

Here is a short list of the most useful channels and what they control:

Channels	Description
The diffuse channel	This defines the color or texture of the surface of the material. It can be a solid color, an image map, or an algorithm-generated pattern.
The specular channel	This defines the glossiness of the material.
The alpha channel	This defines the opacity of the material. It can be a single value, 50 percent opaque for example, or it can use an image map to create variable levels of transparency in different parts of the material.

Please note that Studio refers to the alpha channel as **Opacity**.

So, if we want to change the color of the piping, we need to change what's in the diffuse channel in some way.

Now, looking at the **Diffuse Color** value, we see that it's set to **241 241 241**.

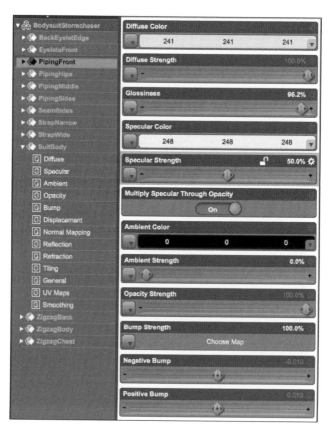

Those numbers are values for the Red, Green, and Blue (RGB) color channels. A color that has the same value for all three channels is a shade of gray. That makes sense, we see some sort of light gray in our Viewport. If we click on the swatch of the color, the OS's color picker will be shown and we can select a new color from there.

The result is immediately shown in the Viewport.

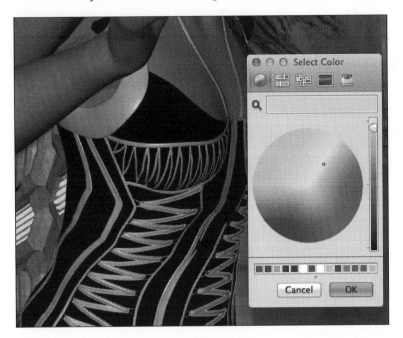

In this case, let's choose a color with values of **241 192 76**. The choice was done by using the color wheel provided by the OS. Mac OS provides a color wheel in the picker; Windows uses a square with several gradients of color. Now we can apply the same change to the other materials involved:

- **PipingSides**
- **PipingMiddle**
- **PipingFront**
- **PipingHips**
- **ZigzagChest**
- **ZigzagBack**
- **SeamSide**
- **StrapWide**
- **StrapNarrow**

Moving on to the vest, the small garment that covers the shoulders, we have the VestPiping material that needs to be set to the same color. Color pickers allow to save a color and recall it from a list of shortcuts. Using this technique, we save some time and set all the materials to the new value in a few seconds. We can also use copy and paste by right-clicking on the specific **Diffuse Color** value and select **Copy Selected Surface(s)**. Then, select the destination diffuse color and apply the symmetrical operation by right-clicking and using the **Paste Selected Surface(s)** option.

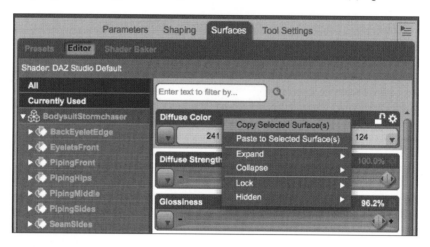

We are in control

The little exercise that we have just done shows us one important concept: we are in control of the materials that we use. While there is a wide variety of products out there, and some of them might be not optimized for Studio, we don't need to let that discourage us. By getting familiar with the **Surfaces** tab, we can easily adjust a material to our liking. This is true also for Studio-specific materials. Just because the author of a product has set a material to be in a specific way, it doesn't mean that the material is set in stone. We might want to dim the color of a texture or make a material shinier. We are in control.

Make sure that you understand the role of the basic channels so that you know where to operate when you need to change the way a material works.

Mixing colors with image maps

If we look carefully, to the left of **Diffuse Color** there is a square with an arrow pointing down.

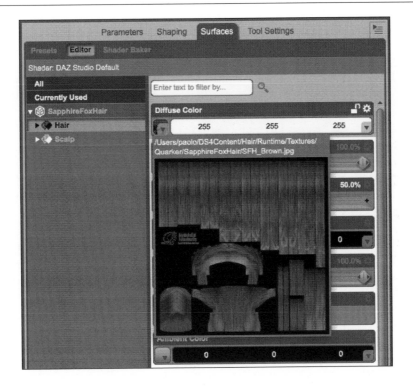

This widget allows us to add an image map to the channel. Image maps in Studio are often referred to as textures, but the term is actually incorrect. A texture is any pattern, solid or otherwise, that is applied to a surface. A solid color is a texture, an image is a texture, and a program-generated pattern, also known as a procedural pattern, is a texture. When we apply an image to a channel, we are using an image map.

We can see that there are several widgets in the Studio material editor that allow us to use an image map together with a color. How these two elements work together is very important.

The color and the image map are multiplied together. To understand how this works we need to introduce an alternative notation for color definition. Up to this point we have used colors using the integer RGB notation. This notation defines a color using three values: the amounts of red, green, and blue. The amounts are expressed with integer values ranging from 0 to 255 because each color channel is saved using a byte and the range for a byte is between 0 and 255.

If you are interested in the reason why a byte has this range, it's important to remember that a byte is defined as a set of eight bits. A bit is a binary digit that can assume only the values 0 and 1. With eight bits, we can express a maximum number of 2^8-1 or 255. The 2 in the previous expression is the numeric base. When we use bits, we work with a binary system, also known as base two. The 8 is the number of digits.

Whenever we need to find what is the maximum number, that can be expressed using a certain amount of digits the formula is: *numeric base^number of digits-1*.

If we were using the decimal system, we would have 10^8-1 or 99999999. Going back to our original expression: 2 to the power of 8 is 256, minus 1 equals to 255.

Instead of using an integer system, most computer graphics programs convert the value to a floating point number for convenience of processing. Each color channel is therefore expressed internally as a value from 0.0 to 1.0. The formula for converting from integer to floating point is simply to divide 1 by 255, and then multiply that value by the channel's integer value. With that formula we can convert our gold color used for the piping to 0.94 0.75 0.3. For example, the red is converted by 1:255 x 241 = 0.945098039, rounded to 0.94.

If we now introduce an image map, we can multiply each RGB pixel of the image map by the RGB color. Since each pixel in the map is itself expressed with floating point values, the result will never go beyond 1.0, and we will obtain a new image map that has a gold cast.

To understand how this works, let's consider a hypothetical pixel in the map having and RGB value of 193 240 95. We then set the diffuse color to be a shade of gray: 142 142 142. The image map pixel is converted to floating point to 0.76 0.94 0.37. Our gray color is converted to 0.56 0.56 0.56. When we mix them together, we obtain 0.76 x 0.56 = 0.42, 0.94 x 0.56 = 0.53, 0.37 x 0.56 = 0.21, or 0.42 0.56 0.21. So, the result of the multiplication of an image map pixel by another color is an image that, in this case, has the same color but half as bright as the original image.

The preceding exercise is telling us, for example, that we can use grayscale colors to dim an image without having to edit the image in an external program. It's convenient to remember that 127 127 127 is medium gray, a color that is half the brightness of pure white. Any image multiplied by 127 127 127 will be half as bright as the original.

By the way, the preceding algorithm explains exactly what the Photoshop Multiply blending mode does.

Since 1/255*255 equals 1.0, it is derived that multiplying an image map to pure white, or 255 255 255, means to multiply each pixel by 1.0 1.0 1.0. In other words the original image is left unchanged.

If we recall that multiplying a value by 0 means to turn that value to 0, we can use that principle to completely remove a color from an image map. For example, multiplying an image map by 255 255 0 will leave the red and green channels untouched but remove every bit of blue from the resulting image map. Pretty handy, isn't it?

So, remember that whenever you see a widget that handles both an image map with a color, the operation that happens between the two is a multiplication, and that you can use it to dim a texture using a gray color or give it a color cast of your choice.

The specular channel

In addition to the diffuse channel we have the specular channel represented by the **Glossiness**, **Specular Color**, and **Specular Strength** values. The specular channel controls the properties that define the shine of a material. When we look at a shiny material there are two main factors that we need to consider: the amount of light reflected and how polished the surface is.

The specular color determines the amount of light that is reflected. More specifically, the brightness of the color controls this property. A brighter color reflects more light, a darker one reflects less. An easier way to demonstrate this is to do a simple exercise.

1. Save the scene that you have so far created, and create a new scene.
2. In there add a sphere primitive by navigating to **Create | New Primitive...** and select the sphere.

3. With the sphere selected, go to the **Surfaces** tab and select the default material.

4. Set the diffuse color to a bright red.
5. Set **Specular Color** to **127 127 127** which is mid gray.
6. Set **Glossiness** to **50.0%**.
7. Make sure that **Specular Strength** is at **100.0%**.

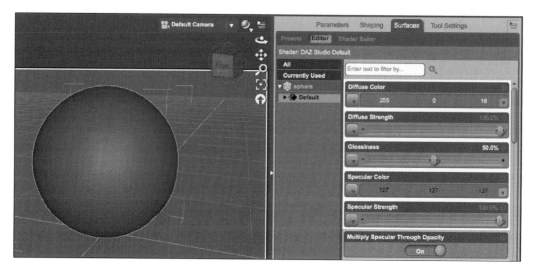

Take note of the result in the 3D Viewport.

8. Now change **Specular Color** to **255 255 255** and notice the difference.

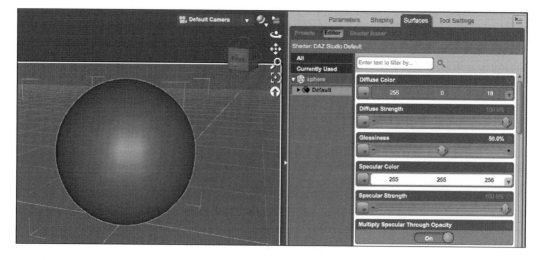

When we change the color to pure white, we keep exactly the same hue, the relationship between the RGB values, but the brightness changes. This is what is making the material capable of reflecting more light.

The **Glossiness** slider controls how polished the surface is. A rough surface can still reflect a lot of light but the light is scattered by the roughness of the surface. For example, a pearl has that property. If we take a piece of rough metal and we polish it, we can get a mirror-like surface. In fact, that's how primitive mirrors were made, before civilizations learned how to master the craft of glass making. The glossiness slider allows us to change how rough or polished the surface of the material is. Higher values indicate higher levels of polish.

Finally, Specular Strength is a simple multiplier that acts on the specular color. If we set **Specular Color** to **255 255 255** and set **Specular Strength** to **50.0%**, we obtain the exact same result of setting **Specular Color** to **127 127 127** and **Specular Strength** to **100.0%**. The slider is just a convenient way of controlling the brightness of **Specular Color**.

Using the alpha channel

The alpha channel is the standard term used in Computer Graphics to refer to the control of transparency. In Studio this is controlled by the Opacity widget, which includes a numeric value and an image map. In its simpler form we can use the Opacity widget to set the level of opacity of a material. Lower values cause the material to be more transparent. For example, the following image shows a sphere that is 30 percent opaque, or 70 percent transparent:

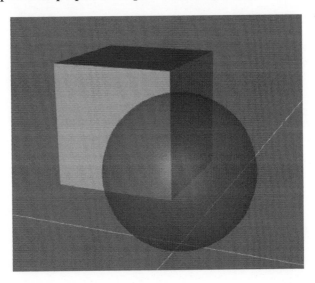

As we can see, the whole material is uniformly made semi-transparent.

On the other hand, we can set an image map to control the transparency. We click on the image map widget to the left of the **Opacity** slider and select **Browse...** from the pop-up menu.

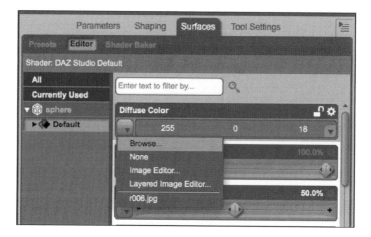

We can then select a grayscale image that is used to control the opacity on a pixel-by-pixel basis. For this demonstration I generated a simple map via Photoshop.

When we apply this map to the alpha channel and set the **Opacity** slider back to **100.0%**, this is the result:

For this effect to work, the image map must be a grayscale image. The map is taken to have numeric values that express the level of opacity for each pixel. For this reason the map needs to be of the grayscale type, otherwise it would be hard to predict which pixels will result in transparent or opaque areas. The black pixels indicate transparent areas or zero opacity. The white pixels indicate opaque areas. The values in between are interpolated to created intermediate levels of opacity. For example, medium gray or **127 127 127** will result in 50 percent opacity.

How is the map painted on the sphere? Is it something that Studio does automatically? No, that is something that has been defined by the author of that specific 3D primitive and is controlled by a special type of map, called a UV map.

Learning UV maps

When the need to paint a 2D image over a 3D surface was analyzed, a solution was found: associate each vertex in the 3D model with a specific pixel inside the image. When we deal with 2D geometry, we generally use the Cartesian coordinate system, which labels the horizontal location with x and the vertical location with y. While referring to a pixel inside an image map used to texturize a 3D model, the symbols u and v are used instead, probably to avoid confusion with the x and y used for the coordinates of the vertex.

UV mapping is the technique of mapping a series of 3D vertices to a list of 2D points. The matrix of 2D points then can be used to project an image map on the geometry.

The following image shows the UV map for the face skin material (`1_SkinFace`) of V4 projected on the original texture for the face.

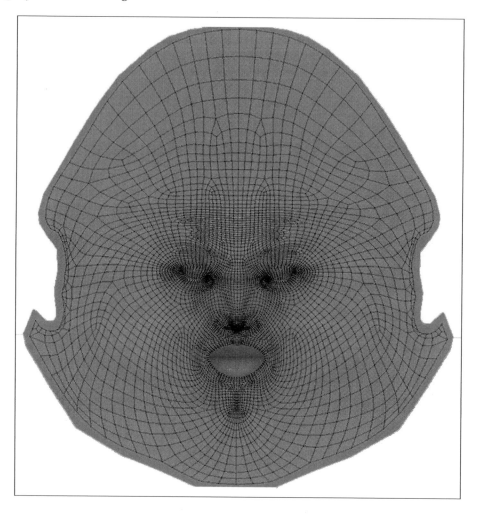

Note that the lips are not part of the map. The material for the lips is mapped separately.

While Studio does not provide tools to manipulate the UV map, it is important to at least be aware of how image maps are projected onto the 3D surface.

Setting the character's skin

Now that we know about material files, we can change the skin of our character. Victoria 4 comes with a default base skin, which uses low quality image maps that show a rather bizarre purple fuzzy bikini. While that gives Victoria a measure of modesty, the bikini shows through several outfits and the basic maps are just too low quality to be realistic. There are literally hundreds of skin replacements for V4. Some of the best are by Danae (Renderosity), Viktohria (Renderosity and RuntimeDNA), and Syyd (RuntimeDNA). There are other authors as well that provide very good alternative skins. The preceding names are just a very small sample. In this example, I have used Danae's Rio. To apply a skin we simply select V4, navigate to the `Pose` folder, and find the folder that contains the material files. Double-click on the right one and we are done. The following screenshot shows the Danae's Rio materials in the content library:

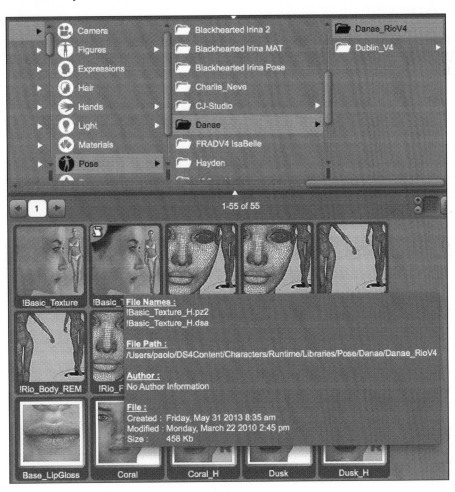

After we apply the material, our scene is ready to go. The only thing that remains to do is to set some good lights and that is the subject of the next chapter.

Final bits

The hair for this scene is an old model, but one that still delivers really good results. It's called **Sapphire Fox Hair**, available at DAZ, and it was actually made for Victoria 3. There are several products in the marketplace that make it fit to V4, and the fitting can be easily done by hand using the scale and translate values.

The monster is the excellent Dynoconda available at DAZ. I just did some minimal adjustments from the default pose, mainly to reposition the neck and tilt the head.

Summary

In this chapter we have seen all the elements that can contribute to creating a full scene. We first started putting together a full environment out of small building blocks, and this showed us how we can combine elements together to create our own environment, beyond what the original product provided.

We have seen how to manage several aspects of fitting a garment to a human figure, including mixing together elements such as boots and pants. We also used the smoothing feature of Studio to remove poke-throughs.

We have seen how to use material presets and how to edit a material by using the **Surfaces** tab. Finally, we learned about channels and how they contribute to the final material.

It's now time to look at how to use lighting artistically, something that we will learn to do in the next chapter. Lighting is probably the single most important element of any scene. Learning how to use it and when to use it is a fundamental skill for any 3D artist. The next chapter will introduce lights, their use, and how to control them.

9
Lighting

Lighting is where the magic happens. This is true for both photography and 3D art.

I have noticed many times that newcomers to the field of 3D art tend to focus on a series of technical issues—texture resolution, antialiasing, SSS, for example—and spend comparatively smaller amounts of energy in learning about lighting. The harsh reality is that great lighting will do more for the final quality of your image than anything else. Great lighting upstages texture resolution and even material definition.

Learning about lighting is, therefore, one of the most important tasks facing a 3D artist, no less important than it is for a photographer.

We cannot condense all there is to learn about lighting in one chapter—it takes years of practice to become proficient in this field—but we will see some of the basic principles that can guide us in the process of learning about the wonderful art of painting with light.

Setting the scene

For this lighting lesson we are going to use a set created by Jack Tomalin, called The Throne of the Skeleton King. Jack has graciously provided the set to be included for free for all the readers of this book. You can find the ZIP file containing the set in the project files for this book. It's the file called TSK.zip in the 3DAssets directory.

Jack is one of the top developers of content for DAZ Studio and Poser, with a vast assortment of exotic and elaborate environments. I invite you to visit his website, www.jacktomalin.com to find more environments that can be used to expand your Runtime.

This set leads itself to very dramatic lighting. Let's first add it to our scene and then add a figure. I'm using V4 with a great armor outfit, the Historical Armor by Arien, to which I applied the **Sisterhood of the Sword** texture package. You can use Genesis or any other figure if you prefer, there are no constraints. The pose for this scene is included in the project files and it can be applied to both V4 and Genesis.

 You can find the complete scene without the figure in the projects files. In the Chapter_09 folder look for the TSK_scene.duf file. To that scene you can add your figure of choice. To pose your character you can use TSK_figure_pose_v4.duf for V4, or TSK_figure_pose_gen.duf for Genesis. These files are provided for your convenience. I invite you to ignore them and recreate the scene from scratch using the instructions in this chapter. But in case you get stuck, you can use the files provided to help understand how the scene should be set. To apply the pose navigate to **File | Merge**.

This is a typical situation for the Studio artists. There is nothing wrong or outdated about V4. I have a lot of content in my Runtime that I have bought over the years, and like thousands of others, I'm not going to throw it away because a new figure is available today. In this specific case, it makes no difference to use V4 or Genesis, so I use V4 because I have the armor for that model, while I don't have anything comparable for Genesis. Trying to adapt the Historical Armor to fit Genesis would be just a waste of time without bringing any benefit.

Our design decisions should not be influenced by marketing. If Genesis is the best choice for the job at hand, use it. But if another figure fits the situation better, reach for that figure and make your life easier. Victoria 4, or even Victoria 3, can be used today to create stunning images, especially in a case like this when we cover most of the character with a suit of armor.

The frame

Here is the frame that we are going to recreate. It's best if you look at the original color file for the projects files—the black and white print cannot give you a complete idea of the direction that we are going to. Look for the file named FinalRender.png.

The camera's focal length is set at **43.51** mm for a nice wide view, which enhances the dramatic effect.

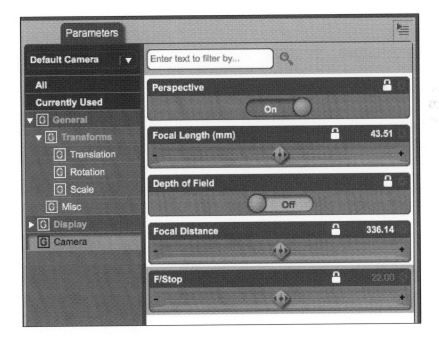

As we can see from the preceding screenshot, the mood is dark, pensive, and the lighting is meant to accentuate that mood with splashes of light on the walls. We want to simulate the lighting provided by torches and flames. The braziers give us the perfect opportunity to place orange-colored lights to suggest the presence of fire.

Adding the required lights

Lighting is not about illumination. Lighting is not about making things visible. Lighting, in fact, is often used to hide things. Take a look at the original Alien by Ridley Scott. Up until the very end we see very little of the creature. The monster is hinted at and kept in the darkness. That's what makes it so scary.

Lighting is an artistic choice. The sooner you stop thinking about lighting as a way of making objects visible, the sooner you will start using it as an artistic tool. Think of each light as a paintbrush that provides a brush stroke of a certain shape, color, and strength.

There is no doubt that there is a great deal of technical detail about lighting. Like any craft, lighting requires some technical knowledge. The same is true for painting, photography, and hundreds of other artistic activities. Even graffiti artists need to know the technical points of how to mix the right type of spray paint and how to use stencils properly. Don't let the technicalities take center stage. Lighting is an artistic choice and that must be our focus in order to be able to use light effectively. The technical information needs to be learned and practiced until it becomes second nature and then it fades in the background. Technicalities tend to become prominent when there is no enough familiarity. Practice transforms what is new into something familiar so it's important that you practice the effects of applying a light until you don't have to think about it.

Before adding a light to a scene we need to know what role it has. Without that piece of information we cannot add a new light; it would just create confusion and provide no benefits. We might not know the exact location, color, and intensity of a light before adding it, but we need to know why we want it in the scene. For example, we might need it to brighten the face of the subject. Or maybe we want to project a shadow in a specific location. In fact, thinking of light as the generator of shadows is actually a very effective way of approaching the lighting problem.

It is possible that after experimenting with a light, we reach the conclusion that we don't need it, and so we end up deleting it. That's perfectly OK, don't let what I said earlier paralyze you from adding a light once a legitimate artistic question comes to your mind. We are human and sometimes we need to try things before we know for sure if they work. The important thing is that we don't start adding lights recklessly; that never works.

Although we work with 3D software, the end result is a two-dimensional image. Shadows play a fundamental role in sculpting the image and providing a three-dimensional, engaging look. In fact, the first light that I generally add to a scene is the one that creates the main shadow. This light is called the **key light**.

The following image shows the position of the key light:

The role for this light is to show the side of the character, which makes for a more dramatic effect than full-frontal lighting, and to project a shadow on the right wall to accentuate and amplify the pose. Press *Cmd + R* (on Mac) or *Ctrl + R* (on Windows) to do a render at this point, the effect should be quite clear.

 Also, note that the light is positioned low, pointing up. That is called a **low key light** and it's normally used for scary or dramatic scenes.

Studio provides several types of lights. For the key light we use a spot because it provides excellent control. In fact, we will see that most of the time we use spots to light a scene. The spot emanates light in one direction, forming a cone that is controllable by the **Spread angle** parameter. The key light has been set to have **Spread Angle** of **39** degrees, **Intensity** at **100.0**%, and **Color** of **255 216 158** (RGB).

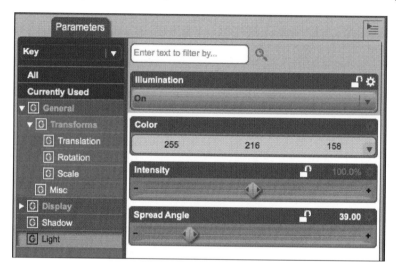

That is a nice, pale orange that suggests light from a fire. The shadow is set to **Raytraced** (this is going to be our default from now on) with a softness of 15 percent.

Renaming objects

When we add lights and other objects to the scene, Studio assigns a unique name to those objects. The name is decided by the program, but it's not set in stone, we can change it. Having a series of lights named Spotlight 1, Spotlight 2, and so on is not helpful to make us understand the role of each light. So, it's best to rename a light as soon as it's been added to the scene. To rename an object, we need to work in the **Scene** tab. The procedure is very simple. We first select the object and then click again on its name. An edit field will appear to let us type in the name for the object. Make sure that you don't double-click on the name. The sequence is click once, wait a second, and click again.

Let's name this first light Key.

Cinematic lighting

Before we continue, there is an important lighting concept that we need to understand. Very often I see that Studio artists try to light a scene based on what they see in real life or in the movies. That approach is not going to work.

Our eyes are amazing in their ability to perceive the difference of light and darkness. They also continuously adapt to variable light conditions without us doing any conscious effort. Film, digital sensors, and 3D renderers don't have the same flexibility. The range of light and darkness simultaneously recorded by a device is called the latitude of that device. Motion picture film and digital cameras, even high-end DSLRs, have less than half the latitude of the human eye.

This means that if you see a given light situation in real life and you want to reproduce it with a digital camera, you will need to enhance the lighting to help the camera capture a comparable image. Latitude should not be confused with the ability to see in the dark. Latitude is about being able to record bright areas and dark areas simultaneously, without overexposing the bright spots and underexposing the dark spots.

For example, a person holding a candle at arm's length will not register enough light to show much more of hand holding the candle, unless the flame is brought next to the face of the subject. Our eyes can see through that dim light, but film and digital cameras cannot do that. The same is for images rendered by 3D programs on the screen.

For this reason movie productions often use trick candles that have two or even three wicks. The additional wicks make the candles much brighter. Even in that case, the amount of light generated by the candles is usually not enough, and supplemental lights are employed. If that was not done, it would be impossible to expose the image correctly. Because of the limited latitude of cameras and film, if there were no additional lights and the scene was exposed for the subject, the flame will be blown out—what we call **overexposing the image**. On the other hand, if the scene was exposed for the flame, the face and the rest of the frame would be in complete darkness—what is called **underexposing the image**.

So, on the set of a movie production the cinematographer and crew add more lights in a subtle and believable way. In the case of candlelight, they might add a large, diffuse light and color it with a plastic sheet, called gel, to make it orange. The diffuse light will decrease the contrast of the scene and it will be perfectly believable. If the light is positioned correctly, it will not be seen out of place because the candle is providing the reason for the light to be seen. In Hollywood parlance, the candle is giving the light the motivation for being there. Unmotivated lights can be added to a scene, but that's a technique that is tricky to execute. If you are not a seasoned photographer or cinematographer, it's better to stick to motivated lights for the time being.

With 3Delight we don't have exposure control; the only way to adjust the brightness of the scene is by using the intensity value of the lights. We will see how that changes while using Reality and LuxRender. For now we are going to use 3Delight as a point-and-shoot camera that adjusts exposure automatically.

The braziers

Those two braziers at the side of the throne are perfect for placing some spotlights to simulate the bright light coming from the burning wood. We want to have the light splash on the wall so that we can see part of it. The first light that we place is on the camera-left brazier. We orient it so that it points toward the wall.

Color for this light is **209 99 4**, **Intensity** is set to **129.7%**, and **Spread Angle** is set to **60.00** degrees. Make sure to rename this light `Left brazier`.

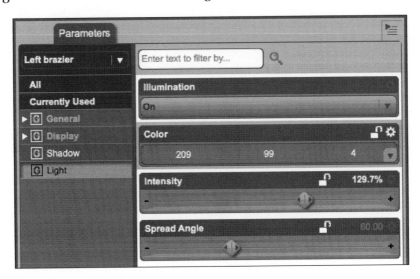

In a similar fashion we add two spotlights to the brazier to the right of the frame. We need two lights in this case because the area of the wall is larger. We could have used a single light with a larger cone, but two lights give us more control. One light is pointed slightly toward the throne, the other is angled in the opposite direction. These lights are named `Right brazier` and `Right brazier 2`. You can see the result up to this point by examining the file named `TSK_intermediate_01.png`.

At this point the scene is very dark in the lower part of the frame, especially in the left corner. It also lacks contrast, which makes the whole combination not very attractive. We are going to fix this by adding some moonlight.

Moonlight

The moon does not emanate light on its own. What we see is the light of the sun reflected on the surface of the moon. So, strictly speaking, we are seeing sunlight. But because of the distance of the moon from our planet, the light that we see is very dim, which is causing a shift of our visual perception. When our eyes have to peer into the darkness, the result is to lose color detail. Everything looks quite desaturated. That's just how our eyes-mind complex works.

Since the invention of color film, photographers and cinematographers have simulated the effect of moonlight using blue light, and that effect has become ingrained in our visual language. We are going to use the same approach for this scene.

To change the color of a light, photographers apply sheets of special heat-resistant plastic called **gels**. Gels come in a range of many colors and intensities. The most common gels are **CTO (Color Temperature Orange)** and **CTB (Color Temperature Blue)**. The quality of light is defined in color temperature and measured in Kelvin degrees. For example, a tungsten lamp has generally a color temperature of 3200 Kelvin (K). Daylight can be anywhere between 5600K and 6500K. Paradoxically, the higher the color temperature, the colder a light is considered. For example, a light bulb (3200K) is hotter than daylight (6500K).

When placing a CTB gel on a tungsten light, which has a color temperature of 3200K, we make that light shift to a colder temperature and it will not turn blue but become a daylight source. In this way we can mix tungsten with natural sunlight without seeing a difference in color. Gels can be layered to accentuate the effect.

With Studio we cannot use gels, but we need to operate on the RGB value. Nevertheless, it's useful to know how things work in the real world.

The first step is to place a spotlight outside, behind the rose window, pointing inside. This setup has limited use, but it gives us the right motivation for additional lighting. To make the light visible, we need to be very careful about the position and intensity of the light. Between the elaborate design of the transparency map used in the alpha channel for the window, and the fact that the light is dark blue, we need to bring the intensity of the spot up considerably. The parameters for this light are: **Color** set to **169 214 255**, **Intensity** set to **500.0%** (you need to disable the limits for this light to apply this value), **Spread Angle** set to **60** degrees, and **Shadow Softness** set to **4.0%**. This light is named Moon outside.

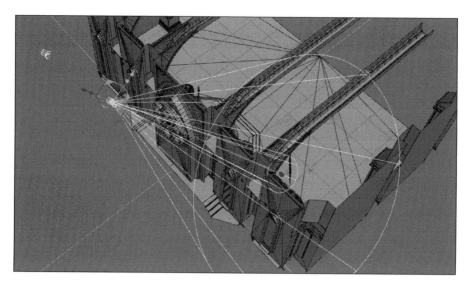

Another spotlight is set to similar settings, and it points toward the long window at camera-right (main camera). This light is named `Moon outside window`. As we can see from this example, there is no need to use short, cryptic names for our objects; we can be quite descriptive. But make sure to not abuse this flexibility. Three words is where generally I draw the line.

To test the result of these lights, it's best to turn off all the other lights and render an image. Isolating the moon lights does two things for us:

- It makes the render go faster so that we can adjust the lights quickly
- It shows us exactly what those lights do for our scene

I included the image named `TSK_moon_lights.png` to show the effect of just those two lights. Light isolation is a great technique to help us during the design of our lighting.

While we have some splashes of moonlight on the floor, we can see that they are hardly enough to convey the right atmosphere. This is where we imitate Hollywood and supplement the light with something more. In this case, what we need is more blue light in the chamber.

When we run test renders for evaluating lighting, it is crucial to have a fast response from the renderer. Unfortunately, 3Delight slows down to a crawl when rendering hair. For this reason, it is best to avoid adding hair to the figure until the very end of the process. Alternatively, we can add the hair and then make it invisible until we are done with the test renders.

To do so we add another spotlight, this time inside the chamber, up near the ceiling and pointing down.

The parameters for this light are: **Color** is set to **169 214 255**, **Intensity** is set to **100.0%**, **Spread Angle** is set to **60.0%**, and **Shadow Softness** is set to **7.4%**. We name the light Moon.

With this light, we get a nice amount of blue splashing on the floor and on the support for the right-side brazier. Most of the window patterns projected on the floor are preserved, and the overall effect of moonlight is much stronger.

Ambient color

Even by increasing the intensity of the moonlight lamps, the window glass looks quite spent, lifeless. This is caused by several factors, such as the fact that Studio has no real simulation for glass. We will see how this can be changed when we examine the Reality plugin and LuxRender.

Instead of spending more time and energy in trying to light it properly, we can use a trick that revolves around a property of the material. We can easily simulate a glow by using a material property called **Ambient Color**. Let's press *M* to switch to the material selection tool, click on the glass behind the throne, and then click on the **Surfaces** tab to examine the material definition. The node selected should be called arch and the material selected should be **arch_glass**. In the **Ambient Color** selector let's choose a light blue, for example, **204 223 255**. Finally, let's set **Ambient Strength** to **87.3%**.

We then need to repeat this for the windows at the side of the throne and we are all done. Now the windows glow brightly as if lit by the moon outside.

Adjusting darkness

While we talk about dark scenes and blue lights, it's important that we address an important issue for any visual arts practitioner: monitor calibration. I see very often images submitted to deviantART or other 3D art galleries that are so murky, so dark to be almost unrecognizable. I'm not talking about images that are partially dark as evident in a film noir. The renders that I saw are all murky, with features barely visible and 60 percent or more of the image approaching black.

This happens because the artists didn't calibrate the computer monitor. Regardless of how expensive your computer and your screen are, they are not calibrated correctly from the factory and the levels of brightness and contrast vary enormously.

I'm sure that those murky renders look better on the authors' monitors, which are probably much too bright and with contrast incredibly out of balance. It's a shame that others will not be able to enjoy those renders.

The solution to this problem is simple, we need to use a calibration tool such as the Spyder4PRO or ColorMunki. These tools are a combination of a hardware sensor and software that tests your monitor. The sensor is placed on the screen and it analyzes objectively the levels of the screen, including brightness, contrast, white balance, and color levels. Once the calibration program runs the full battery of tests, it adjusts the monitor parameters and saves the new values on a special file that will be loaded by the OS from that point on. This operation guarantees that we work with a monitor that reproduces images in the most accurate way possible.

From this point on, we need to repeat the calibration process every month or so. Monitors change over time and periodic recalibrations ensure that we keep having good image reproduction.

Checkpoint

This is the perfect time to turn on the lights that we switched off before and do a render of the scene. The result is in the file named `TSK_intermediate_02.png`. This is almost right. We have our key light with the big, ominous shadow, we have the light from the braziers, and we have the moonlight to contrast the fire with its coldness.

What is not working at this point are two things: the face of the subject is too dark and the left-hand side of the frame is just a big black blob. It's important that we understand the difference when darkness gives atmosphere and when it's just too much. One of the parameters that we can use is balance. The left-hand side of the image is such a large portion of black that it skews the balance of the scene. Our eyes go automatically there, but there is nothing to see there. Clearly, we need to break that block of black with some light.

Let's take care of the face first; this is an easy fix. We are going to add yet another spot to brighten that zone. To make the spot fit the scene, we are going to color it orange (RGB set to **255 179 24**). This light has the role of making us see the face a little better. The face has already quite a bit of light. This additional face spot is present just to reduce the darkness of the shadows and brighten the face a bit. For this reason we need to keep the **Intensity** low at **28.6%**. We also need to reduce the spread of the light so that it doesn't spill to the rest of the scene. **Spread Angle** is set to **15.52** degrees. Rename the light `Face`.

This is another example of painting with light. This spot is another "brush stroke" that we deliver. As with all brushes, we have freedom to apply a certain force to the stroke, not just color and direction. Remember to consider the intensity of the lights. It's the rhythm of light and shadow that keeps the image interesting.

Finishing touches

The next light that we are going to add is used to break that big block of darkness on the left of the frame. Let's place another spot at camera-left, just outside the frame. This light is almost at the same position of the key light: positioned low, pointing toward the left brazier and the back wall. **Color** is set to **255 204 92**, **Intensity** is left at **100.0%**, but **Spread Angle** is set to **33.25** degrees to avoid spilling the light on the parts of the frame that don't need it. We assign the name `Left rim` to this light.

We see the result in the following image, which you can examine in glorious color by opening the file `TSK_intermediate_03`:

We are very close, but the rim light now illuminates the back wall in a way that is too obvious, too direct.

Cookies

We can solve this problem with a simple trick, something that is used in movie productions every day. What we need is something that breaks the light, something that gives a bit of rhythm to the spot so that it's not so obvious. In theater and movie production there are panels of plywood, foam core, or other rigid materials that have cutouts of various shapes. These panels are placed in front of a light to break it up and project interesting patterns of light and shadow on the set. The original name for one of these panels is **Cucoloris**, usually nicknamed **cookie**.

We can make our own simple cookie in Studio. First of all, we add a plane primitive to our scene. Then, we move it close to the Left rim light and we resize it so that the **Z Scale** parameter is at **8.0**%. Now let's add a new plane; select the first one and press *Cmd + C* (on Mac) or *Ctrl + C* (on Windows) to copy its position and size. Select the new plane and press *Cmd + P* (on Mac) or *Ctrl + P* (on Windows) to paste the attribute of the first plane. The second plane jumps to the same position of the first one. Now let's call the Universal tool by pressing *U* and move the second plane down a bit, just enough to leave a slit between the two planes.

Let's repeat the sequence two more times until we have four blinds spaced apart. The effect is good, but we want to be able to move these four planes as a single entity, so that it's easy to position them in the right place. This can be easily accomplished by using the group primitive of Studio.

From the **Scene** tab, let's click on the first plane and then press and hold the *Cmd* (on Mac) or *Ctrl* (on Windows) key. While holding the key pressed, we then click on the other planes one at the time until all four are selected. At this point we can let go of the *Cmd* (on Mac) or *Ctrl* (on Windows) key. With the four planes highlighted now, let's navigate to **Create | Group...** from the Studio menu. When prompted for the group's name, enter the word Blinds. The four planes have disappeared and in their place there is a new entity called **Blinds**. If we click on the disclosure triangle at the left of the group's name, we see our four planes there. In fact, we see that they have not moved from the 3D Viewport.

What happened is that we grouped those four objects together, so that now we can select the group in the **Scene** tab and then use the Universal tool to move all four blinds together as a single unit. This is what you should see:

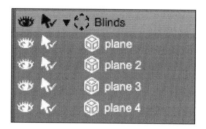

The cookie is now ready to be positioned in front of the light. If we place it close to the light, the shadow that it projects will be blurry. If it's positioned closer to the wall, the shadow will be sharper. We want to break the light with some blurry shadow, so we place the cookie fairly close to the Left rim light.

Now we can do our final test render and the light is scattered a bit, giving us the right effect. See the file named `FinalRender`. If we don't like the position, we can use the **Blinds** node to rotate or move the whole group as a single entity.

No lights in the frame

In this lighting exercise all our lights are not visible by the camera. Make this way of working your habit. Photographers have no choice but to be ingenious about placing light in a way that is not visible by the camera. The fact that we can make a light invisible by a trick of the software should not be something that you rely on. Because we are used to not seeing lights in the frame, if a source of light is in the frame and we can't see it, that will be potentially jarring for our brain. It will not look correct.

Recently, I was playing a videogame on my PS3, my character on screen crawling inside an air duct. In the middle of an intersection between two ducts, I noticed a much brighter splash of light. I looked for the source—maybe there was an opening in the duct or maybe there was a light installed—but I could not find any light source. Nevertheless, a spotlight was clearly placed above my head. Even professional game developers fall into the trap of invisible lights. Be very careful about this. Unless you are simulating ambient light with one or more distant lights, if you want a light to be invisible, move it out of the frame.

Summary

There is much more about lighting, but the procedures described here should give you a good idea of the approach used while lighting a scene. The key concept here is to think about a source of light as something that we can control and shape to our will. Placing objects in front of a light will scatter it and make it create interesting shadows. Speaking of shadows, remember that they are the main tool with which we create a sense of depth in a bidimensional image.

In the next chapter we will delve deeper into the realm of realistic lighting by using an alternative renderer, LuxRender, via the Reality plugin. With Reality we will be able to change the Studio materials to simulate real materials such as metal, glass, and water. The world of photorealism is within reach.

10
Hyper-realism – the Reality Plugin

For many 3D artists, achieving photorealistic results is the Holy Grail of 3D technology. Up to this point we have rendered our scenes using 3Delight, the renderer that is integrated in Studio. Although this situation is convenient, it doesn't mean that it's the only way to render a Studio scene. High-end 3D programs such as Maya or Blender have the option to switch renderers, and it's common for users of those programs to choose a renderer based on the desired result. This is done because each renderer has a different look and provides tools that might be more appropriate for a certain workflow. We will see in this chapter that we have the same opportunity with Studio.

LuxRender is an open source, physically accurate renderer that delivers extremely realistic images. Studio can render with Lux via the Reality plugin, a fully featured render interface that converts materials and geometry from Studio to Lux.

Using the Reality plugin we can achieve levels of realism that, not long ago, were only attainable with programs costing thousands of dollars. In this chapter we will see how to use this plugin and how to achieve photorealism in Studio.

I'm the author of the Reality plugin and I will do my best to keep the information objective and informative.

LuxRender

Since the beginning of computer graphics, realism has been one of the most important goals facing artists and programmers alike. Jurassic Park, released in 1993, became a landmark moment in cinema history because it showed the whole world that 3D computer-generated images could be rendered realistically. It changed the movie industry forever.

On the surface it might seem that we have reached the target: computer-generated images can be realistic. In reality the solution is not at all that simple. Even with powerful software, achieving realism is very difficult. A typical Hollywood blockbuster using a lot of **Computer Generated Imagery (CGI)** requires the dedicated work of many experts for years in order to achieve any level of realism. Movies such as Avengers or Iron Man cost north of 200 million dollars to be realized and a lot of that cost is in paying CGI artists for their time and expertise.

It would be reasonable to think that hyper-realism is out of reach for the hobbyist or small-business owner. Thanks to modern technology and the open source software model, however, that is not true anymore.

One way to approach realism in CGI is to design software that simulates the behavior of light and materials exactly in accordance with laws of physics. LuxRender is that kind of software. The following image is illuminated by a single light, a physically accurate sun, and it uses physically accurate metal simulation by Lux. The result is highly realistic without needing to spend hours in defining materials.

The vast majority of renderers, including 3Delight, don't employ a realistic model of light. The material definition of 3Delight does not include mathematical models of how real materials such as glass or metal react in the real world. This is typical of most renderers.

LuxRender, on the other hand, calculates light exactly as it behaves in the real world, including how light bounces off objects or how reflections are caused by surrounding objects.

Lux is able to calculate the attenuation and color shift caused by the light traversing a volume of glass of a certain thickness and containing a fluid in it.

LuxRender's materials include physically accurate models for metal—with presets for gold, silver, aluminum, and others—glass, velvet, silk, mirror, and others.

Instead of defining a complex network of material properties trying to simulate glass, the Reality user can simply select the glass material for Lux and the result will be extremely realistic.

There's still a lot of flexibility for the artist to manipulate the result, but the high-level materials of Lux make it possible for the 3D artist to avoid being bogged down in the minutia of shader definition.

Interfacing with Lux

The limitation of Lux is that it does not read any file format from other 3D programs. For example, it does not read Studio or Poser files. In fact, Lux does not read even standard interchange file formats like OBJ.

This was a deliberate decision based on the fact that Lux needs a very particular material definition that cannot be easily connected to file formats such as OBJ or Collada. As a result Lux has its own file format, which is documented in LuxRender Wiki (`http://www.luxrender.net/wiki/Scene_file_format_overview`).

To use Lux we need a program that takes the geometry and materials of the base application, like Studio, and exports the data using the Lux scene definition format.

Reality is the program that exports the geometry from Studio to LuxRender.

Creating Reality

I learned about LuxRender in 2009. At that time the program was virtually unknown in the world of Studio and Poser. It became clear to me that the incredibly realistic results of Lux would be the perfect complement for the vast library of models available in the market. Interesting enough, nobody was talking about this possibility. The forums at Renderosity, RuntimeDNA, and DAZ had no mention of Lux, so it seemed like a good opportunity to take.

In January 2010, I started writing a plugin that would take all the materials, lights, and objects in a Studio scene and export them to Lux. The plugin would then launch Lux and obtain a Lux-rendered version of the Studio scene as framed by the Studio camera. In addition, the plugin would allow the user to edit all the materials in the scene so that they could be changed to use any of the materials supported by Lux. Lastly, this plugin needed to be artist-friendly so that using Lux would become easy and fun.

I named that plugin **Reality** to highlight that its function is to enable the Studio artist to attain realism. Reality was released in August 2010 and became one of the most successful plugins for Studio. Today, there are versions for both Studio and Poser, and Lux is one of the most desired options for 3D artists using premade content. Today, there are a few thousand Reality artists who produce amazing work that is used in many fields of illustration, is featured in CG sites like deviantART, and is even used in the production of Hollywood blockbusters.

In this chapter, we will see a preview of the new version of Reality for Studio, release 3, and explore what this plugin has to offer to the Studio artist who wants to achieve hyper-realism.

Understanding LuxRender concepts

LuxRender works in a very different way to other renderers. When we use 3Delight, we see the render appearing one line at a time, starting form the top. Lux instead renders the whole scene in one single pass, showing the user the full frame in a few seconds. This rendering is very grainy at first, and it gets refined continuously until the grain, called **render noise**, goes away.

The following screenshot shows Lux at the very beginning of the rendering process:

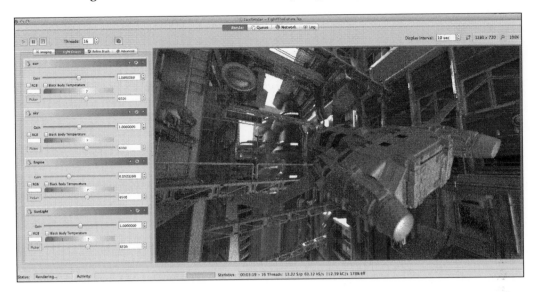

 Notice that the image is visible in its entirety, but it's still noisy. The noise will progressively disappear as Lux computes more light samples.

This workflow is very convenient since we are able to verify important aspects of our scene in a matter of few seconds or minutes. Wardrobe poke-throughs are easily visible; lighting can be verified without having to wait until the scene is fully rendered.

The render never stops

Unlike other renderers, Lux never stops rendering. The program continuously refines the render, and it will continue to run until we stop it. It is the responsibility of the user to stop Lux when the image has reached a satisfactory quality. At that point, we can simply close the program and the image will be available in a file saved on disk.

Lights and exposure

Lux allows us to set the exposure of the scene as we do with a real camera. This is a tremendous artistic tool that adds many possibilities. The brightness of a photo is determined by the exposure that the photographer uses. Many renderers don't provide access to the exposure controls forcing the artist to change the brightness of a scene only via the intensity of the lights. That is a very limiting way of working. Lux instead has control for all the usual exposure parameters: ISO, shutter speed, and aperture. We will see later what these terms mean.

In a similar fashion, Lux allows the artist to change the intensity and color temperature of groups of lights while the render is running. Again, this is an incredible feature that is not available in many commercial and expensive programs.

LuxRender has features that you can find in programs such as V-Ray or Maxwell while being completely free. The software is available for Mac OS, Windows, and Linux, and it can be used to create a renderfarm with unlimited numbers of nodes, with each node using every CPU core. In comparison, commercial renderers often have a licensing scale based on the number of cores that are enabled by the software. Using more cores costs more money.

So, we see that Lux is a very desirable renderer. Reality makes it possible to access all that power with ease, right inside Studio.

A renderfarm is a group of computers connected together via a network and participating in a common render task.

With a renderfarm, an image is sent to several computers at the same time with the assignment to render a portion of the image, and then send it to a central computer that gathers the render results. This division of tasks helps render complex images in shorter times.

Renderfarms are used by special effects houses that create scenes for movie studios. Motion pictures have a frame rate of 24 frames per second. Creating CGI effects for such movies, or animations like the ones created by Pixar, requires generating thousands of frames, each frame at a resolution of 2,000 or 4,000 vertical lines. The rendering quality of such frames is so high that a single computer could take hours or even days to finish rendering one image.

Companies like ILM or Pixar manage renderfarms with thousands of computers that render overnight whole batches of frames. For example, Pixar's Monsters Inc. was rendered with a renderfarm including 3,500 processors, with some frames taking up to a full day to render because of their complexity.

Installing Reality

LuxRender is available at `http://www.luxrender.net`. As mentioned, there are versions for Mac OS, Windows, and Linux. The Mac OS version is 64-bit only. For Windows, there is a choice between 32-bit and 64-bit. You should download Lux at the same bitness as your OS.

The second option for Windows users is to select the OpenCL or non-OpenCL version. OpenCL is built inside Mac OS, so there is no need to choose if you use a Macintosh. LuxRender for Mac includes support for OpenCL, which is a technology that allows programs to execute instructions in parallel using the **Graphics Processing Unit (GPU)**, which is another name for the video card. Modern GPUs from AMD and NVIDIA can be used to accelerate some types of processing. Lux has some options to use the GPU. In case you are not sure if your GPU is OpenCL-enabled, download the non-OpenCL version. You can always change your mind later.

OpenCL should not be confused with OpenGL or CUDA. OpenGL is the **API (Application Programming Interface)** used for displaying 3D images on the screen. Every GPU in the market today supports OpenGL, which is now also implemented in portable devices such as iPhone and iPad. OpenGL is the cornerstone of 3D modeling programs and video games alike.

OpenCL is an API defined recently, and released as an open standard, dedicated to the task of making it easier to run tasks in parallel while using multicore GPUs and CPUs. Most GPUs from AMD and NVIDIA support OpenCL. Intel has also added OpenCL support recently for their Xeon Phi coprocessors. OpenCL is a multiplatform, vendor-independent open standard.

CUDA is a technology similar to OpenCL, but it's proprietary to NVIDIA and does not support parallelization on both the GPU and the CPU.

So, you need to download LuxRender, which is free, and then install it on your disk. On a Macintosh, the program is usually installed in the `/Applications/LuxRender` folder. On Windows, it generally goes to the `C:\Program Files\LuxRender` directory. Those are just suggested locations; you can install the program in any folder of your liking.

Reality is a commercial product that, at the time of writing this book, costs less than $40 and is often on sale. It can be purchased at Renderosity, RuntimeDNA, and through the site of my company, Prêt-à-3D, which is `http://www.preta3d.com`.

Reality is available for both Mac OS and Windows. Because this is a plugin, which is an extension of Studio, the bitness of the plugin must match the one of the main program. This means that if you run a 32-bit version of Studio, you must install the 32-bit version of Reality. If you use a 64-bit version of Studio, you must install the 64-bit version of Reality.

The installation process is very simple. Reality is distributed as a ZIP file that contains the full program with instructions in a `Readme.txt` file. There is also a very detailed *Reality User's Guide* (also known as the *RUG*), a PDF book that explains how to use the program in detail. The up-to-date installation instructions are included in `Readme.txt` and RUG. Just follow the steps in there and you'll be up and running in a few minutes. The RUG is also available online at `http://preta3d.com/reality-documentation`.

Running Reality

Once installed, Reality is always available and can be called from Studio by navigating to **Render | Reality Render Editor** or through the keyboard shortcuts *Cmd + Shift + L* (on Mac) or *Ctrl + Shift + L* (on Windows).

The following screenshot shows the User Interface (UI) of the upcoming Reality 3 for Studio while editing the materials for the character Dawn by HiveWire3D:

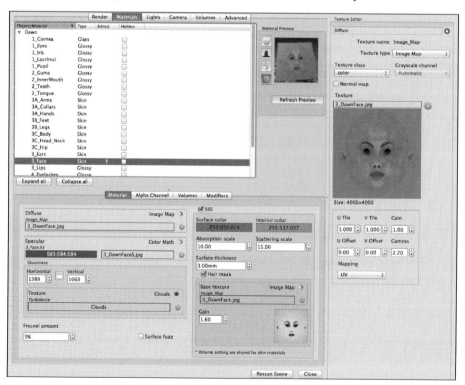

Dawn is a new character that has been designed by the original creator of Victoria, Chris Creek. Chris is the cofounder of HiveWire3D, a new content distributor. Readers of this book have access to Dawn for free, thanks to HiveWire3D. For more information, visit `http://hivewire3d.com`.

In the preceding screenshot we can see the list of materials that have been found for the figure. Each material is listed with its name and the type (**Glossy**, **Glass**, **Skin**, and so on). The lower part of the screen shows the properties for the selected material. The diffuse channel, for example, contains a reference to an image map. The image map is shown on the right-hand side of the UI, called the **Texture Editor**.

Reality is designed to provide all the options for controlling the render process in one single convenient location. The UI is divided into tabs that group specific functions. For example, the **Materials** tab contains the material editor where all the materials of the scene are listed, grouped by object.

Reality automatically converts the materials from Studio to its own representation, which is compatible with LuxRender. The original materials are left untouched, Reality creates its own materials separate from the Studio ones. This step is only the beginning. Because Studio doesn't provide information if a given material is designed to simulate glass, metal, or any other physical material, Reality cannot select a material type automatically. The material editor allows us to do so and take advantage of all the features of Lux. In addition, we can change any property of a material to fit our artistic vision. For example, we might want to increase the glossiness level of a surface or lower the intensity of the bump map. The Reality material editor allows us to do every modification that we need.

The **Lights** tab groups all the parameters for the lights in the scene. We can edit the light parameters in Reality independently from Studio. Lux provides many options for lights that are not present in Studio, so this arrangement is very convenient.

Having the parameters for Lux grouped in a separate window avoids cluttering up the Studio UI as well, which is already quite busy.

Rendering

To render a scene with Lux, we simply need to click on the **Render** tab and then click on **Render Frame**. Reality will spend a few seconds exporting all the geometry and materials from the scene to a series of files on the disk written in the Lux scene file format. When it's done, Reality will immediately launch Lux instructing the program to load the exported scene. Lux will start rendering the scene in a few seconds.

Lux will show the scene in its window right away, and then it will refine the image progressively with every pass. Unlike when we render with 3Delight, Studio is free at this point. We can let Lux render as long as it takes and we still have access to Studio. In fact, we can change the same scene that we are rendering without problems.

Using realistic materials

I mentioned a few times that Lux provides physics-based materials. Let's see how some of those work. The following scene uses the same elements that we have seen in the previous chapter: the Throne of the Skeleton King environment and one V4 figure with the Historical Armor suit:

If we look at the rendering of the metal of the armor or the blade of the sword, we see a realism that is unreachable with Studio's renderer. The reflections on the sword are so faithful, so perfect, to make us believe that we are looking at a photo.

If we look at the Studio definition for one of the materials of the suit of armor, we see that it's composed of a very long list of properties. I have created the following composite just to show all the properties in one single screen:

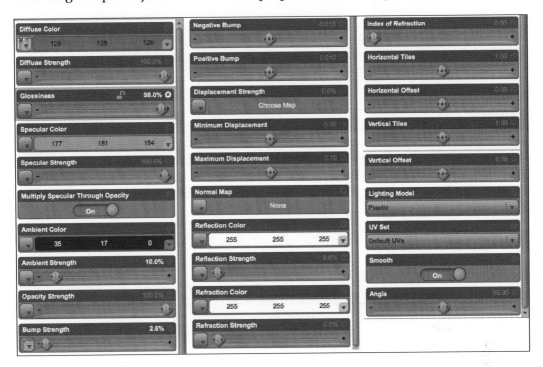

The list is in fact so long that it doesn't fit on a 30-inch display. Despite being so complex, this shader does not produce a convincing emulation of metal.

In comparison, the Reality metal material is disarmingly simple.

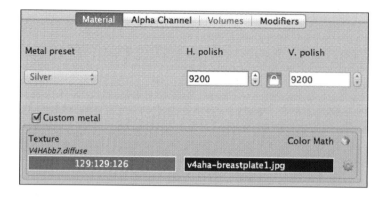

Lux has a material of type Metal and when we select that type, the renderer will simulate the metal based on scientific data, which takes into account the angle of incidence of the light and the point of view of the camera. We don't need to micromanage the shader and be experts in how a metal reacts to light. Lux does the work for us and Reality gives us the interface to set the specific properties for the material.

In the preceding panel we see the presence of metal presets. Reality provides physically based presets for aluminum, cobalt, chrome, copper, gold, lead, mercury, nickel, platinum, silver, titanium, and zinc.

For the armor, though, we used the **Custom metal** option because the original material from Studio provided a texture, and we want to create the illusion of a metal that has been decorated. The custom metal option allows us to use any image map as the source of the color for the metal.

Lastly, we have the controls for the level of polish of the metal. This is a straightforward concept. The higher the number, the higher the polish. The vertical and horizontal levels can be unlinked for creating special effects of shine.

That's all that there is about defining metals in Reality. The plugin also groups the alpha channel in its own tab. Bump map, displacement, and subdivision are found in the **Modifiers** tab. In this way, if we don't need to deal with those parameters, we don't have to be bothered by their presence on screen. This arrangement keeps things well organized and simple to read.

Converting materials

Studio doesn't provide any information about the nature of its materials. Simply by examining the list of properties of a shader, we cannot tell if the material is supposed to be metal, human skin, glass, or wool. As a consequence, Reality often converts a Studio material to the generic **Glossy** type. We can easily change this and select any of the specialized materials available. To do so, we right-click on the material name and select the new type.

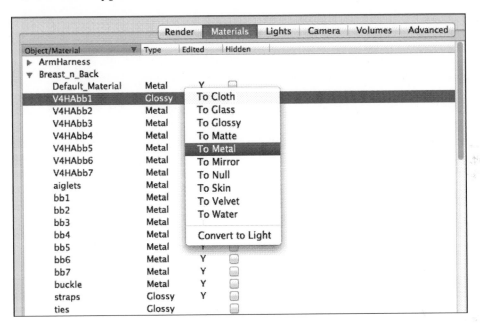

The preceding screenshot shows all the material types available in Reality. Each material type has its own series of parameters. As the properties are specific to a material, they are easier to understand than a series of generic parameters because they have a context. This makes the combination of Reality and Lux capable of producing more realistic images, while at the same time being easier to use than the default Studio material system.

Using glass

The glass material gives a very dramatic example of what Lux can do. Here is a simple scene that shows a glass vase on a stand:

This vase is a free prop by DominiqueB available at ShareCG:
http://www.sharecg.com/v/61278/view/5/3D-Model/Crystal-Vase.

You can find the full-resolution color image in the projects files for this chapter in the file named GlassVase.png. If you look carefully, you can see the vase catches reflections of itself and some reflections of the cloth. You'll be very hard-pressed to find anything like that in any render made with Studio's built-in renderer.

The material has been converted to glass in Reality. When we do that, we are presented with a panel that lists the relevant properties.

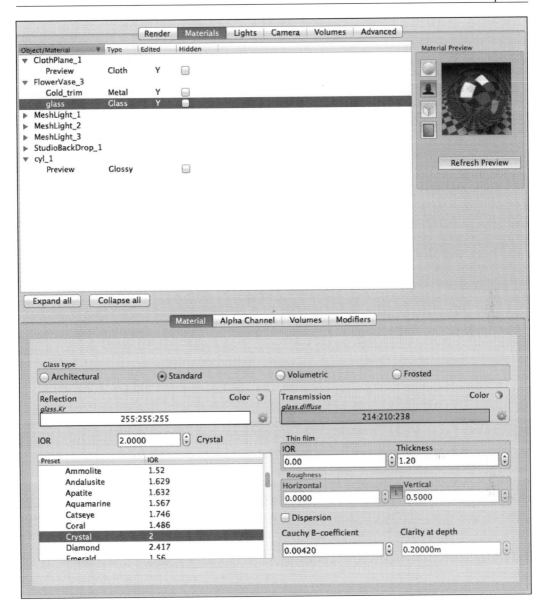

The glass material controls four types of glass: **Architectural**, **Standard**, **Volumetric**, and **Frosted**.

The Architectural glass is a simplified version of glass that can be used for things such as small windows or car headlights; basically, for all the situations where we need some reflection visible, but we don't want to spend too much computation time because the detail is not that important.

The Standard glass is the most widely used type, and it provides an excellent representation of glass that looks very realistic. This type of glass takes into account the **Index Of Refraction (IOR)** specified and the thickness of the volume. A thicker glass will show up darker and with more refractive distortion than thinner glass. In the case of this vase, I used the crystal preset, which gives me an IOR of 2.0. We can enter the IOR by hand, if we want, but Reality includes presets for dozens of liquids, glasses, and gems.

The reflection color controls how much light is reflected by the material. Brighter values cause the surface to reflect more light. The transmission color controls the tint of the glass. There are other parameters but those are more rarely used. You can find all the details, if you want, in the *Reality User's Guide*, which can be downloaded from http://preta3d.com/reality-documentation.

At the top-right of the Reality window, we can see a handy material preview that lets us know how the material will look when rendered. The preview is updated automatically whenever we change a material property.

The glass produced by Reality and Lux is photorealistic. It takes almost no effort to create an image with absolutely astounding glass. On the other hand, you could struggle for hours, if not days, with the Studio shaders and not come close to generating believable glass. That is the power and convenience of using a physics-based renderer.

Lighting with Reality and Lux

Another area where Lux shines is in the way it simulates light. To understand how light works, we can consider how a standard digital photo camera works. In real life light is emanated from a source, it hits objects nearby, and it's reflected by those objects. The light reflected bounces off other objects, and it becomes tinted based on the colors of the surfaces touched. Finally, the light rays reach the camera, they are gathered by a lens, and hit the image sensor where they will be converted to digital data.

The camera lens has an iris that works similarly to the human iris; it adjusts the aperture of the eye, the pupil. A smaller pupil keeps excessive light from hitting the retina. A smaller lens aperture does a similar job; it reduces the amount of light that hits the image sensor.

We know that cats can see in the dark better than humans can. The cat's eye has a higher sensitivity to light. In a similar way, the camera's sensor can be adjusted to be more sensitive to light by boosting its electrical charge, which results in amplifying the signal from the sensor. It's a technique very similar to turning the volume up on a radio. The sensitivity of a sensor is called ISO or the ISO speed. It is expressed using integer numbers such as 100, 200, and 800. The higher the number, the more sensitive to light the sensor is.

Cameras don't expose the image sensor all the time. A cover is placed in front of the sensor to block light from hitting it. This cover is called the shutter, and is lifted for a very short time to expose the sensor to light every time we take a photo. The cover then shuts back in place, hence the name shutter. The shutter moves generally at speeds of $1/125^{th}$ or $1/250^{th}$ of a second, but it can be changed to stay open to any amount of time from 30 seconds to something like 1/1000 or 1/2000 of a second. Longer shutter times let more light hit the image sensor and so they generate brighter images. For example, a shutter speed of $1/125^{th}$ of a second will bring twice the amount of light as $1/250^{th}$ of a second.

All these parameters define the **exposure** of the image. Every camera works with these parameters, even camera phones. Some cameras calculate the parameters automatically, while professional or prosumer cameras allow to control them manually.

What is important to remember is that the exposure determines how bright or dark an image will appear. In other words, changing the brightness of an image while using a camera is normally done by adjusting the exposure, instead of changing the intensity of lights. If we consider real-life situations, such as shooting a scene lit by the sun or by street lights, we see how important it is to have that level of control in the camera. We cannot dim the sun, but we can close the iris of the lens or adjust any of the other parameters.

Lux provides that level of control because it computes light using full spectrum information, not just RGB. LuxRender calculates the light and then applies the same ISO, aperture, and shutter speed combination of real cameras to bring the light into the range of visible colors. Like commercial cameras, it has a point-and-shoot mode that calculates the exposure automatically, and it has a manual mode where we can adjust every parameter to our liking.

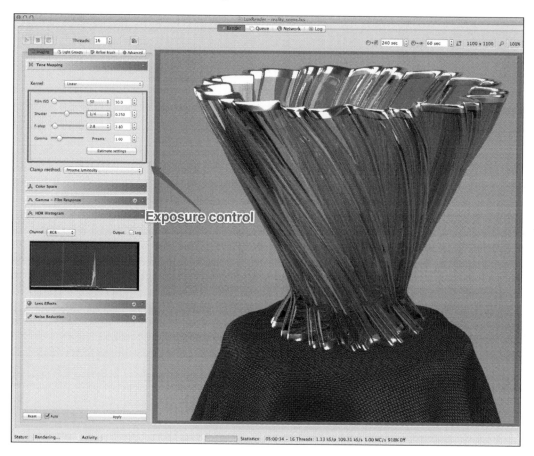

What this means is that we can change the exposure of the scene while it is rendering. We don't need to stop the render and start over. We can change the exposure while the render continues to be refined. This is something that we can't find in numerous software costing several hundreds of dollars, let alone in something that is free.

But the surprises don't stop here. Lux allows us to change the intensity and color of the lights in the scene while the render runs. It's truly fantastic.

Lastly, we can stop the render, close Lux, and then restart the render even days later without loss of data. Lux will resume from where it stopped and continue to refine the image.

This level of control is very useful, and Reality provides all the support that you need to access those features with a simple point-and-click UI.

Creating water

Reality provides a very realistic water material, complete with ripple control.

Water, like glass, is very hard to simulate correctly without a physics-based renderer. Reality includes a water plane prop that can be used to add water to most scenes. The water prop is simply a plane primitive that has been divided into small polygons so that they can be displaced to create ripples.

Adding water to a scene is generally a matter of adding the water plane, adjusting the color of the water and the amount of ripples, and then rendering.

As it is in the spirit of the program, Reality makes it very easy to adjust the water material by providing a very simple UI that controls the necessary properties.

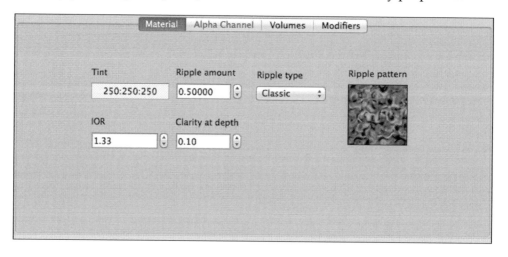

This is typical of how Reality works. It manages all the gory details behind the scenes, and it provides the level of control that is necessary to the artist using terminology that is easy to understand. The **Tint** property is the color that the water will have. The **Ripple amount** property is self-explanatory. The **Ripple type** property provides a few different patterns of ripples to choose from. Each selection is illustrated with a sample of **Ripple pattern** shown on the right-hand side of the panel. The **IOR** property is, like with the glass material, the Index Of Refraction. Finally, the **Clarity at depth** property indicates how far we can see inside the water volume. The distance is expressed in meters.

Reality in production

In the course of three years, Reality has been used in many different situations by artists of all extractions. Recently, I have been contacted by Sam Kennedy (http://preta3d.com/blog/2013/06/24/whos-using-reality-sam-kennedy-professional-illustrator-and-teacher/), a professional illustrator who has worked for the gaming industry for 12 years. Sam's work has been used for games like Medal of Honor and the Tom Clancy series, just to name a few. Sam uses Reality for Studio in his professional work. In fact, Sam is so impressed by Reality that he teaches how to use it in his Rapid Illustration class at ZBrush Workshop.

Ron Mendell (`http://www.ronmendell.com`) is a veteran of Hollywood productions, as his extensive IMDB credits show. Ron creates props and gadgets for movie productions, and he uses Reality to provide a 3D mockup of the prop that needs to be created. Ron recently used Reality in the production of Jurassic Park 4 and Hunger Games 2.

Summary

There are many other powerful features of Reality, including procedural textures, mixed textures, animation, and more. This chapter is meant to just give you an overview of the capabilities of the program.

With Reality and LuxRender, we can access a level of realism that was previously restricted to 3D applications costing thousands of dollars.

Since I started working with computers, 30 years ago, I have been intrigued by how technology can enable people to do extraordinary things. Reality is an example of what technology can do. Because of the generosity and genius of the developers of LuxRender, we have a renderer today that can generate physically accurate images for free. This, in turn, made it possible to write an inexpensive program like Reality, which makes this kind of technology extremely affordable.

With all the content available in the market today, the Studio artist has access to almost limitless expressions. We can build entire worlds from premade assets and populate them with people, creatures from other worlds, animals, monsters, and props for all occasions.

With Reality and LuxRender now, we can make those worlds believable.

In the next chapter we will explore the exciting world of content creation. Up to now we have used content made by other people. It's now time to look into the process of creating our own wardrobe.

11
Creating Content

There are times when we cannot find the type of content that we are looking for. Other times we might have an idea for a product that could be introduced in the market.

Studio can be easily extended using standard 3D modeling applications. In this chapter, we will see how to create clothing for a base figure and how to package and distribute the final product. Finally, we will see how to connect with some of the brokerage services that we discussed before, this time with the purpose to sell content through these companies.

This chapter is not meant to be an in-depth tutorial about modeling clothing. We would need a full book just dedicated to that subject. Instead, we will see all the steps that are involved in the process so that we don't get bogged down by the minutia of technical issues. In this way we get a clear view of all the steps involved, from the beginning to the delivery of the final product to the broker.

Creating clothing

Creating clothing for 3D characters presents a very fascinating challenge. The problem is twofold: on one side we need to design and model the new garment, something that fits the base figure that we chose, on the other we need to also define how the garment will move and how it will follow the figure.

Clothing in real life is often made of a fabric of a certain thickness and stiffness. Depending on the shape and amount of fabric used, the garment can drape or cling to the body. Silk, for example, is soft, thin, and light. It naturally drapes around the body. Denim, on the other hand, is thick, doesn't bend quite as easily as silk, and it's much stiffer.

When we model a garment, we don't have a selection of fabric. The founding block of all geometry is the polygon, a shape that has either three or four sides. Most of the time, we will use four-sided polygons, also known as quads. Quads don't have the qualities of fabric. We cannot say "these polygons are made of silk and the other are made of velvet."

There are programs or plugins that allow to create dynamic, draping clothing based on parameters that simulate the properties of fabric, but that kind of software comes in place much later in the pipeline, not during the development of the garment.

3D modeling with modo

To create clothing or other accessories, we need to step out of Studio and work with a program that allows us to assemble polygons together and to manipulate them in any way possible, so that we can create a shape.

The practice of creating shapes out of geometry primitives, like polygons, is called 3D modeling. Studio does not provide any 3D modeling feature, so we will use a program called modo, by Luxology.

modo (notice the all-lowercase name) is used in many professional situations and is also the program used to create Victoria 4 and Genesis. It's an incredibly powerful application that can create any geometry shape via very sophisticated tools. We will see just a subset of the program. You can try modo free for 15 days by downloading the program from `http://www.luxology.com/trymodo`.

After you download your trial version of modo, you should follow a few basic and entertaining tutorials that show you how to use modo. There is a Navigation Basics tutorial at `http://www.luxology.com/tv/training/view.aspx?id=648`, which is really well done and extremely useful. Once you have learned the basics on how to move inside modo, you should watch this tutorial about the tools available for creating basic shapes, such as cubes and cylinders: `http://www.luxology.com/tv/training/view.aspx?id=649`.

Finally, you will need to watch the following video to learn everything about selection of polygons, edges, and vertices: `http://www.luxology.com/tv/training/view.aspx?id=650`.

You can use any other 3D modeling program if you prefer. For example, Blender, which is free, can be used as an alternative. ZBrush is also a great program to create clothing. In fact, modo and ZBrush can be used together in a workflow that is very effective and that leverages the best features of both programs.

I use modo because it's a very powerful 3D modeler that retains a very usable user interface, despite the complexity of the task at hand.

Rigging a figure

Once we create a shape for a garment, we still have a lot of work to do to make it function as a piece of clothing. There is a very precise logic behind the behavior that makes a piece of clothing move together with a base figure. This kind of behavior doesn't happen automatically, it needs to be defined.

Each figure is divided into groups of polygons based on their function. For example, the polygons that define the left thigh are grouped together. The same is for all the other body parts, down to the fingers, each one divided into three phalanges. In this way, each part can move in a very precise range of motions. For example, the first phalanx of the index finger has three types of motion: twist, side-by-side, and bend. Each motion has a defined range so that the finger does not bend in an unnatural way. All these parameters are defined by the author of the figure and they define the **rigging** of the figure.

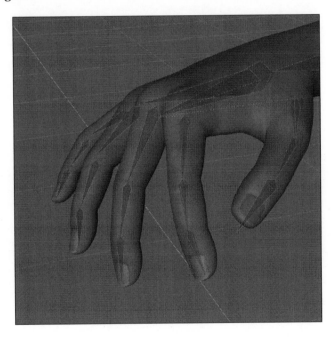

If we want to create a piece of clothing that moves together with a figure, we need to create a relationship between a portion of the garment and the corresponding part of the base figure.

The ability to make a garment follow the base figure was originally created for Poser by Larry Weinberg, in collaboration with Poser's product manager, Steve Cooper. The idea they had was to connect two figures that used the same rigging and make them move in synchronicity. If figure A (the clothing) is linked to figure B (the person) and figure A defines a polygon group that has the same name of a polygon group in figure B, any movement of a group in figure B can be duplicated for the corresponding group in figure A.

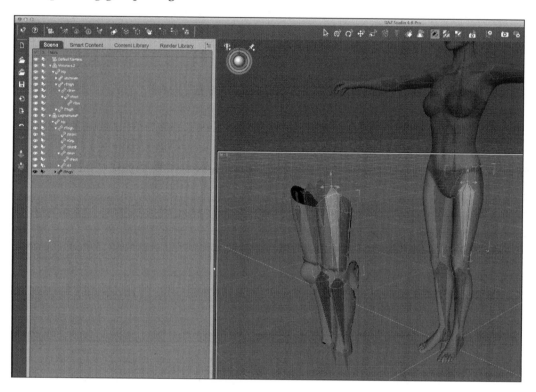

In the composite image shown in the preceding screenshot, we can see the rigging made visible. The pyramids inside the figures are called bones and they control the movement of the connected geometry.

We can see that both the legs of Victoria and the suit of armor use the same configuration of bones. We also see that the exact same names are used in the scene hierarchy for both V4 and the armor. The naming scheme is what allows for the synchronized moving of conforming wardrobe.

The reality of the system is more complex than this simplified explanation, but this is the logic behind the way conforming clothing works.

Box modeling or retopology

There are two main ways for defining a piece of geometry based on a model. We can use retopology or box modeling. Retopology means that we define a new geometry based on the surface of a reference model using a different organization and layout (topology) of polygons. Retopology works well for clothing that is really close to the skin of the model, such as wetsuits, gloves, and tight pants.

Box modeling is based on creating a cube or box that partially encloses the figure. The cube is then divided into sections and adapted to create the desired shape. Box modeling provides a very flexible way of creating clothes that are free to drape and move around the figure with a high degree of freedom. While it seems counter-intuitive at first, we will see in this chapter how easy and efficient it is to use box modeling for creating a simple dress for a female figure.

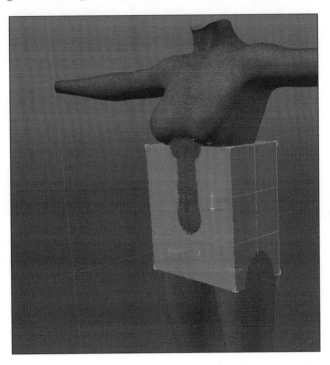

From the preceding screenshot, we can see an example box modeling in action.

Dawn of a new era

As you are reading this chapter, I assume that you are interested in making content and possibly sell it via one of the marketplaces that we saw in *Chapter 6, Finding and Installing New Content*. The market for Studio figures is a pretty small one. This is not the iPhone market where there are millions of users. The number of people actively buying content for Studio are a few hundreds of thousands. It's also a fairly crowded market with a lot of competition and a few well-established names. For all these reasons, you want to maximize your opportunities to sell to the largest public. This means to target both Studio and Poser users. In fact, sites such as Renderosity and RuntimeDNA predominantly sell Poser products, as Poser users represent the largest portion of the buyers of premade content. It makes sense to target that section of the market or at least to keep that option open. This is similar to what I do for the Reality plugin. While I used Macintosh for my work, I develop my software for both Mac and Windows, as a large amount of potential customers use Windows machines. When it comes to business, we need to be pragmatic and fair.

Reaching the largest market means that we need to be careful about the figure that we use as the base of our product because clothing is not interchangeable. For example, clothing for Victoria 4 does not work, without adaptation, with Genesis. Clothing for Victoria 3 does not work with Victoria 4. Each figure has different geometry and rigging.

Victoria 4 has the largest market today and the figure works in both Studio and Poser without modifications. Genesis only works in Studio. There is a plugin to load it in Poser, but the software doesn't work very well; it's extremely slow and has a lot of issues. Also, a lot of Poser users resent the need to use a plugin to load a figure; they want a native figure for their program.

Recently, a new figure has been introduced in the market, her name is Dawn. Dawn is the creation of HiveWire3D (http://hivewire3d.com), a company created by a group of ex DAZ employees, including the creator of the original Victoria 1 figure.

Dawn is a modern figure that uses more advanced rigging than V4; in fact, it uses the same weight-mapping techniques used in Genesis/V5. Unlike V4, Dawn has articulating toes, a more advanced neck rigging, and she uses the modern weight-mapping system instead of the old-style rigging. Dawn works as a native figure for both Studio and Poser, and it has received an overwhelming support from the majority of the industry. Because of all these factors, I thought that it would be a good idea to see how to start creating clothing for Dawn, so that's what we are going to do. You can use the techniques shown in this chapter with any figure of your choice. If you prefer to use V4 or Genesis, just load that figure instead of Dawn.

Our goal is to create a simple dress for Dawn using box modeling. We will then use the tools in Studio to rig the dress, so that it will move naturally when we pose the base figure.

A surprise for you

The fine people at HiveWire3D have given you a special bonus. Actually two. You can get Dawn for free by going to the HiveWire3D website (http://hivewire3d.com) and using the coupon code **DAWN4FREEPCBK13** while adding Dawn to your shopping cart. In addition, they have provided the coupon code **DAWNSTK25PCBK13** for a 25 percent discount for the Dawn Starter Stack, a bundle that includes a morph pack, hair, jeans, tank top, combat boots, and a pose package.

Layout of the tutorial

I wanted to make this section of the book meaningful for all readers, regardless of their experience with modo. This means that I will explain the commands used, but that I will also keep the explanation pretty generic and at a high level so that the lesson doesn't get lost in the minutia of keystrokes and mouse movements. In this way, hopefully, you will be able to transpose the concepts to another modeler in case you need to do so. The detailed use of figures and explanation of the steps involved should make the reading of this chapter useful even if you don't do any modeling.

Making a dress for Dawn

Making even the simplest garment for a 3D character can be a daunting task if you have never done it before. A whole book could be dedicated to that process, if we had to cover all the techniques in detail. On the other hand, we can cover the basics in a few pages, if we keep our target simple. The following tutorial is based on a very simple dress. Don't expect high fashion. We are going to keep things very, very simple so that we can see all the steps involved from zero to the finished product. After we are done with this chapter, if you find the matter interesting, you can look for more tutorials about modeling.

Let's begin.

Obviously, we need to have the base figure loaded in modo so that we can model a dress around it. modo does not read the Studio file format, but it can import many standard 3D file formats, such as OBJ. Unfortunately, Studio does not use the OBJ format for its figures as Poser does. A Poser character file, or CR2, is a file that refers to an external OBJ file for the definition of the geometry of the character. The CR2 file then adds all the rigging information and all the deformation parameters such as scale and rotate. Because of this we can make clothing for Poser figures by directly loading the base OBJ referenced by the CR2 file. For Studio we need to add a small step into our workflow.

We can do two things to import Dawn in modo:

- Load the figure in Studio and then export it as an OBJ file
- Load the OBJ file included in the Poser version

Being able to edit any 3D asset that we can load in Studio is definitely useful, so let's see how we export a figure using OBJ.

Exporting a figure as an OBJ file

We begin in Studio by loading the figure that we need to export. For Dawn the authors have prepared a special version to be used in the creation of clothing. Instead of loading the full version, we navigate to **Dawn | Clothing | Resource Kit** in Studio **Content Library** and load the ClothingresourceBase object. This model appears as a red figure without head, hands, and feet. In addition, the model is slightly different from the original, with the gluteus smoothed and some other portions of the geometry highlighted to make the design of clothing easier. This is a very welcome addition and a sign of the effort behind the design of Dawn. In the following image we can see some of the differences side by side:

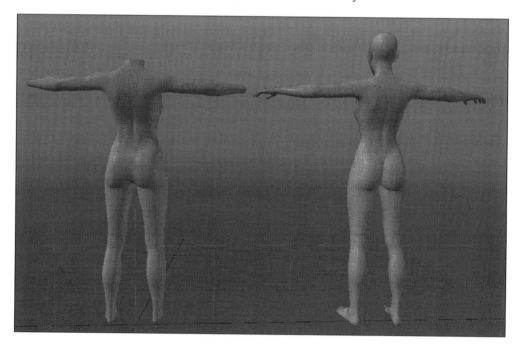

1. With the figure loaded in Studio, we go to the menu and navigate to **File | Export**.

2. A window will show up and in there we select **WaveFront Object (*.obj)** for the file type and enter the name `DawnCRKit`. Make sure to select a suitable folder for the file and make a mental note of the name of that folder. Let's use **3DRefenceModels** inside the home folder.

3. Once we select a name for the file, a window will be displayed to let us select all the options that control how the OBJ file will be written. We don't need to learn all those options now; we can simply use one of the presets available. We will select the modo preset, which gives us the following configuration:

4. From here, we simply click on **Accept** and the file will be written.

The modo preset ensures that the OBJ file is written at the right scale. We mentioned this when we looked at the opposite operation, importing OBJ files into Studio. An OBJ file doesn't specify the unit of measure used in the application that generated it. The data in it is written using generic units. For example, a polygon can be one unit tall. There is no indication if that unit is one meter, one centimeter, or one inch. Studio uses centimeter as its unit of measurement. modo, on the other hand, uses meter. If we write the OBJ file using the Studio units, a person that is 1.80 meter tall—or 180 centimeters—will appear in modo as being 180 meter tall, the equivalent of a building 65-story tall. We don't want that. Let's click on the **Accept** button and we have a standard OBJ file that we can open with any other 3D application, including modo, ZBrush, Blender, and many others.

5. At this point we can launch modo and load the Dawn's OBJ file in a new scene.

6. To do so we navigate to **File | Import,** navigate to the directory that we used in the previous step, **3DReferenceModel** in my case, and select the `DawnCRKit.obj` file.

7. modo asks us how we want to import the mesh. Let's select **Import as Static Mesh**.

    The object will be loaded in the scene and now we can start creating our new model.

    In the scene we can see the standard object called **Mesh** and the new entry called **DawnCRKit**. We don't want to create the dress as a mesh of the original Dawn figure, so we need to make sure that the **Mesh** object is selected in the **Items** tab.

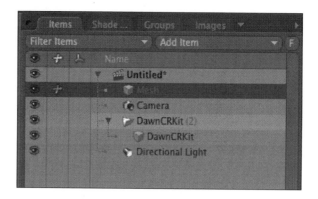

Better yet, let's rename that object to be called `Dress`.

8. With the item selected, we click one more time and then change the name.

9. This is now a geometry item called **Dress** with no geometry yet defined. It's basically a placeholder for the polygons that we are going to create.

10. In the **Model** tab—top-left of the window—we click on the **Cube** primitive to activate that tool, and we start drawing a square starting just below the right breast and ending just outside the left hip. Don't press Q or Space bar yet, as those keys will drop the cube in the scene. We need to change its properties before we continue. This is what we have on the screen so far:

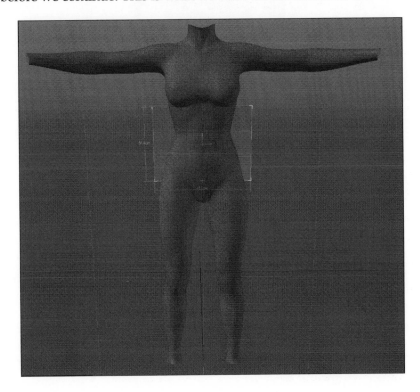

11. The cube is rather flat, but that is going to change soon. The edit panel for the cube is where we enter some crucial data.

12. First, we need to set the origin on the x axis to **0**. This is absolutely vital. Then, we select to have two divisions of the cube along the x axis, three along the y axis, and two along the z axis.

13. The divisions are defined in the **Segments** section.

14. A few divisions give us a cube that can be deformed a bit instead of being a monolith. We can apply divisions later, and in fact we will, but this is a convenient starting point.

15. With the cube still active, we then go to the Viewport and use the controls identified by the * to size the box so that it encloses the torso from below the breast and up to the pubic area. It's better if the sides sink inside the base figure a bit, as it's easier to pull them away later. If you move the sides, make sure that the **X** position is always at **0** by entering that value after the change. Similarly, it's better if the gluteus sticks outside the box than to make the box so large as to enclose it.

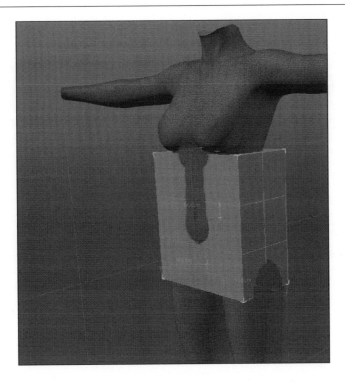

16. At this point, we can press Q to drop the tool and make the cube defined with the parameters that we have specified. From this point on we will have to modify it by pushing, pulling, rotating, scaling, and extruding.

The next step will be to change the cube to be a more irregular shape that encloses Dawn a little better.

Editing a piece of geometry relies heavily on our ability to select a portion of that geometry and apply some sort of transformation. For this reason modo has excellent selection tools. We can select groups of vertices, edges, polygons, depending on what is most appropriate. Refer to the basic training referenced at the beginning of this chapter for lessons on how to use the selection tools; they are well worth the time.

1. We start by selecting the two front-upper edges of the cube. Check the procedure on how to do so in the videos referenced earlier. As a reminder, we press 2 to switch the selection to edges.

2. We then click on the upper-right edge of the box.

3. Press and hold the *Shift* key and then click on the upper-left edge.

4. We can now let go of the *Shift* key.

5. Then, we press *W* to call the move tool and move the edges out to be past the breast. We repeat the same operation on the rear bottom edges so that we move the lower edge of the cube just past the gluteus.

   To make sure that our dress is perfectly symmetrical we can engage the symmetry tool of modo, which replicates on one side of our 3D object the modifications that we do on the opposite side. This way of working is incredibly helpful; it ensures perfect symmetry of the model and speeds up our workflow considerably.

6. To activate symmetry we need to look at the top of the modo window and locate the toolbar where the **Symmetry** menu is located. It's to the right of the **Action Center** menu.

7. Click on it and select **X**. Now every transformation that we make on one side of the dress will be mirrored to the other side automatically.

 Please note that the **Symmetry** settings are not saved with the modo scene. This means that if we close the scene and we reopen it at a later time the symmetry will need to be reset manually.

Now, we can select the bottom-right edges of the cube and move them out. The same will happen to the opposite side. So, let's start moving the right-hand side edges at the bottom and see the left-hand side edges adjust as well. The goal is to obtain something like this:

Now we need to extend the box down to cover part of the legs and up to cover the chest up to the base of the neck. We are going to use the **Bevel** tool to do so. The Bevel tool, when applied to a group of polygons, extrudes the geometry along one axis as far as we pull. Let's switch the selection mode to Polygons by pressing *3* and select all the faces at the top of the cube.

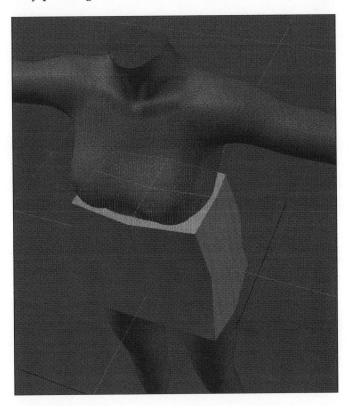

8. Now let's press the *B* key and click in the Viewport.

9. Two handles will appear next to the selected faces. One blue handle points up and it's similar to the move tool. The other is a red handle and it resembles the scale tool.

10. Click-and-drag the move handle up, toward the neck; you will see that new faces are created. Drag until the new polygons are approximately as tall as the others, and then press Space bar to commit the change.

11. At this point, the Bevel tool is not active anymore but the faces that we selected are still selected. Let's press the *B* key again, click on the Viewport, and extrude a new set of faces up to a point just above the neck and then press Space bar again.

12. With the polygons still selected, press *W* to move the area back a little bit, just enough to have the faces centered around the neck.

13. Press *Esc* to deselect the faces.

    Now we do the same thing, but for the polygons facing down.

14. We select them, press the *B* key, click on the Viewport, and then pull the blue arrow. As you click-and-drag, the polygons will be extruded down. Use the scale handle to size the area, if needed, and then press Space bar to confirm.

    Extrude once more with the Bevel tool until the box is just above the knees. Scale the extrusion up a bit and then confirm it. You should have something like this:

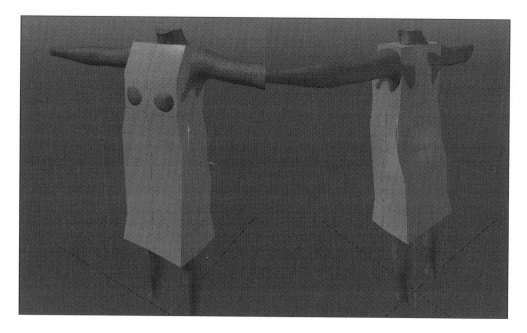

This is still very boxy, but we are approximating a rough shape and we have done this in a few minutes and with very little effort. It's now time to treat this shape as a piece of clay, and push and pull the elements until a better shape is obtained.

Before we continue, let's delete the polygons at the base. This is a going to be a dress, not a sack.

1. Let's press *Esc* to deselect any elements that could be selected.

2. Select the polygons at the bottom and press *Delete* on the keyboard. Now our box is open and legs can move naturally. We will see later how to deal with the same issue with the neck.

The Transform tool

We could use Move, Rotate, and Scale to make our modifications to the dress, but that requires the usual cycle of select, call the tool, transform, and commit. There is a faster and more immediate way of applying many small transformations to a mesh: the Transform tool.

We enable this tool by pressing T. There is no need to click on the 3D Viewport, the tool is immediately ready to work. Now, let's hover with the mouse over the dress for a few seconds. We see that faces, edges, and vertices can be highlighted depending on where the mouse cursor is. With the Transform tool, we don't need to activate a specific selection mode.

Make sure that Symmetry is active and move the mouse over the median edge that splits the side of the dress and over the third vertex from the top. When the vertex is highlighted, click-and-drag the vertex out. This is what you should see:

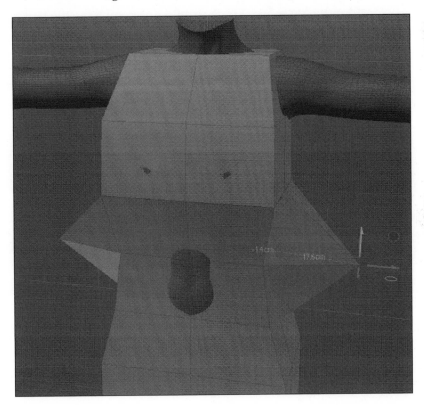

The vertex is pulled out and the equivalent vertex in the opposite side is moved by the same amount and in the opposite direction. Let's press *Cmd + Z* (on Mac) or *Ctrl + Z* (on Windows) to undo this and then T again to reactivate the Transform tool. Practice a little bit using the Transform tool so that you get the hang of it. Try moving vertices, edges, or faces. The only limitation of this tool is that we cannot select multiple elements for the transformation. If we need to do that, we must use one of the other tools, such as Move, Rotate, or Scale. But, the immediacy of the Transform tool, coupled with Symmetry, makes it an invaluable instrument to apply "freehand" transformations to a mesh.

The secret of turning this extended box into a dress is to move the rough geometry in a way that follows the body in the most natural way. This requires a bit of imagination, as we have big squares instead of a nice, flowing mesh. On the other hand, the coarse geometry makes it possible to make large changes without being bogged down into moving a large set of polygons.

Just use the Transform tool to move things around until you have the best fit possible. You should get something like this:

The shape is approximating what we need, but it's obvious that this is way too blocky. For example, the breast area doesn't have enough flexibility to follow the shape of the body without making that area baggy and bulky. We need finer, more detailed geometry there. This can be achieved by adding some edge loops, which are edges that cut the geometry all around in a certain direction or loop.

1. Let's press *Esc* to make sure that nothing is selected. Then, we click on the **Edge** vertical tab to select the tools to create and manipulate edges.

2. In the **Edge** tab, we click on the **Add Loop** button. Then, hover with the mouse over one of the vertical edges of the breast area until all the polygons in that ring are highlighted.

3. Click on the rig of polygons and then press Space bar to create a new edge loop and drop the tool. Now we can use the Transform tool to adjust the shape so that it covers the breasts.

4. Press *Esc* to deselect the edges. Press *T* to enable the Transform tool. Move the polygons, edges, and vertices until you get something like this:

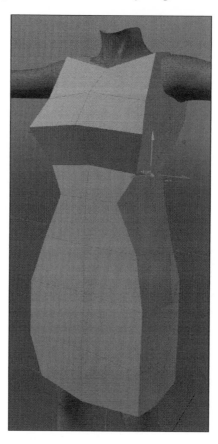

The front of the dress is too coarse and we need to add a couple of edge loops to it. We are going to use the Bevel tool to do so. Press 2 to activate the selection of edges. Double-click on the vertical edge in the center of the dress to select the whole loop. Press *B* and look at the left of the screen in the panel that lists the properties for the **Bevel** tool. Make sure that the **Round Level** value is set to **1**. The **Sharp Corner** option is not important. It can be enabled or disabled for this.

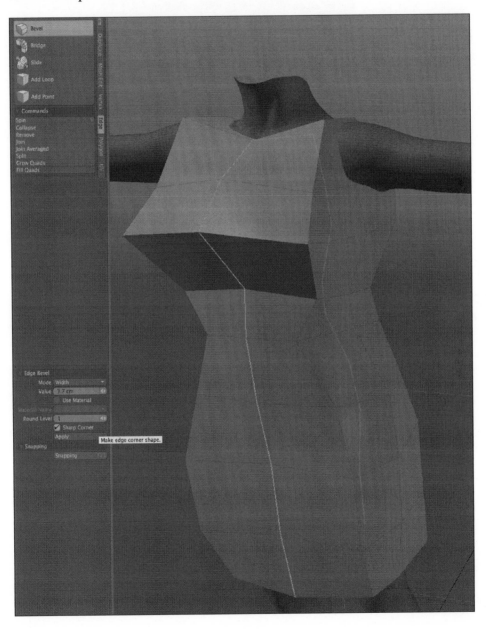

Now click on the selected edge loop and drag sideways. You will see two edge loops being created. Position them centered in their sections and then press Space bar and *Esc* to drop the tool and unselect the edges. With the added resolution, we can make more adjustments to the shape until we get a better approximation of the dress shape.

This is closer to the final result than you might think. Here comes the magic; press *Shift + Tab*. All of a sudden we have a much smoother shape than before.

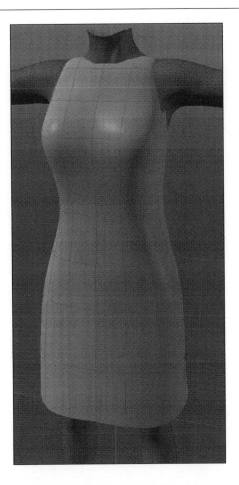

Tab or *Shift* + *Tab* enables subdivision in modo. *Shift* + *Tab* uses the Pixar subdivision algorithm, which is generally more advanced than the one activated by *Tab* alone. They both generate very smooth geometries from a coarse mesh. We can press *Tab* again to go back to the original mesh. We can edit the mesh in either mode. In many cases, it makes sense to use the coarse mesh because it's easier to make large changes to it and then quickly check the result by pressing *Shift* + *Tab* again.

The next thing to do is to cut openings for the neck and the arms. Let's switch back to the coarse geometry and add an edge loop using the **Add Loop** tool as we did before. Make sure that no element is selected and then click on the **Add Loop** tool. Hover with the mouse over the row of polygons in the upper chest area, about where the collar bone — the clavicle — is. Move the mouse until all the polygons are highlighted. Click and then press Space bar to drop the tool. The arrow in the following image shows you which loop has been added.

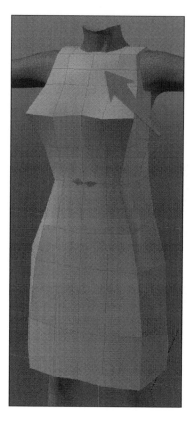

Now, if we look at the top of the dress, we see that there are four polygons right at the base of the neck. We want to remove those faces and the top two in front of the clavicle. Press *3* to enable selection by polygon, click-and-drag with your mouse to select those six faces, and press *Delete* to remove them.

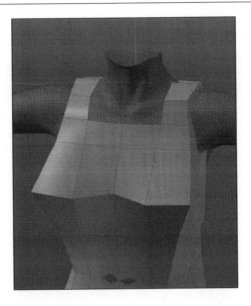

This will give us a nice hole for the neck and a nice cut out for the front. We can new use the Transform tool to grab that center vertex and drag it down a bit to create move of a V-shaped scoop.

Now, let's go to the side and select the four polygons where the arm emerges. Press *Delete* to remove them, and now we have the real shape of the dress in place.

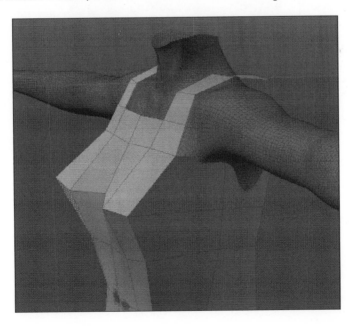

From here we need do some adjustments to move things around and shape the dress better. The shoulder straps need to be adjusted to avoid having the dress sink inside the character. This is done best with the Transform tool while using subdivision (press *Shift + Tab*). Move all the elements until the dress has a nice shape, no parts of the figure are poking through, and everything flows naturally. Remember to save the scene every now and then.

At the end you should have something like this:

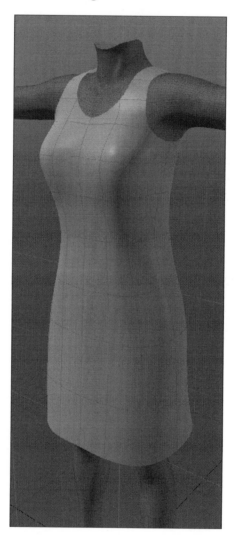

Not bad for a few minutes of work. This exercise shows that we can define a shape that follows another one with just a very coarse geometry. We don't need to define and push a large amount of polygons.

Assigning a material

Now that we have our geometry, we can assign a material to it. A material defines how a certain number of polygons are painted in the final render of the scene. Defining a material in modo is very simple. First, make sure that no vertices, edges, or polygons are selected. To do so press *Esc* a couple of times. Make sure that the **Dress** item is selected in the **Items** tab and then press *M*. A window appears asking us to name the material and define some properties such as the color.

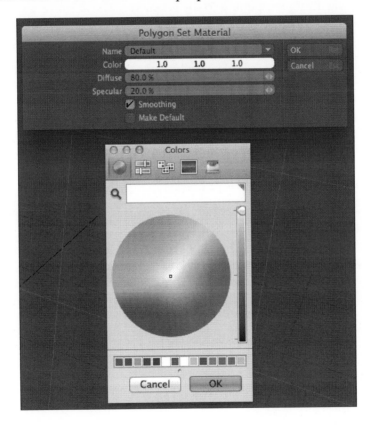

We call this material **Dress** and click on the color swatch to select a color. I use a bright green to make the dress stand out, but you can use whatever color that you prefer. It's not really important at this point. Once we confirm our choice, the dress appears with the new color.

Defining UV maps

At this point we need to define the UV map for the dress. We talked about UV maps in *Chapter 7, Navigating the Studio Environment*. A UV map describes how we can project an image onto a piece of geometry. This is done by mapping the vertices of the geometry to a specific point inside a square image. It's a procedure analogous to peeling an orange without breaking the skin and then laying out the skin on a flat surface. We need a UV map if we want to project an image on the dress.

To create our UV map we will stay inside modo, which has excellent UV mapping tools. Before we begin, make sure that you have saved the scene.

A UV map is created by defining seams that cut the geometry into separate zones. There is no actual cutting happening to the geometry. The seams are simply defining areas of the geometry that can be isolated and then projected into a flat image surface. It's easier than it sounds. Let try it.

First of all, let's press 2 to use the selection by edge. Now let's double-click on one of the edges in the middle of the side of the dress. This operation selects the whole seam on the side of the dress. If we have symmetry still active, the corresponding seam will be selected in the opposite side. Now, with the selection still active, let's orbit the camera around the dress so that we can see the shoulder strap clearly. Press *Shift* + click on the edge in the middle of the shoulder. This operation adds the edge to the current selection. Now we have defined a seam that cuts the dress into two separate sections, one for the front and one for the rear.

Let's click on the **UV** tab at the top of the modo window. When we do this, the mesh for the Dawn base figure turns into a different color. This is how modo tells us which mesh is active for UV mapping and which one is not. On the left-hand side of the window, we see a grid. That's where the UV map will appear once it's defined. In the top-left area of the window, there is a button to select the Unwrap tool. Click on it and then click on a point in the grid. The Unwrap tool has done what its name suggests. Based on the seams that we have defined, the tool cuts the geometry and then lays the polygons flat on the UV map.

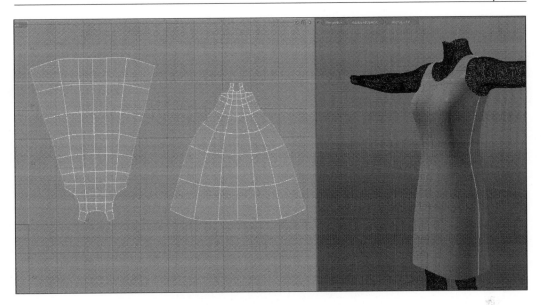

 Notice that if you hover with the mouse over one of the edges in the UV map, modo highlights the corresponding edge in the dress in the 3D Viewport.

This shows us the relationship between the UV map and the geometry. This relationship makes it possible to project an image onto the geometry. We will see in a few minutes how that works. What we can see from the UV map is that the rear piece is upside-down and the front piece shows heavy distortion in the form of strong compression in the upper chest area. This will result in an uneven distribution of the texture and stretching or compression.

We are going to fix this quickly, but we are not going to make this UV map perfect. The point of this exercise is to show you the basic operations and the workflow involved in the definition of UV map. A lot more can be done, but let's keep things simple at this point. A way to relax the tension in the map is to add more seams in strategic point. Looking at the map it's clear that the lower part of the dress is much larger than the top one. So, if we separate those two sections, they will be free to move independently. That's exactly our strategy. We are going to add a seam just below the breast, like this:

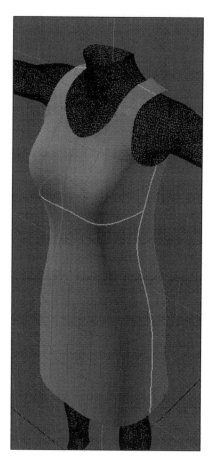

Select those edges and then use the Unwrap tool again. The UV map will be updated to be something like this:

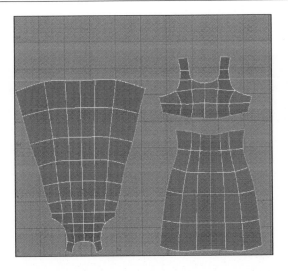

We are almost there. The different colors—shades of gray in print—indicate different levels of distortion in the map. We are not going to be concerned about that right now. The little bit of distortion that we have is acceptable for this example. What is important to note is that the UV map can be edited in the same way we edit a 3D mesh. So to rotate the rear section by 180 degrees, we can switch to selection by polygon and double-click on one of the faces in the UV map. Then, we press *E* to activate the rotate tool. At this point we can either use the mouse to rotate the section of the UV or enter 180 in the **Angle** field of the **Transform** panel to the left of the modo window. Press *Esc* when done to deselect the faces.

Lastly, let's select the top-front part of the dress, activate the **Move** tool, and move it so that the center edge aligns with the center edge of the lower portion of the map. This is the change:

The UV map generated by modo is just an automatic suggestion by the program. It's not written in stone. We can change anything about it if that makes sense. For example, the top and bottom edges of the large frontal piece don't need to be wavy; making those edges straight will make the painting of textures much easier. So, let's press 2 to select by edge and select the bottom edge. In the left-hand side of the modo window there are a few tools that can be used to align the UVs. We are going to use these two:

The one with the arrow pointing up aligns the horizontal edges to be all at the same level, based on the highest edge. The other tool performs the same action but in the opposite direction. With the lower edge selected let's click on the **Align Bottom** tool. Let's press *Esc* and select the top edge and align that one too. We will also align the bottom edge of the top piece and finally align the bottom edge of the rear panel. Ideally, we want to have both pieces from the front of the dress to align closely so that it will be easier to paint a seamless texture. We can do that by using the Transform tool. After all these transformations the final result is this:

The edges of the two front sections have been made to overlap. This makes it easier to paint seamless textures.

It's time to see what is the result of all this work. We want to paint a texture in Photoshop (or equivalent program) and see that the texture is being projected correctly on the dress. The first step is to export our UV map as an image, so that we can use it as a template. To do this we navigate to **Texture | Export UV to EPS...** in modo. The only request for this function is a filename. I entered `DawnDress_template` and modo will generate an **Encapsulated Postscript (EPS)** file. EPS files use vector primitives to draw their content. This means that the image can be scaled up to any dimension without any aliasing (jagged edges). The downside is that EPS files are more complex to use. It's generally better to have a JPEG file. This is easy to do if we have Photoshop. In Photoshop load the `DawnDress_template.eps` and the program immediately asks you at what size you would like to rasterize the content. Let's select **1024 x 1024**. The image created is a perfect replica of the UV map template at 1024 x 1024 pixels, which can be easily distributed to artists who can then create patterns for the dress. The only issue is that Photoshop shows the template against a transparency grid. We just need to add a layer, move it to be the base layer and then fill it with white. Save the image to JPEG and you're all done. Close the image and then load the file saved, `DawnDress_template.jpg`. Navigate to **File | Save as...** to save it to `DawnTexture_01.jpg`.

Now we can paint. Our goal is to verify that the UV map works and specifically that we can paint a texture that overlaps the two sections in the front of the dress without seeing a seam.

Let's add a layer and make it the top layer, so that the UV template is at the bottom. Make the top layer 50 percent transparent and add your graphics of choice. I used a classic Yin-Yang symbol scaled big enough to cover both sections. The image is included in the project files. Then, I copied the symbol twice for the rear section. In this way we can verify that the UV map works for both the front and the back of the dress. Obviously, we don't want to show the UV map grid, so we need to delete the base layer. When we do that, the three symbols stand out in the middle of an image that is completely transparent. As the background for the symbols is white, we just need to add a new layer, move it at the bottom, and fill it with white.

This is the final result:

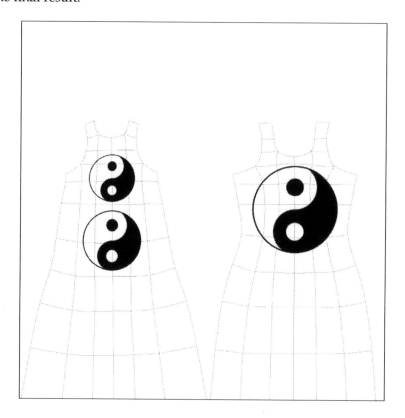

The border and UV frame are shown just for illustration; they are not included in the actual image.

Now we can test this in modo.

Click on the **Model** tab at the top to exit the UV map editor. At the top-right of modo window, click on the **Shader Tree** tab and click on the disclosure triangle for the **Render** item. In there you should see a subitem called **Dress (Material)**. Select it. At the top-right of the window, there is a drop-down menu named **Add Layer**. Click on it and navigate to **Image Map | (load image)**.

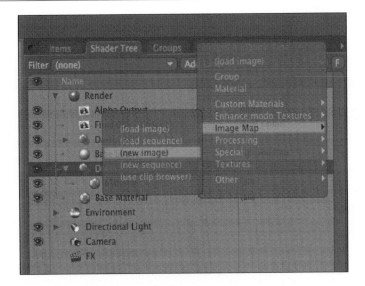

Navigate where the file `DawnDress_01.jpg` is and select it. The texture should show immediately in the Viewport.

Congratulations! You have modeled a dress and UV-mapped it. Now we need to get the object out of modo, inside Studio and rig it so that it can move with the figure.

Getting the dress out of modo

Our target is to export the dress model using the OBJ format so that we can import it in Studio. To do so, we need to perform two operations before we navigate to **File | Export**. First, we need to delete the base model. modo does not have a selective export feature and so it exports every model that is in the scene into a single OBJ file. Obviously, we don't want to have the base figure of Dawn in our dress file. In the **Items** tab of modo, right-click on **DawnCRKit** and select **Delete** from the pop-up menu.

The second modification that we need to do is about the geometry of the dress. Up to now we used the subdivision to smooth out the lines of the dress. Unfortunately, that strategy does not work when exporting to OBJ. The exported file will only contain the coarse geometry. The solution is very simple, though. Press *Tab* to return the dress to the original coarse geometry. Now press *D* a couple of times. This command actually subdivides the geometry. Each time that we press *D* we split every polygon into four smaller polygons. In my version of the dress I have 204 base polygons. After pressing *D* once, I have 816 polygons. With the second subdivision I obtain 3,264 polygons. Now we can export the dress. Subdivision should be handled with attention. Every level quadruples the number of polygons and that poses a heavy burden on the memory of the computer. Use subdivision judiciously.

Navigate to **File | Export As...** and select a folder and filename. I save my file on the Desktop with the name `DawnDress.obj`. In the window you need to select what file format you want to use for the export. Select **Waverfront OBJ**. Close modo *without* saving the file so that you can return to it if necessary.

Rigging the dress

We are almost at the end. At this point we need to import the dress in Studio and rig it. Rigging means creating the bones that are used by Studio for moving a piece of geometry. Think of the geometry mesh as the skin of the character. Without bones a figure would just bend unnaturally. When we create bones for a mesh, we identify which parts of the geometry move and which range of motions those movements will have. You can relax immediately; we are not going to spend any time tweaking angles or doing any math. In this section we will see the essentials of rigging so that you can get the general feeling for what is involved in the process.

Importing the dress

The first thing that we want to verify is if the dress actually fits the Dawn figure inside Studio. So, let's start Studio and load the full Dawn figure. Then, we navigate to **File** | **Import** to import the OBJ as we did before. Make sure that the modo preset is selected in the **Import** window.

If everything worked out well, you should see something like this:

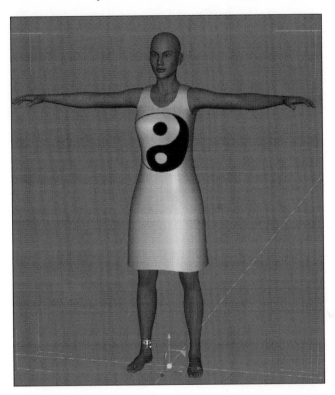

While the imported object fits the figure, if you pose Dawn in any way, you will see that the dress doesn't follow the movements. Up to this point we just have an object superimposed on Dawn. To turn it into a conforming garment, we need to rig it to add bones to its geometry. This operation used to be very laborious in the past, but Studio 4 makes it very easy. Let's take a look at what 3D bones look like. Select **Dawn** and click on the Joint Editor tool in the toolbar. The following screenshot shows the Joint Editor tool in the selected state:

When we do that, Studio draws the bones on the selected geometry. We don't really need to do anything with the Dawn's bones, but this little exercise is useful in visualizing the relationship between bones and the geometry. When we pose a model, we actually move the bones and then the associated geometry is moved in the same way.

If we create the same number of bones in the dress and we name them exactly in the same way, Studio can move the bones in the dress every time we move the bones in Dawn. For example, if we take the **Chest 1** bone and bend it a bit, Studio looks up if the dress has a bone called **Chest 1**; if it's found, it gets bent by the same amount. As the dress' bone is bent, the associated geometry is deformed with the net effect of making the dress follow the base figure.

So, all that we have to do is to create the bones in the dress with the exact same names and connect them to equivalent groups of polygons. It's actually easier than it sounds.

From the Studio menu, navigate to **Edit | Figure | Transfer Utility...**. The window that appears is the **Transfer Utility**, a tool that takes the bones and polygon groups from one figure and applies them to a target object.

> Note that Transfer Utility only works with weight-mapped figures.
> V4 and previous figures, which don't use weight mapping, cannot
> use Transfer Utility. For those figures a slightly more complex
> routine is necessary. Refer to the documentation for *Context Creation
> Toolkit* from DAZ.

In our case, we want to take the bones and corresponding polygon groups from Dawn and copy them to our new dress. In the **Source:** panel we select **Dawn** as the value for **Scene Item:**. In the **Target** panel we select **DawnDress** for **Scene Item:**. Then, click on the **Show Options** button to expand the window to show all the options involved in this operation.

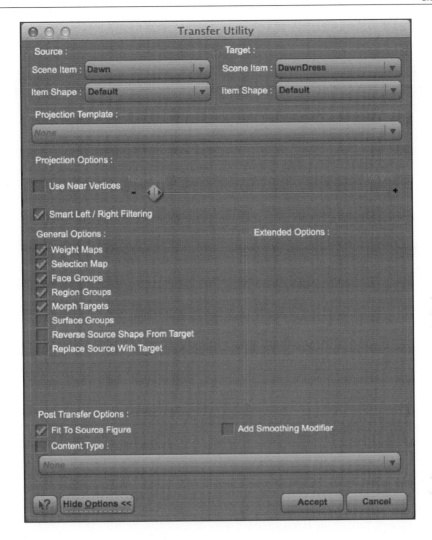

Click on **Accept** and Studio will do the rest. After two or three seconds, the dress will be changed to be a conforming figure. In the **Scene** tab, you will see that what was a simple object before is now a complex figure with all the nested nodes (bones) that you would expect. If you move Dawn, the dress now follows the figure. You have now created a dress and rigged it to follow a figure. Congratulations!

Distributing your work

At some point you might desire to let others use your work, either for profit or for free. If you are just starting to make clothing for Studio figures, I suggest giving the first few examples for free so that you can gather feedback from the users. When people pay money for a product, they demand a certain level of quality and that can only be achieved after a bit of experience.

To distribute content we need to know how to package it. We need to make someone else, who doesn't have a single file of our product, able to add that product to his/her scene. It is necessary to be thorough and precise. Fortunately, Studio has all the tools to help us.

Choosing a file format

When we create objects, files, and other elements that define a product, like the dress in this chapter, the process happens incrementally and we rarely make the decision to keep an inventory of all the files that are necessary for making the same product work on a computer.

Notice that I said files, plural. The first concept to assimilate is that we cannot distribute our product as a single file. It's a collection of files, even when it's just a simple dress like the one that we have just created.

This collection includes files that define the geometry, files that define the figure properties, its materials, UV maps, and so on.

At the center of the process there is a file with the extension `.duf`. For example, `DawnDress.duf`. The `.duf` extension is a bit of an unfortunate double acronym. It stands for **DSON User File**. **DSON** itself means **DAZ Studio Object Notation**. Studio 4 uses a file format called DSON, which is a way of describing 3D assets using a text file. The format is itself an extension of one of the exchange file formats that has become a de-facto standard of the Web: JSON. JSON is a file format defined to allow multiple diverse applications to exchange data. The **JSON** format (**JavaScript Object Notation**) defines collections of properties and their values. It is a simple file format that has received worldwide adoption by many organizations. DAZ has extended that file format for its own use and named it DSON. There are several files in the Studio **Content Library** that are defined using the DSON syntax. When we save a figure to be used in Studio, that figure, in this case, our new dress, is saved as a DSON User File or DUF.

Let's see how it's done. In the **Scene** tab we select the DawnDress figure. Then we navigate to **File | Save As | Support Asset | Figure/Prop Assets...**. The first thing that Studio asks is the name and location of the file. I created a folder DawnDress in my Desktop folder and I'll save this file with the name DawnDress in that folder. Once we confirm the name of the file, Studio shows the window for the tool that saves the selected object as a loadable asset. In that window we need to make some decisions, which will affect how the product will be packaged.

The **Asset Directory:** field value is the location where we want to store the geometry data of the dress. This includes the geometry itself, the UV map description and other files that are used by Studio. Keep in mind that up to this point the dress is only defined in memory and it's not saved to disk. If we were to close our scene, all the data for the dress would be lost. That's why Studio is asking for a location to store the geometry. While we have the model in OBJ format, Studio is not going to use that file; it needs to store the model in its own format. The asset directory is the base directory where the model's data will be stored. This field is a drop-down list of the directories configured for Studio. For example, in my case I have /Users/paolo/DSContent. The /Users/paolo directory is my home folder on my Macintosh. In Windows it would be something like C:\Users\paolo.

Select the folder that you want and take note of what it is, you will need it later.

Vendor Name: is very important. Make sure that you pick a good name and that you will hold to that name consistently. The vendor name will be used to create a subdirectory for your content so you want something short and possibly without spaces. Spaces in file and directory names are often troublesome and it's a good idea to avoid them as much as possible. For this example, we are going to use the fictitious name MegaVendor. **Product Name:** is also going to be used to create a subdirectory, so we are going to use DawnDress. **Item Name** is going to be DawnDress again. If we had a package with multiple pieces, like a coordinated belt, we would keep the product name the same for all items—DawnDress—but then assign a different item name to each piece.

The **Set Content Type:** checkbox enables the setting of the metadata for our product.

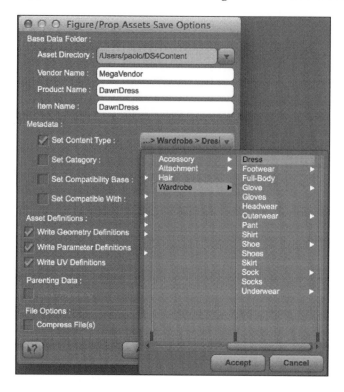

The term metadata is used for data that describes data. In general it's a series of properties that describe a digital asset. For example, digital cameras place metadata in each photo describing the date and time, the exposure parameters (ISO speed, shutter speed, and aperture), and, if the camera is equipped with GPS (that is camera phones), the geographic location. In the case of Studio, the metadata is used to place the dress in the appropriate folder in the **Smart Content** tab. You can see my settings in the preceding screenshot.

All the other parameters are kept as a default except for the last one. I disabled the file compression because I want to be able to review the file before delivering it, and make sure that it doesn't have hardcoded paths to files that are on my machine.

By default, Studio compresses its files using the gzip algorithm. This operation doesn't gain anything except making the files smaller. It doesn't make them faster to load or take less memory. The .duf files need to be decompressed in memory for Studio to use them, and the text in them needs to be parsed completely. If we want, we can resave the file later on in a compressed format after we verify that everything is in order. DSON files are just text files, so we can load them in a text editor and verify their content as long as they are not compressed.

Click on the **Accept** button, and then a new `DawnDress.duf` file will be created together with a thumbnail. Look in the folder that you have selected and both files should be there.

Now look in the folder specified in the **Asset Directory** field. You should see a directory named `MegaVendor` with the `DawnDress/DawnDress` subdirectory, which should contain a `DawnDress_1833.dsf` file. The number in the name might be different in your case, it's not important. This file is also in DSON format, although it has the extension `.dsf` instead of `.duf`. It contains the description of the geometry.

When we want to distribute our products, we need to include both the `.duf` file and the supporting hierarchy, including the `MegaVendor` directory.

The distribution hierarchy

Now we have all the files that we need, but they are not organized in a way that can be distributed to another user. We need to package them into a structure that can be used by Studio.

All products for Studio must follow a certain hierarchy of directories in order to be installed correctly. Starting from the folder that contains the product, in our case `DawnDress` in the `Desktop` folder, there must be a folder named `data`. In that folder we need to copy the `MegaVendor` folder that we have created in the previous step.

When we distribute clothing, the product must be inside a directory structure that connects the product to the figure for which it's designed. Studio defines this relationship at the filesystem level by using the following structure:

- At the beginning there is a directory called `People`
- Inside `People` there is the name of the figure, `Dawn` in our case
- Inside `Dawn` we need the name of the category, in this case, `Clothing`
- Inside `Clothing` we add a directory with the name of the product, `DawnDress`
- Inside `DawnDress` we have the actual files that make up the product

This is how it should look:

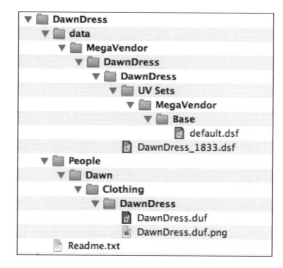

Note how I added a `Readme.txt` file. This file can give instructions on how to install and use the new garment.

Now we can zip the top `DawnDress` directory and distribute it.

Getting down to business

Let's say that you have mastered the art of 3D modeling and gained quite a bit of experience in rigging and packaging content. Now you want to enter the exciting world of 3D commerce. The business model used for the resale of 3D assets is called brokerage and it's similar to what Apple uses for its App Store. The content creator sells through an intermediate company, the broker, and they both split the profit in the middle, 50 percent to the author, 50 percent to the broker. While 50 percent can sound like a lot, and it is, the reality of the market is that many products are sold at a very low price, often below $10 and rarely above $20. The only way anybody can make any sort of money with such a low price is by selling large quantities. The broker provides advertising, storage, web bandwidth, and it processes the payment for you. The broker also pays the credit card fees, which are significant, and provides tools for tracking sales. All in all, the broker does a lot of work for you. The 50-50 split is standard across the border, so your only alternative is to sell by yourself, which can limit your ability to reach the market dramatically.

What a broker offers is a large market and the means to reach it. That's why I sell my Reality plugin via that system. While with software there is more flexibility than with content because of the cost of writing and supporting applications, the advantages of using a broker are several. A broker will advertise your product in their mailing list, which reaches a vast public.

I have used all the major brokers in this market and my suggestion is to go with either Renderosity or RuntimeDNA. The reasons for this choice are market reach and service. When you sell through an intermediary, you want to be sure that the company provides you with good tools and good service. The two companies mentioned above are the best in the market in my opinion.

Renderosity has probably the largest circulation in the market. Because of the large number of vendors already on board, you will have to compete with others to gain the attention of the viewer. The best way to be noticed is to be original. For example, there is an overabundance of sexy lingerie and suggestive outfits. These types of products are not going to make you noticed. The old saying says that "sex sells", but the truth is that a lot of people are actually turned off by those kinds of outfits because they are in a line of work that does not include erotica. There is a large untapped market of potential buyers of high-quality outfits to be used in a much larger series of scenarios. The same is for fairies, dragons, and fantasy themes. That market has been flooded for quite some time now. Be original, exploit niches that are neglected and you might be able to gain good customers.

RuntimeDNA is a smaller outfit, which means that they reach fewer users, but this fact also means that you will be competing with fewer vendors. In addition, they have more personal relationships with their vendors. RuntimeDNA is also more selective about the content that they publish, and they tend to prefer material that is unusual. RuntimeDNA, at this moment, does not have much architectural material so that could be a great niche to explore. Create great environments that can be used in many different situations, and you can have a good chance to succeed in that market. The additional benefit of architectural modeling is that you can target both the Studio and Poser user base, expanding your offering and your potential revenues. Two customers are better than one.

My advice is to try both Renderosity and RuntimeDNA, with different products, and see which one suits you better.

To become a vendor (Renderosity) or merchant (RuntimeDNA), you can apply online. After you are signed up, you will then be asked to submit a product, which can be done via the web interface of the broker. You will need to create ZIP files for the distribution of products, similar to what we have seen in this chapter. The products will be tested by the QA team (Quality Assurance) and then released a few days later if there are no issues. If there is anything that needs to be changed, you will be notified of it and you will have the opportunity to resubmit the files. All brokers provide detailed information on the delivery format that they need.

Both brokers have excellent sales reporting tools that you can use to monitor your sales in real time. At the end of the month, the payment will be sent to you. You can be paid with a personal check or via PayPal. The latter option is preferable; once the broker posts the payment, you get your money immediately without waiting for the mail to be delivered and without trips to the bank.

Summary

We have seen how to create a new garment from scratch, based on the new character Dawn. Dawn is a promising figure that works for the whole market of premade content for both Studio and Poser, which provides the widest market appeal.

From the steps described in this chapter, you can see what's involved in the creation of new clothing: modeling, UV mapping, exporting and import in Studio, rigging, and final packaging.

There is a lot more about making clothing, there are special morphs to be added, there are figure variations to be added, and material presets to be included with any sellable figure. But those are details that can be explored on your own once the big picture is understood. That was the purpose of this chapter, to give you a bird's eye view of the process from far up so that you can get an understanding of how to get to the finished product from the blank page.

In the next chapter we will look into the final piece of the Studio puzzle: animation.

12
Animation

3D animation is very popular today. Pixar has made it so with its incredibly successful movies. Studio provides several tools that are needed for creating 3D animations, but there is a lot more to animation than the tools.

The subject of animation is very complex and it would require a book in itself to just describe the tip of this very large iceberg. Instead of giving you an incomplete presentation of animation techniques, in this chapter we will see the essential workflow elements involved in the production of an animation, and how they all work together in Studio. This type of coverage will give you an overview of what is involved in any animation project, what steps are appropriate, and what is best avoided. For example, a lot of newcomers in this sector render animation as movie clips. We will see why that is not the correct approach.

After you have read this chapter, if you want to dig deeper into this subject, you can look for books specialized on this topic or enroll in animation classes like the ones offered by Animation Mentor (`http://animationmentor.com`).

The topics covered in this chapter are as follows:

- Animation concepts
- Frame rates
- Keyframing and tweening
- The Studio timeline
- Tools for animation – keyMate and aniMate2
- Animation rendering
- Editing
- Exporting the movie
- Adding music and sound effects

Understanding animation

Animation is based on a phenomenon called **persistence of vision (POV)**.

> *Persistence of vision is the phenomenon of the eye by which an afterimage is thought to persist for approximately one twenty-fifth of a second on the retina.*
>
> *— Source: Wikipedia*

Refer to `http://en.wikipedia.org/wiki/Persistence_of_vision`. In other words, if an image flashes in front of our eyes and then goes away, it sticks to our brain for about 1/25th of a second. This means that, if we see 25 images in a second, they will seem to be part of a seamless sequence with no gaps in between. This is exactly the principle behind every motion picture and animation work. The frequency of images flashing in front of the viewer is designated with the term **frames per second** and generally abbreviated as **fps**.

Understanding frame frequency

25 fps is the frequency of the PAL TV system widely used in Europe and Japan, among other places. 24 fps is the frequency used by motions pictures. NTSC, the American standard for TV, uses 30 fps.

It might seem strange that motion pictures are shot at 24 fps when we just said that the POV rate is 1/25th of a second. The exact reason for this is not completely known. In any way, we are talking about a difference of just one frame per second. The 24 fps rate was decided long time ago by the people running the film industry and it is still in use today.

This means that if you want to create an animation, you have to draw 24 images for each second of the movie. That is a lot of work. Walt Disney, the pioneer of full-length animations, made a fundamental discovery at the beginning of his career. He found out that if you take the same frame and you show it twice, you can create animations by drawing 12, instead of 24, frames, and still provide a very smooth effect. The early classics of Disney, Snow White (1937) and others, were all made with this technique. Don't think that Disney was being cheap. All those frames were drawn by hand by a small army of artists. The chief artists, the people in charge of deciding the look and feel of the movie, usually drew by hand the starting and key frames of each sequence, especially when expressions where involved. A group of more junior, but still very capable, artists were in charge of drawing the frames in between the key frames. Those artists were nicknamed in **betweeners** or **tweeners**, and the technique of filling the gaps between key frames became known as **tweening**. Once drawn, the frames were then placed on a special camera and shot one by one on a roll of motion picture film. Think of this operation as the equivalent of modern time rendering.

Today's animations are made with computers, but the same principles apply. When we want to create a motion from a point to a destination, we plot the motion and then define positions at key points in the sequence. Those key points are our key frames, which from now on will be spelled keyframes. The software, Studio in this case, will do the tweening automatically. Tweening is done in a very literal and linear way by the software. Don't expect common sense. Unlike with humans, you cannot expect a level of understanding of the subtleties of movement from a program. For example, if you need to raise the arm of your character, you might have a rotation of 30 degrees at the shoulder joint. If you create a keyframe at frame 1 for the starting point and then create a keyframe at frame 12 for 30 degrees of movement, the computer will have to create 10 intermediate frames, each one rotating the shoulder joint 2.5 degrees. If you need to add some twitch or other irregular movement, you will have to craft that by hand.

So, the quality of an animation depends heavily on the skillful placement of the keyframes; that is, how often you add a keyframe and what kind of content is in it. Keyframes guide the software. This is the concept to keep in mind. It's also important to remember that a character that moves her limbs in perfectly uniform increments will look like a robot and not like a person. Something can be done by the software by marking target keyframes for ease-in or ease-out tweening. An ease-in modifier will instruct the software to create an animation that gradually slows down as we reach the next keyframe. An ease-out keyframe causes a gradual increase of motion as the animation moves away — or out — from the keyframe.

This is important, for example, for camera moves. If you move the camera between two points, you want that motion smooth and natural. If the camera starts moving from perfectly still to full speed with no transition, it will look mechanical and the effect will make the viewer aware that she is watching through a camera.

> The ease-in and ease-out terms don't appear in the DAZ Studio documentation and user interface. Nevertheless, they are often used in many other animation and motion graphics tools, and it's important to be aware of these concepts.

Part of the art of making a motion picture is to create the suspension of disbelief that immerses the viewer in the story. If our camera moves with a jerky motion, the whole illusion goes away. Real cameras have inertia. Hollywood cameras from the 1920s or 1940s were huge, weighed several tens of pounds, and they moved slowly. You could not whip them around like an iPhone. This created a movie language based on fluid motions through elegant arches. They made movies look beautiful. The upshot of all this is that viewers are used to that visual language and so we have to respect it in order to create animations that look realistic and engaging.

As human beings we do move with inertia. Even when we turn our head the movement has a slow beginning, a full speed, middle, and a slow down phase. Cameras in our animations need to work in a similar way.

Of course, we can also fine tune the frames manually after they are generated by the automatic tweening. These are just some of the fundamental concepts about animation. There is a lot more about it.

The work of an animator is both artistic — it requires aesthetic sensibility and sense of timing — and technical; it deals with a myriad of small technical issues. If you cannot count on the help of other people, you should expect to spend a week, eight hours a day, to create a few seconds of animation, without counting the rendering. That's about 56 hours of work for anywhere between two and five seconds of footage, depending on the complexity of the scene.

I don't say this to discourage you but simply to give you a frame of time, so that you know what to expect before tackling such a task. Planning is essential for every animation work. The animation project starts with rough sketches of how the animation will progress. You can make the sketch with stick figures if you don't have the skills for drawing. It doesn't matter how crude your sketch is, as long as it depicts the key points of the animation and how it progresses. This will allow you to anticipate problems before you're committing many hours of hard work. We call this series of sketches the storyboard of the animation. You can download a free storyboard template from `http://karenjlloyd.com/blog/free-storyboard-template-downloads/`.

Load the template in Photoshop, or any other drawing application of your choice, and roughly sketch the action as you see it in your mind.

Delving into the frame ratio

We talked about frame sizes before. When we create an animation, we need to consider that the work will be shown on a TV set or, at the very least, it will be watched by people who are used to watching this kind of shows on a TV. This means that the aspect ratio of the frame needs to be locked-in at the beginning. The exact resolution of the animation can be changed later, but the aspect ratio determines the framing of each and every frame, and so it needs to be determined before the first frame is created.

The vast majority of TVs today are set at HD resolution, which has an aspect ratio of 16:9. As we mentioned before, we have two basic resolutions that fit that aspect ratio: 1920 x 1080 and 1280 x 720. I suggest to start with the lower one, 1280 x 720 because it makes the rendering of test frames faster. We can change the resolution later on. In fact, we can use something like Ultra HD resolution (3840 x 2160) without affecting anything but the render time. All these resolutions, 720p, 1080p, or Ultra HD have the same 16:9 ratio.

The Studio timeline

Look at the bottom of the Studio window. You should see two tabs named **Animate Lite** and **Timeline**. Click on the **Timeline** tab. The timeline is where we control our animation. It is also the place were we set the animation parameters. If we look at the bottom left of the tab, we see three input fields:

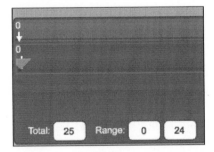

The **Total:** field is the total number of frames in this shot. The **Range:** lists the starting frame, 0, and the ending frame, 24. Numbering of frames starts at 0 not 1. It's weird, it's a bit of computer jargon that slipped through and there is nothing to do about it. We just have to remember that.

Studio always sets the animation to last for a second of time using whatever frame rate is used when the program starts. Actually the animation is, in this case, one second and one frame. We can make longer animations by simply changing the total number of frames. For example, if we want a 15-second animation, we need to enter 360 (24 fps times 15).

At the bottom-right of the tab, we find two other fields: Current and FPS. The first field indicates our current position, the frame that is currently shown and that can be edited. When we scroll through the timeline, an operation that is called scrubbing, Studio updates the Viewport to show the animation frame. The FPS field is the most important and needs to be set before we start working on the animation. It indicates, of course, the frames per second used in our animation. Strangely enough, the default used by Studio is 30, the NTSC format. We need to set it to 24 so that it conforms to the motion picture frame rate. Once we enter the value 24, we will see that the tick-marks at the top of the timeline change to adapt. Try changing the fps value a couple of times between 24 and 30 to see the effect on the timeline. Then, make sure that it's set to 24.

Scrubbing

The orange triangle pointing down is our timeline cursor. Try dragging it to the right. As we drag the cursor, we see the **Current** field changes with the value of the current frame. When we have a bit of animation in our scene the operation of scrubbing will show the result for each frame.

To make the job of navigating our timeline easier, let's add a few keyboard shortcuts. Having to move the mouse just to scrub is quite counterproductive. We will add three shortcuts: one to start and stop the animation playback, one for moving to the previous frame, and one for moving to the next one.

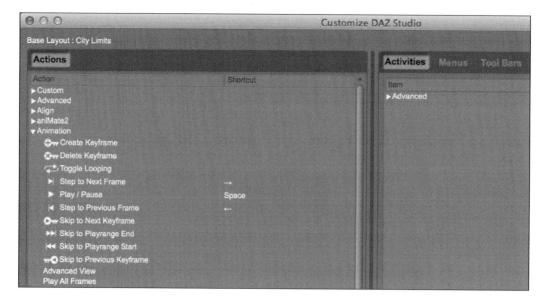

This is how we do it:

1. Press *F3* to call the UI customization window.

2. In the left panel, labeled **Actions**, find the **Animation** group.

3. Click on the disclosure triangle to open the group. You will find three actions: **Step to Next Frame**, **Play / Pause**, and **Step to Previous Frame**.

4. Select the **Play / Pause** action.

5. Right-click on it and select **Change Keyboard Shortcut**.

6. Press Space bar. The window will reflect your choice.

7. Select the **Step to Previous Frame** action.

8. Right-click on it and choose **Change Keyboard Shortcut**.

9. Press the left arrow key.

10. Repeat the operation for **Step to Next Frame** using the right arrow key.

Now we can start and stop the playback of the animation by pressing Space bar, and we can move frame by frame in the logical way by using the arrow keys. Give it a try.

A simple animation test

Let's see how the principle of keyframing works with a simple exercise. Start with a new scene. The idea for this exercise is to change a figure from the standard T pose to a more natural one. So, let's add Dawn to our scene. You can use any other figure if you like. Make sure that the timeline cursor is at frame 0 and that the animation is set for 24 fps.

Activate the Universal tool, go to frame 15, grab the left arm by the forearm, and drag it down until it is alongside the body. Repeat the operation for the other arm. This is the position that we should have:

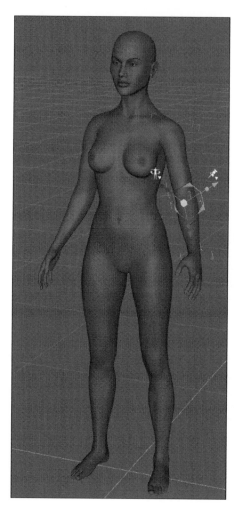

Now drag the timeline cursor back to frame 0, you should see the animation playing back. Studio has created the frames in between frame 0 and 15 automatically, moving all the body parts in the right way to create the transition from T pose to the pose that we have created at frame 15. While we have simply dragged a limb, several other body parts have been affected by the movement, and the parameters for those body parts have been recorded. All the variations of those parameters have been stored in the keyframe at position 15. Also, note that we didn't have to do anything special for creating the keyframe; the simple act of moving things around caused the new keyframe to be recorded.

This logic is called autokeyframing and can be a good or a bad thing. It's good because it makes things easy, but on the other hand we cannot disable this feature and sometimes we want to move objects around without creating keyframes. Just keep in mind that we cannot disable it and that it affects your cameras as well as any other object in the scene. Very often it can happen that we move our camera to look around the scene and then the camera moves all around the place while playing the animation back. This is one of the cases where it is useful to use the perspective camera because, by not being a real camera, it is not affected by the keyframing.

Controlling the keyframes

Let's go back to frame 15 and look at the head. Since we only moved the arms, the head should be more or less unchanged. Let's go to frame 20 and then rotate the head to look at the camera. We need to rotate the head and possibly a bit of the neck as well.

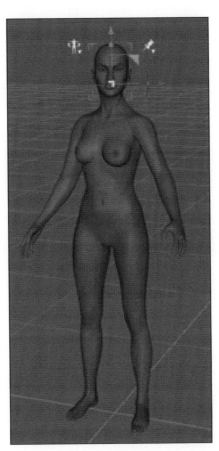

Let's go back to frame 0 and scrub our timeline. Now we can see that the head starts moving right from the third or fourth frame. Why is that? We clearly verified before that the head was not moving up to frame 15. What happened is that we created a keyframe at frame 20, and since there were no other keyframes, Studio starts the tweening from the first keyframe, frame 0, and it divides the increments evenly until it reaches frame 20. At frame 3 or 4 the first movements are noticeable. If we wanted to keep the head still up to frame 15, we need to set a keyframe at frame 15 to hold the head still so that the movement runs only from frame 15 to 20.

Editing keyframes

The Studio timeline is pretty rudimentary and editing keyframes in it is not easy. I'm not saying this to criticize the product but to make clear that this is not the state of the art in this area of technology. Other 3D programs have more advanced and easier to use timeline editors that allow the user to do a whole set of operations on keyframes. We will see a solution to this problem shortly. To fix our head animation issue, we would ideally copy the keyframe at frame 0 to frame 15. This is not possible with the Studio timeline so we have to resort to some other trick.

Make sure that the head is selected and go to frame 20. The timeline should show a small black triangle pointing down. That is a keyframe. At the bottom-center of the **Timeline** tab, there is a series of buttons. Find the one that shows a key with an x. Hover with the mouse cursor over it and see if the tool tip says **Delete the keys at the current time**. Then click on it and the keyframe will be deleted. Repeat the operation for the neck if it had been affected when setting the head position. Click on the neck, check the timeline at frame 20, and if there is a keyframe, delete it as well.

Now the animation for the head has been returned to the original state, when we had no movement for it. Hit Space bar to play the animation. You should see just the arms moving. Let's move to frame 15, select the head, and then click on the button that creates a new keyframe. It is the one with a plus sign on the icon of a key.

Do the same for the neck as well. Now go to frame 20 and turn the head again as you did before. When we play our animation now, we can see that the arms get lowered first and then the head turns.

Doing it the Studio way

Most 3D programs that handle animation show us all the tracks that have keyframes simultaneously in the timeline editor so that we can see at a glance where data is stored. Studio, by default, does not do that. The program shows only the keyframes of the selected body part. This makes it quite difficult to edit animations as it requires us to guess where the keyframes have been added. We can spend quite a bit of time clicking around and trying to find the right limb. Even when the right element is found the options to edit a keyframe are very rudimentary. A better option is to buy the keyMate plugin. keyMate provides a much improved timeline editor that lists all the nodes that have been affected by the animation, and allows us to modify the placement of keyframes by simply dragging them along the timeline. keyMate is still not as sophisticated as the timeline editor of modo or Poser, but it's a vast improvement compared to what is available in Studio. If you are going to do any animation work in Studio, buying keyMate is a no-brainer. You can find it at the DAZ store.

One of the great advantages of keyMate is that when we click on a keyframe in the timeline the corresponding element is highlighted in the Viewport. For example, if we select the keyframe for the left shoulder then that part of the body is highlighted.

Understanding the logic behind animations

The basic concepts of animations are contained in the keyframing techniques explained earlier. As you can imagine, there is a lot of tweaking and adjusting involved in building a fully polished animation.

One thing to keep in mind is that the camera is one of the actors involved in each shot, and its animation dramatically contributes to the overall feeling of the animation.

Clothing needs to be animated as well. As we move a figure from frame to frame, the clothing needs to follow in a natural way. This might be done adequately by Studio, but most of the times we will need to make manual adjustments. Same thing is for hair. The devil is in the details.

I suggest that you perform a few dozen tests on several types of animations in order to acquire the right amount of practice. Don't worry about rendering the animations and obtaining a finished video clip. The focus with this exercise is to become proficient in animation techniques and develop the muscle memory necessary for efficient work.

Organizing your project

Before you start any animation project, you should have a basic checklist to help you set things right. It's far easier to start right than to have to retrofit your project after you have added some content. The following is a short list of the things that you should have ready before starting any animation work:

- Storyboard
- Shot list
- Frame rate
- Frame size
- Camera data

The last point is about the camera's focal length. It's very likely that we will not always use the same focal length. Some shots will be wide, others will be close ups or medium shots. Again, the storyboard is the tool that allows us to plan ahead this kinds of actions. While preparing a storyboard, it will be clear what parts of the animation will require the camera to frame wide shots or close ups. When we change the focal length during an animation we zoom in or out.

Annotating the storyboard or writing information in a shot list can help in keeping things organized. The focal length might not be easy to decide until you start working inside Studio, don't worry about that. But it does help to write down the information once you have it. It can help you with subsequent shots or if you need to add shots later on.

The shot list

Any motion picture, from full-length features to 30-second commercials, is meticulously planned and divided in shots. A shot is an uninterrupted sequence of frames. While shooting with live actors, there can be multiple tries for a shot. Those are called **takes**. Multiple shots can create a sequence.

For example, we can have a scene of the hero running through a crumbling temple trying to save himself. The first shot has the camera facing the hero frontally; he's running furiously towards a gap in the floor. The second shot is a close up of the foot, as it steps at the edge of the gap and springs up for a strenuous jump. The third shot has the camera inside that gap, which is actually a bottomless pit. The camera is 10 meters down inside the pit and points up to frame while the hero jumps mid air. The fourth shot has the camera at floor level, just behind the edge of the pit, as the hero slams on the inside wall of the pit and his hand grasps at the floor trying to get a grip to avoid falling to his death. The face contorted into a grimace of pain, fear, and so on. Those four shots and the ones that show us how the hero gets to safety, altogether form a scene.

Before starting work on an animation, it's important to have the scenes clearly designed and sketched. The storyboard helps you in this, before you commit a lot of time in creating shots that might not cut together well.

Often the storyboard is digitized and loaded in a **Non Linear Editor** (**NLE**) to verify how it plays. It doesn't matter that the frames are rough and spaced apart. Even that crude previsualization can give very important clues on how the animation will flow. The change between each camera angle or each shot is called a **cut**.

With a storyboard you identify the shots, the uninterrupted sequences of frames. Each shot is given a name. For example SC04SH01 is Scene 4, Shot 1. Consistent shot naming translates into consistent file naming, which will help you greatly in finding the right group of files once you are in the thick of your production.

Defining NLE

Cutting is an art in itself and is done with the aid of a video editor such as Final Cut X, Adobe Premiere, or iMovie. Those programs are called NLEs because they allow editing of footage without having to spool and unspool a film reel. In the days of film, the only way to edit was done by literally cutting two pieces of negative and gluing them together. That's why the word cut came into use in movie production. The term is still used today.

aniMate2

Another tool available for animation is the aniMate plugin. aniMate takes a higher level approach to animation by providing blocks of premade animations that can be dropped into a specialized timeline. This timeline runs in parallel with the Studio timeline, but is dedicated to the handling of aniblocks, as the elements of aniMate are called.

Aniblocks apply a complex animation sequence to a character. For example, there are aniblocks that move a character form standing to sitting down. Other aniblocks provide running sequences, fighting moves, or runway walks.

Aniblocks can be placed one after the other on the timeline. They can be spliced, inverted, slowed down, and accelerated. The software comes with a few premade aniblocks and more can be bought at the DAZ store. Many aniblocks provide rather natural and convincing movements, and the software performs quite well.

The danger in using this kind of approach is that the movements of the figures can look canned. If we repeat the same aniblock in several situations in the story, it will be obvious that it's a premade routine. And because the same aniblocks can be purchased by other people, you risk making your animation similar to the work of others, which is really not what you're looking for. For example, there are groups of aniblocks with dance moves or fight moves. While they are entertaining to use privately, for a short while, I would avoid using them for anything that will be watched by the public, such as YouTube viewers. They are too recognizable and quite hard to fit in a storyline.

aniMate shines in the use of mundane activities, such as sitting down, running, walking, and waving. While using those, you have a great help in making great sequences in short time.

Aniblocks can also be trimmed, joined together, and even edited. In that regard the aniblocks can be considered as a good starting point that leads to more custom-made sequences. This is definitely an attractive solution because we can use the aniblocks to create the bulk of a complex movement, and then personalize the sequence with changes that reflect the particular storyline that we are developing.

Spline editing

aniMate provides the ability to edit the movement of a figure by editing a spline directly in the 3D Viewport. A spline is a line created by segments that are joined by nodes. You edit the spline by dragging the nodes around, creating new shapes. With aniMate, you can add an aniblock to the timeline and then edit the path created by that block for any element of the figure. Let's see it in action.

1. First we add Victoria 4 to the scene.
2. With the figure selected, we add an aniblock such as **sit in chair**.
3. Then, from the Studio menu, we navigate to **Window | Panes (tabs) | Tool Settings**. This action shows the **Tool Settings** pane. We can dock the pane to any part of the UI, either left or right.
4. The **Tool Settings** pane provides the controls to fine tune several tools available in Studio. For example, it can be used to change how the Universal tool appears and behaves. In the top portion of the pane, there is a drop-down menu that can be used to select the tool to be edited.
5. Let's click on it and select **aniMate2**.
6. From the **Pose Splines** group, let's enable the **head** checkbox.
7. Now let's scrub the timeline until we are at frame 17 of the **sit in chair** block. We should see something like this in the Viewport:

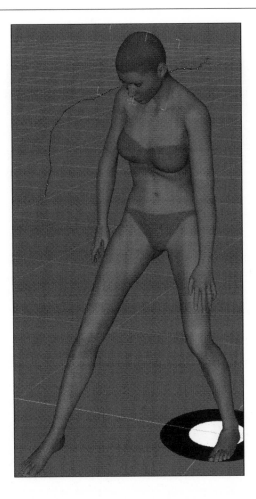

Notice that the spline that shows the trajectory of the head. By dragging the nodes of the spline, we can change the direction of movement of the head to better suit the mood and situation of our story.

aniMate is included in Studio as a limited version called aniMate lite. Once you buy the license for aniMate2, the serial number provided unlocks the full functionality of the plugin. You can use the lite version to see the basic functionalities, and then decide if this can be of help for your animation work.

Rendering

Once our animation is completely defined in Studio, the next step is to render it so that it can become a standalone video. This is the equivalent of shooting a take for a real-life movie. The rendering of the shot is not the final product, it's just the beginning. A rendered shot is just one element of the whole animation.

While creating a motion picture, the raw footage is taken from the camera and stored on a server. In the days of film the 11-minute reel was sent to a lab for development and then divided in shots. Film reels were limited to the amount of film that could be fitted in them and that was generally equivalent to 11 minutes of camera time.

When we render an animation, the result is directly ready for editing, as long as we have used consistent and organized naming for our scenes and shots.

With all the shots collected, it is then time to start editing the movie. During editing we can do cuts between shots, we can create transitions, we can add sound, music score, and special effects. Editing is where the movie is made. Finally, once the whole movie is completed, the final step is to color-grade it and add titles and credits.

The reason to avoid movie clips

It is extremely important that the footage acquired is in a format that helps preserve the quality throughout the edit process. It also needs to be NLE-friendly, which is not always the case with video formats. For example, compressed video formats such as MPEG, WMV, or AVI must be avoided at all cost while preparing shots to be edited. This is because those formats are designed for playback and they are very inefficient in editing.

Also keep in mind that we will need to export the footage from the NLE to a format that is distributable for playback. We will need to obtain a QuickTime or MPEG file from our sequence in the NLE. This requires generating a compressed video file. If the input for editing is already compressed, we will be forced to apply a compression on top of another.

Video compressions are all lossy; they degrade the quality of the image up to a certain level. Generally one level of compression, if done correctly, will not degrade the image in a perceptible way. But when we stack those compressions on top of another, the degradation becomes visible. That's why we see so many low-quality YouTube clips. They have gone through multiple aggressive compression phases. The process of converting a video clip from one encoding to another is called transcoding. If you care at all about your work you want to avoid transcoding as much as possible. In the following sections we will see how we achieve that.

There is another reason for avoiding movie clips as the format for rendering our shots: efficiency. Let me give you a couple of real-life scenarios that happen much too often.

Horror story 1

Let's say that you have a two-minute shot that you want to render from Studio. You decided to render it to a movie clip. Two minutes of footage at 24 fps gives us 2,880 frames. Let's say that you are using the highest quality of rendering, and that it takes about a minute and a half to render each frame. This is a rather optimistic scenario. High-quality rendering can take a lot longer even on a high-end machine. But for this scenario, we are going to assume a rather optimistic estimate. 2,880 times 90 seconds (one and half minutes) is 259,200 seconds or 4,320 minutes, or 72 hours. So, you leave your machine running for three days straight. This is not an unusual scenario.

After about 50 hours of rendering, your machine crashes and the movie file is completely lost. There are millions of reasons for this to happen: the cat walked over your keyboard, the power went down, the OS or Studio crashed, or Windows updates decided to reboot your computer. Now you have lost 50 hours of rendering, you have to start over and there is no assurance that something like this will not happen again. When we render to a movie file, if anything happens before the file is completed, the whole clip is lost, no matter how many hours have been spent.

Horror story 2

Same premise of Horror story 1 but this time the render completes. You load your soon-to-be-transcoded-and-shredded-to-smithereens clip in the NLE and find out that 10 frames of the clip have the feet of a character in the wrong position. All the rest is fine. You could fix the problem by just re-rendering those 10 frames. No problem, we can do that in Studio, but how can we find the exact point in the timeline where those 10 frames are? What frame numbers are those? The process can be rather laborious. In addition, we have to splice the footage in the NLE and hope that the compression of the re-rendered clip is consistent with the original one. Finally, even if you fix all that, you will have a compressed clip that will get transcoded.

Escaping the horrors

The preceding scenarios have happened and continue to happen because so many people don't use the simplest solution, the one that is also used by professional animators and motion graphics artists everywhere: rendering a sequence of frames.

A sequence of frames is a set of image files, one per frame, each one independent and self-standing. Each file has a common prefix and a number that identifies the frame on the timeline. For example, if we use the prefix `temple-escape-`, each frame will be saved as `temple-escape-000.png`, `temple-escape-001.png`, and so on. We use PNG files as the format for each frame. PNG uses a lossless compressions and supports the alpha channel, which can be used for chromakey effects. This means that the image is pixel-by-pixel the same of the image renderer by Studio, no loss caused by the compression. PNG files can be imported in the NLE and edited as much as we need without any loss of quality. We can export a sequence from the NLE to something like **After Effects** for Visual Effects work (**VFX**), and then import it back in the NLE, again, without any degradation of the image.

If a crash happens during the render for any reason, all the frames rendered up to the moment of the crash are saved to disk; all that we have to do is to restart the render from the point of the interruption. No time is lost. Because the filenames have the exact frame number, it is trivial to scrub to the point of the interruption and restart rendering exactly from there.

Sequences of frames are the way to go about rendering animation. Any NLE worth our money knows how to handle them.

Lastly, if we need to make some change to a subset of the shot, we can simply re-render the affected frames and the files will be replaced on disk. Once that is done, the NLE will refresh its own sequence without the need to splice anything.

Color grading

Every movie is color graded before the final delivery. Grading refers to applying a specific look and feel, a way of adjusting contrast, brightness, and color tonality to the whole movie. This technique is used for the vast majority of movies, including several documentaries. You can see an example of how grading was used to achieve the look of The Lord Of The Rings in this YouTube video: `http://youtu.be/M4zRMLbZZxw`.

To grade a movie, we need to export it to a program like After Effects. As you can imagine, the export must be done in a way to preserve the quality of the footage. Frame sequences are, again, the solution for this. We export from the NLE using PNG or TIFF frame sequences and then import the footage in After Effects.

Adding music and sound effects

Often, we need to add all kinds of sound elements to an animation. Characters might have dialogs, in which case, we will need to record those dialogs with actors performing **Voice Over (VO)** services. The actors could be friends and family members, but the final result will be the same: a series of sound files that need to be synchronized with the video sequences. This is another field where NLEs shine. Given their flexibility in editing, shifting, cutting, and controlling the movie timeline, NLEs provide the ideal environment for adding sound.

In addition to dialogs, we will also need a music score and special sound effects, such as glass breaking, cars starting, and doors closing. The reproduction of those sound effects is called **Foley** (`http://en.wikipedia.org/wiki/Foley_(filmmaking)`) and it is a fundamental part of making the movie believable and entertaining. Again, perfect timing is crucial, and an NLE is the ideal application for synchronizing Foley sound clips with the video.

Exporting for playback

So, we have rendered all our frames, edited the animation in the NLE, graded the footage, added the music, the titles, and so on. It is release time. What do we do? Selecting the right export format for playback is extremely important. Unfortunately, the subject is rather complex and it can be daunting to understand all the options.

As it happens with still images, for which we have several formats (JPEG, PNG, TIFF, and so on), the same happens with video formats. There is a large number of them and the options for storing video are complex enough to confuse veterans of the industry.

Playing video, which also has to have synchronized sound, is a very complex operation that requires a lot of CPU power. Think about it. The software has to read a large amount of data from a file, decode 24 or 30 frames per second, and play them on the screen in that second. Also, it has to read and decode the sound data and play the sound in perfect sync with the video.

For example, with HD video at 1920 x 1080, each frame is made of 2,073,600 pixels. If we multiply that by 24, our frame rate, we obtain a massive 49,766,400 pixels per second. As each pixel requires three bytes, one per each red, green, and blue channel, it gives us 149,299,200 bytes (approximately 149 MB) per second. And that doesn't include sound.

Even with all the advanced hardware that we have today, this is a massive amount of data to move around. Obviously, we need some way to optimize that operation. The optimization is obtained by using clever algorithms for storing and retrieving the video. These algorithms are called codecs. The term codec is a contraction of coder and decoder. The choice of codec is crucial. When we select a codec, we select not only the capability of the video playback, but also who is going to be able to watch our video or if the video will be easy to be edited. Not all codecs are available on every computer.

For example, if you use Windows, you might have seen files in the AVI or WVM format and so you might decide to export your clip in that format. Big mistake. You want your animation to be viewed by the largest group of people around the world. Those video formats are specific to Windows and will not play on Macintoshes, iPhones, iPads, iPods, and PlayStation 3. I'm not sure about Android devices, but I don't expect them to be able to play those formats as well. You also want to maintain good quality of an image with a fairly contained file size.

A good solution is to use the MPEG4 codec and file format. MPEG4 is multiplatform, recognized by almost every computer system and OS, including game consoles, iOS, and Android devices.

An even better solution is to use the H.264 codec. H.264 is a variant of MPEG4 and it provides a very high-quality image while keeping the file size under control. H.264 is not a file format though. For the file format we can select QuickTime. QuickTime is the industry standard for distribution of videos. The format is actually a container that can use a number of codecs. The following screenshot shows the QuickTime codecs that are installed on my computer:

```
Animation
Apple FCP Uncompressed 10-bit 4
Apple Intermediate Codec
Blackmagic 10 Bit
Blackmagic 8 Bit (2Vuy)
Blackmagic RGB 10 Bit
DV - PAL
DV/DVCPRO - NTSC
DVCPRO - PAL
DVCPRO HD 1080i50
DVCPRO HD 1080i60
DVCPRO HD 720p50
DVCPRO HD 720p60
DVCPRO50 - NTSC
DVCPRO50 - PAL
H.264
HDV 1080i50
HDV 1080i60
HDV 1080p24
HDV 1080p25
HDV 720p24
HDV 720p25
HDV 720p30
MPEG IMX 525/60 (30 Mb/s)
MPEG IMX 525/60 (40 Mb/s)
MPEG IMX 525/60 (50 Mb/s)
MPEG IMX 625/50 (30 Mb/s)
MPEG IMX 625/50 (40 Mb/s)
MPEG IMX 625/50 (50 Mb/s)
MPEG-4 Video
Photo - JPEG
Sheer
Sheer RGB[A] 10bf
Sheer RGB[A] 8bf
Sheer Y'CbCr 8bw 4:2:2
Sheer Y'CbCr[A] 10bv 4:2:2[:4]
Sheer Y'CbCr[A] 10bv 4:4:4[:4]
Sheer Y'CbCr[A] 8bv 4:2:2[:4]
Sheer Y'CbCr[A] 8bv 4:4:4[:4]
✓ Uncompressed 8-bit 4:2:2
XDCAM HD 1080i50 (35 Mb/s VBR)
XDCAM HD 1080i60 (35 Mb/s VBR)
XDCAM HD 1080p24 (35 Mb/s VBR)
XDCAM HD 1080p25 (35 Mb/s VBR)
XDCAM HD 1080p30 (35 Mb/s VBR)
Xiph Theora
```

The advantage of QuickTime is that it works both on Macintosh and Windows machines. It is also supported natively by all iOS devices. Each Mac comes with QuickTime built-in and it can be downloaded for free for Windows machines in seconds by going to `http://www.apple.com/quicktime/download`.

Many people already have it installed because QuickTime is part of iTunes. Given the popularity of the iTunes music store, the iTunes app is already installed on a lot of computers.

Once you install QuickTime on your computer, generally all NLEs will pick it up automatically and they will provide the H.264 export option. You need to select the QuickTime format, and then look for a button or other control in the NLE exporter that allows you to select the codec.

H.264 settings

Years ago I shot, edited, and published a series of webisodes titled 2nd Unit, which was a fun series of interviews with the people in Hollywood who work behind the camera: cinematographers, lighting technicians, grips, and so on. The episodes were published on a self-hosted website. As you can imagine, keeping the file size to a minimum, without compromising quality, was a very important factor.

Our target audience was formed of independent filmmakers, and many of them constantly asked me how I managed to keep image quality high, with skin tones natural, vivid colors, and no pixelation, while keeping the file size manageable. Here is how it's done:

1. Select **QuickTime** as your export format.
2. Select the **H.264** codec.
3. Call the window to specify the codec options.
4. Set **Frame Rate:** at 24 or **Current**.
5. Set **Key Frames:** at 48.
6. Enable **Frame Reordering**.
7. Set the **Quality** to **Medium** and **1/5**.
8. With the mouse cursor hovering over the quality value (do not click), press the *Option* (on Mac) or *Alt* (on Windows) key. The **Quality** label will change to **Temporal**. Set that value to the same of **Quality** (approximately).
9. Set encoding to **Best quality (Multi-pass)**.
10. Set **Data Rate:** to **Automatic**.
11. Click on **OK**.

Here are the settings all together:

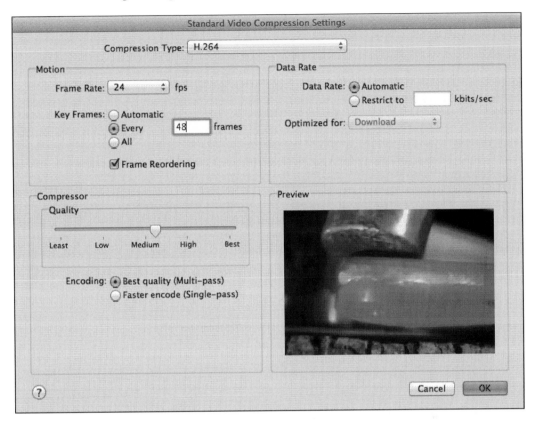

The preceding settings will give you excellent quality and manageable files size, and they will produce a video file that plays on a very large range of devices.

You can also generate multiple versions of the same video for maximum compatibility. For example, you can create an additional MPEG4 video for the devices that cannot play QuickTime files. It will not have the same quality of H.264, but it will give you wider coverage.

Summary

Animations bring together a whole set of disciplines. We have posing, lighting, and framing, just as for still images, but multiplied many times. By using keyframes in a smart way, we can create animations with the least amount of work.

As we saw, we don't have just one way of creating animation but several. We can control the timeline accurately by using the keyMate plugin, and we can complement it with the aniMate plugin for quick building of complex animation using aniblocks.

As with any motion picture work, planning makes the difference between success and failure. Hopefully, the checklist and techniques illustrated here, such as storyboarding, will help you in tackling this complex task.

We have explored all the major aspects of using DAZ Studio for the production of 3D art, from loading 3D figures and props to fully lighting and rendering a complex scene. We have customized Studio for faster workflow, and we have learned how to add more content to the Studio library. We have seen how it's possible to create a completely new character by using morphs. Finally, we have looked at photorealism with the Reality plugin, and we have created our own assets by tailoring a dress for Dawn in modo. Speaking of Dawn, we have looked at how this new figure represents a great new opportunity for content creators. Don't forget to download her, you have a special coupon to get this figure at no cost.

In the movie industry people say that a movie is made three times: the first time when the script is written, the second time when the movie is shot, and the third time when the footage is edited. Editing is a crucial step in the production of the animation and it starts with the selection of the right format for rendering our animation. By using sequences of frames, we obtain the highest amount of flexibility and we minimize the risks involved with lengthy rendering.

With the accurate selection of the delivery format, we are guaranteed to reach the highest group of viewers while keeping the quality of our work intact.

The only ingredient that is missing in this picture is a great story, and that is where I step off the stage and you, dear reader, step right in the spotlight. Good luck!

Installing DAZ Studio

Installing a program is an operation that can confuse a lot of people. The source of confusion is often the lack of understanding of reason for the installation and what is required for our computer. In this section of the book we will see all the details necessary for a successful installation of DAZ Studio.

The reason for installing software

A program is a set of instructions that tells the computer to perform a given task. This set of instructions has to be stored somewhere in order to be used. We store data on a computer using files recorded on a hard disk. Programs are stored in special files. On a Macintosh, a program is stored inside a folder that has a special name. On Windows, programs are saved in files that have the extension .exe. Regardless of the format used to store a program, the idea is that a program is stored in a file on the disk.

 Filenames are made by a name and a suffix, called **extension**, which is separated from the name by a period. For example, DAZStudio.exe is a file that has the name DAZStudio and the extension .exe.

To run a program, the computer—the operating system actually—copies the instructions from the disk file to the memory (RAM) and starts executing the instruction set from the beginning.

Even after more than 30 years since personal computers started becoming popular, there is a bit of confusion about what the term **memory** means. Sometimes, it is used to indicate disk storage and that is simply not correct. Memory refers to **Random Access Memory (RAM)**, which is a temporary storage implemented using electronic components. RAM is directly usable by the processor, and it's where the program instructions are kept during execution. When we turn off the computer, the RAM is erased. On the other hand hard disks, called permanent storage, retain data no matter if power is provided or not. In fact, we can even remove a hard disk from a computer and install it into another machine, and no data will be lost.

So, if we don't have the instruction set, the program, that forms DAZ Studio, we need to add it to our computer. In other words, we need to install it. That's the beauty of programmable computers; they can be extended to perform an unlimited number of tasks by simply adding programs.

When we buy a Macintosh or a Windows PC, the machine comes with a set of programs that are preinstalled at the factory. This is just a convenience and there is nothing special about that process. We could replace the original hard disk with a blank one and install the operating system (Mac OS or Windows) from scratch, and the result would be the same. This is the idea, for example, behind PCs running the Linux OS.

Using the Install Manager

Studio is free to be downloaded from DAZ. The reason for the $0 price tag is that DAZ's business model is based on selling content. They see the software as a platform for using the content that they sell. As the company collects 50 percent of every sale that they make on behalf of content authors, the brokerage of content provides the business model to pay for the development of Studio.

So, the first step is to go to www.daz3d.com and look for DAZ Studio, which is generally under the **Products** or **Software** menu. The program is not directly downloadable; we need to create an account with DAZ and then add the product to the shopping cart. There are no charges, so no credit card information is needed.

Once the order is submitted you will see the following page:

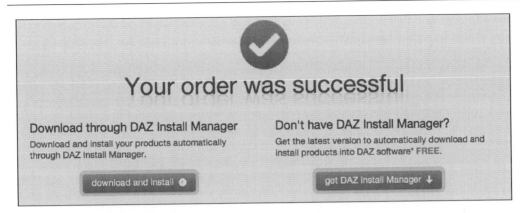

All software from DAZ now is installable via the **DAZ Install Manager**, also known as **DIM**. It is possible to download and install every package directly, but for the sake of simplicity, in this section we will see how to use DIM. If you don't have DIM already installed on your computer, you will need to click on the **get DAZ Install Manager** button.

It might seem confusing to install an installer. Consider that anything that is performed by a computer is a program. For example, the drawing of the mouse cursor, the arrow, on the screen is performed by a program, or more precisely by a subroutine of the operating system. DIM is just another program whose task is to fetch DAZ products from their file server and install them on a computer. As DIM is not preinstalled on our computer, we need to install it ourselves.

This action will cause the download of the DIM installer to the directory of your choice. Note that the Mac OS version is delivered as a ZIP file and the Windows version is delivered as an EXE file. The Mac archive can be expanded by simply double-clicking on it from the Finder. Mac OS has built-in support for ZIP files and the program contained in the archive will be extracted in a few seconds. At the time of writing this book, the extracted program is called DAZ3DIM_1.0.1.81_Mac32. Double-click on that file and the installation process will start.

For the Windows version, simply double-click on the downloaded files and the installation process of DIM will begin.

In both cases the installation process of DIM will be done in a few seconds. After that, you will be able to access DIM from either the /Applications/DAZ 3D/ DAZ3DIM1 folder (Mac OS) or the C:\Program Files\DAZ 3D\DAZ3DIM1 folder (Windows). If you are using the 64-bit version of Windows, DIM might be located in the C:\Program Files (x86) folder.

Once DIM is installed, you can use it to install Studio and all the content that comes from DAZ. Run DIM and enter your DAZ account.

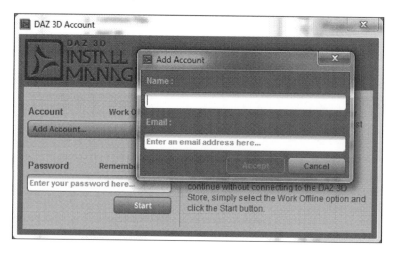

32-bit and 64-bit versions

The Install Manager will show you all the products that you can download and install.

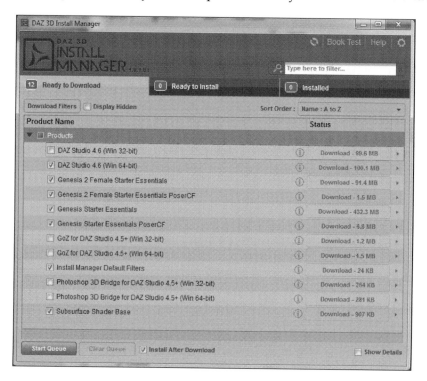

Notice that there are 32-bit and 64-bit versions of Studio. This is important. If we run a 32-bit OS, we cannot use the 64-bit version of a program. If we run a 64-bit OS and install a 32-bit application, that setup will work but it will not be optimal. The application might run slower than expected and it will not have access to all the memory that is available from the OS.

Any Macintosh or PC made in the last three years should be 64-bit capable, but if you don't know for sure, do a Google search on how to determine if your computer is running at 64-bit.

If you have a 64-bit OS, install only the 64-bit version of Studio. From the preceding screenshot, you can see that not all the options have been selected. This is intentional. Studio comes with a series of additional components that can be useful, depending on what other programs are installed on your machine. For example, if you don't use ZBrush, a very powerful 3D modeler, there is no reason for installing the GoZ plugin. If you don't have Photoshop, there is no need for installing Photoshop Bridge. The options that are enabled in the figure are the ones that should be installed by every user.

 Note that the **Install After Download** checkbox is enabled. This option will start the installation of the program or content immediately after it has been downloaded.

All that we have left to do is to click on the **Start Queue** button. DIM will start downloading Studio and all its components. Once the files are downloaded, the installation process will start automatically.

The installation process with DIM doesn't prompt the user for any destination path. This is a radical departure from the past, when we could specify where Studio would be installed. It is still possible to run the individual installers manually and gain more control of the final destination of the files, but if you are totally new to the Studio world, the basic installation via DIM is the easiest option.

Running DAZ Studio

Once Studio is installed it will be ready to be run. On a Macintosh you can find the program in the /Applications/DAZ 3D/DAZStudio4 folder. The program is called DAZStudio.

On Windows it will likely be under C:\Program Files\DAZ 3D\DAZStudio4. The program is called DAZStudio.exe.

In either case, simply double-click on the name of the program and it will start. The first thing that Studio asks, on its first run, is for the serial number. This number confirms that we have an authorized copy of the program. The serial number is found in the **My Serial Numbers** page of your DAZ account. We can simply copy and paste it and the program will be ready to run.

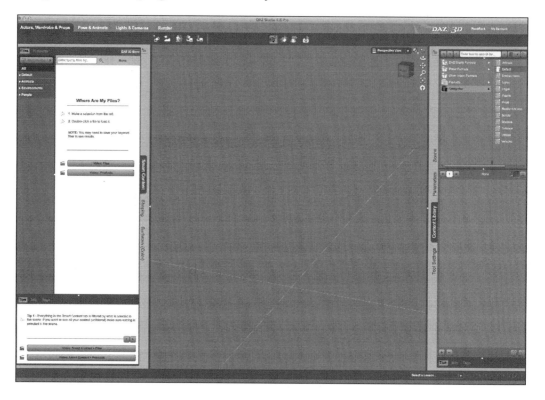

That's all there is to install and run DAZ Studio.

Index

C

camera
  choosing 92-94
  moving 158
Camera: Frame tool 84
category
  assigning, to object 170
CGI 165, 226
channels
  about 176, 193
  alpha channel 194
  diffuse channel 194
  specular channel 194
  using 193-196
character
  adding 184
  creating, with morphs 83, 84
  dressing 186-191
character's skin
  setting 205
checkpoint 220
cinematic lighting
  about 213
  Ambient Color 218
  braziers 214, 215
  checkpoint 220
  cookies 221, 222
  darkness, adjusting 219
  finishing touches 220
  moonlight 215-218
clothing
  adding 16, 17
  creating 247, 248
clothing, creating
  3D modeling, with modo 248
  box modeling 251
  figure, rigging 249, 250
  new era, beginning 252
  retopology 251
ClothingresourceBase object 254
color grading 310
colors
  mixing, with image maps 196-199
common mistakes
  avoiding 64

Computer Generated Imagery. *See* **CGI**
content
  adding 15
  buying, from DAZ 118-122
  clothing, adding 16, 17
  DAZ Studio 116
  finding 113, 114
  free models, downloading 132-134
  Genesis 116
  hair, adding 18
  installing, in Studio 134
  managing 166
  purchasing, from Renderosity 122-127
  purchasing, from RuntimeDNA 128-132
  sources 117
  Studio, configuring for 144-146
Content Library tab
  about 166
  organizing 167-171
content, managing
  Content Library tab 166
  Smart Content tab 166
cookies 221, 222
CTB (Color Temperature Blue) 216
CTO (Color Temperature Orange) 216
Cucoloris 221
CUDA 231
Current field 298
Customize Installation option 135
cut 305

D

darkness
  adjusting 219
Dawn
  about 252
  dress, making for 253, 254
DAZ
  content, buying from 118-122
  URL 118
DAZ Install Manager. *See* **DIM**
DAZ Studio
  about 116
  customizing 8-13
  running 321, 322

mesh 153
Mesh Resolution property 154
models
  importing 171
  importing, from other applications 171
models, importing
  OBJ file, importing 172-177
  scaling issues 172
Model tab 280
Modifiers tab 236
modo
  3D modeling, using with 248
  URL 248
monster factory
  within 84-88
moonlight 215-218
morphs
  about 75-78
  character, creating with 83, 84
  saving 83
Mouth Height parameter 87
Move tool 277
movie clips
  avoiding 308-310

N

Navigation Basics tutorial
  URL 248
Neck parameter 66
Neck Size parameter 82
new era
  beginning 252
new faces
  creating, premade morphs combined 79-83
new layout
  saving 36, 37
NLE
  defining 305
Node selection tool 38, 160
nonconforming clothing
  fixing 20-22
Non Linear Editor. *See* NLE

O

OBJ 171
objects
  renaming 212
OBJ file
  figure, exporting 254-262
  importing 172
Opacity 194
OpenCL 231
overexposing image 213

P

Parameters tab 154, 156, 162, 187
persistence of vision (POV) 294
playback
  exporting for 311-314
point lights 165
point of view (POV) 102
polygons
  about 149-151
  finding, in scene 152, 153
  number of polygons, finding 152, 153
  subdivision 153, 154
pose
  creating 49, 50
  nonconforming clothing, fixing 20-22
  saving 72, 73
  striking 19
pose, creating
  bodies, without limits 62-64
  image size, deciding 56-59
  position, setting of surfboard 59
  reference image, using as backdrop 56
  scene, setting up 51-55
  shot, planning 51
  surfer pose, setting 60-62
Pose Presets 46
position
  setting, of surfboard 59
premade morphs
  combining, to create new faces 79-83

Thank you for buying
The Complete Guide to DAZ Studio 4

About Packt Publishing

Packt, pronounced 'packed', published its first book "*Mastering phpMyAdmin for Effective MySQL Management*" in April 2004 and subsequently continued to specialize in publishing highly focused books on specific technologies and solutions.

Our books and publications share the experiences of your fellow IT professionals in adapting and customizing today's systems, applications, and frameworks. Our solution based books give you the knowledge and power to customize the software and technologies you're using to get the job done. Packt books are more specific and less general than the IT books you have seen in the past. Our unique business model allows us to bring you more focused information, giving you more of what you need to know, and less of what you don't.

Packt is a modern, yet unique publishing company, which focuses on producing quality, cutting-edge books for communities of developers, administrators, and newbies alike. For more information, please visit our website: www.packtpub.com.

Writing for Packt

We welcome all inquiries from people who are interested in authoring. Book proposals should be sent to author@packtpub.com. If your book idea is still at an early stage and you would like to discuss it first before writing a formal book proposal, contact us; one of our commissioning editors will get in touch with you.

We're not just looking for published authors; if you have strong technical skills but no writing experience, our experienced editors can help you develop a writing career, or simply get some additional reward for your expertise.

PUBLISHING

Learning Adobe Edge Animate

ISBN: 978-1-84969-242-7   Paperback: 368 pages

Create engaging motion and rich interactivity with Adobe Edge Animate

1. Master the Edge Animate interface and unleash your creativity through standard HTML, CSS, and JavaScript

2. Packed with an abundance of information regarding the Edge Animate application and related toolsets

3. Robust motion and interactivity through web standards

Keyshot 3D Rendering

ISBN: 978-1-84969-482-7   Paperback: 124 pages

Showcase your 3D models and create hyper realistic images with Keyshot in the fastest and most efficient way possible

1. Create professional quality images from your 3D models in just a few steps

2. Thorough overview of how to work and navigate in Keyshot

3. A step-by-step guide that quickly gets you started with creating realistic images

Please check **www.PacktPub.com** for information on our titles

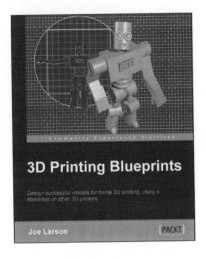

3D Printing Blueprints

ISBN: 978-1-84969-708-8   Paperback: 310 pages

Design successful models for home 3D printing, using a Makerbot or other 3D printers

1. Design 3D models that will print successfully using Blender, a free 3D modeling program

2. Customize, edit, repair, and then share your creations on Makerbot's Thingiverse website

3. Easy-to-follow guide on 3D printing; learn to create a new model at the end of each chapter

Blender 3D Basics

ISBN: 978-1-84951-690-7   Paperback: 468 pages

The complete novice's guide to 3D modeling and animation

1. The best starter guide for complete newcomers to 3D modeling and animation

2. Easier learning curve than any other book on Blender

3. You will learn all the important foundation skills ready to apply to any 3D software

Please check **www.PacktPub.com** for information on our titles

Produced by Amazon
Printed in Japan
落丁、乱丁本のお問い合わせは
Amazon.co.jp カスタマーサービスへ